The American Fighter Plane

The American Fighter Plane

Illustrations by Ted Williams

Text by Amy E. Williams

BARNES & NOBLE BOOKS

NEW YORK

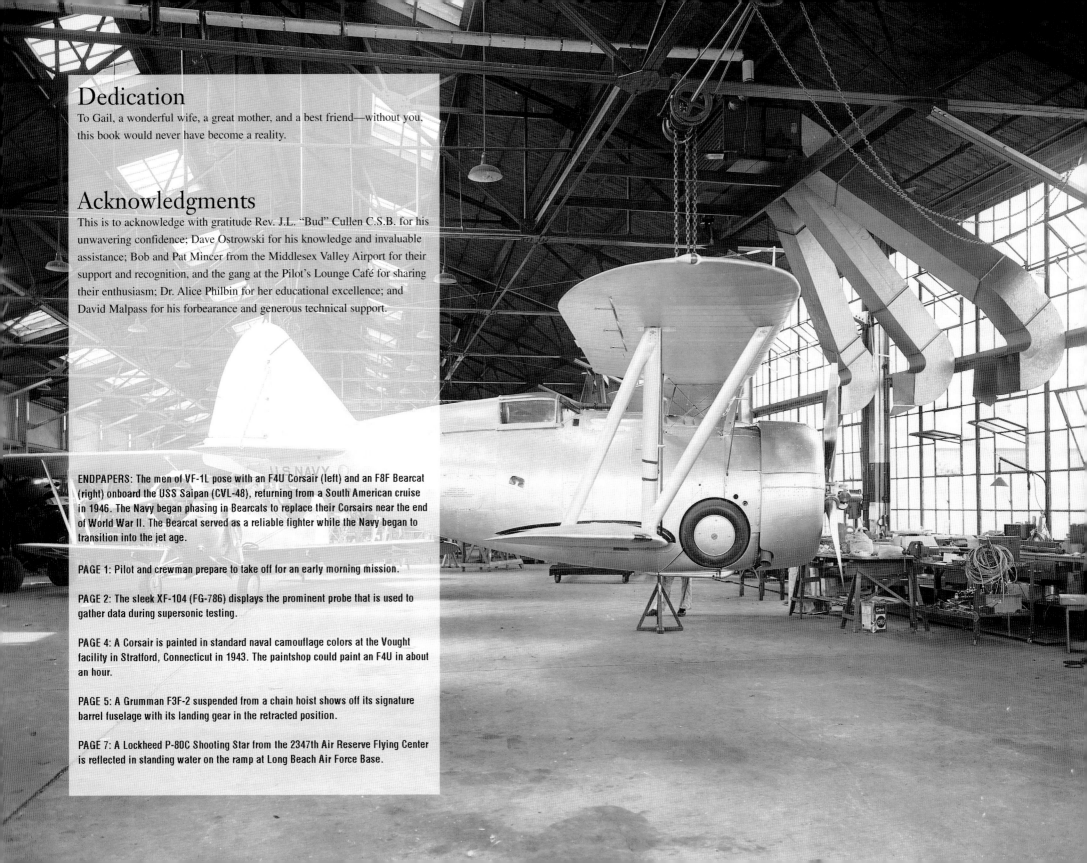

Dedication

To Gail, a wonderful wife, a great mother, and a best friend—without you, this book would never have become a reality.

Acknowledgments

This is to acknowledge with gratitude Rev. J.L. "Bud" Cullen C.S.B. for his unwavering confidence; Dave Ostrowski for his knowledge and invaluable assistance; Bob and Pat Mincer from the Middlesex Valley Airport for their support and recognition, and the gang at the Pilot's Lounge Café for sharing their enthusiasm; Dr. Alice Philbin for her educational excellence; and David Malpass for his forbearance and generous technical support.

ENDPAPERS: The men of VF-1L pose with an F4U Corsair (left) and an F8F Bearcat (right) onboard the USS Saipan (CVL-48), returning from a South American cruise in 1946. The Navy began phasing in Bearcats to replace their Corsairs near the end of World War II. The Bearcat served as a reliable fighter while the Navy began to transition into the jet age.

PAGE 1: Pilot and crewman prepare to take off for an early morning mission.

PAGE 2: The sleek XF-104 (FG-786) displays the prominent probe that is used to gather data during supersonic testing.

PAGE 4: A Corsair is painted in standard naval camouflage colors at the Vought facility in Stratford, Connecticut in 1943. The paintshop could paint an F4U in about an hour.

PAGE 5: A Grumman F3F-2 suspended from a chain hoist shows off its signature barrel fuselage with its landing gear in the retracted position.

PAGE 7: A Lockheed P-80C Shooting Star from the 2347th Air Reserve Flying Center is reflected in standing water on the ramp at Long Beach Air Force Base.

Contents

Foreword

Fighter plane! The very words elicit images of danger, power, speed, and agility, a creation of talented engineers, designed and constructed to be a superior fighting machine. Born of necessity in a world that sometimes erupts in conflict, the fighter plane pits man against man in the ultimate duel, a battle of skill and determination in which the plane with the technological edge greatly improves its pilot's chance of success.

Anyone fascinated with the best of the best—the fastest, the most powerful, the most maneuverable—is drawn to fighter planes, which incorporate the most successful characteristics aviation designers have to offer. Even the names of these aircraft—Hawk, Wildcat, Lightning, Thunderbolt, Sabre—hint at their speed, power, and predatory nature.

American fighter planes are the product of a blending of private enterprise with government assistance and oversight. In 1915, the U.S. government established the National Advisory Committee for Aeronautics (NACA, now NASA) to conduct research and advance the science of aeronautics. Information obtained from this extensive research effort coupled with the results from military tests and development projects are freely provided to aircraft designers and manufacturers. This system has allowed for a continuous improvement in fighter plane technology. Aviation, and fighter plane development in particular, has always attracted people who want to push the envelope, who thrive on challenges, who won't take "no" for an answer, who will always find a way to achieve the impossible.

Competition has also played a major role in the American system of fighter plane development. Once our military services establish a requirement and a design specification for an advanced fighter plane, manufacturers are invited to compete for the contract. A "paper competition" in the form of proposals usually comes first, followed by the flight-testing and evaluation of prototype fighters. Finally, the much-sought-after production contract is awarded to the winner.

In austere times, such as the period between the world wars and, in particular, during the Great Depression, fighter plane production runs have been small. During World War II, however, many manufacturers turned out large quantities of fighters; a feat that is unlikely to be repeated with today's modern, highly complex, and extremely expensive jet aircraft. But each production run furthered the advancement of fighter plane technology and each new design or refinement of an existing model improved upon its predecessor. This approach has resulted in some truly great fighters, and the story of their development and evolution is a fascinating one.

OPPOSITE: To create an aircraft rendering, Ted begins by making pencil sketches of the subject in different positions and perspectives (Top). Choosing the right angle is important to the presentation. In the case of this P-6E, a full side-view was necessary to show a comparison to another plane. On page 25, an F11C is laid out in an identical position to highlight the subtle, and not so subtle, differences between an Army Hawk and its navalized version. Next, using the pencil sketch as a guide, the hues are established and an appropriate color palette is created for the aircraft (Center). It is often difficult to discern hues in black-and-white photographs and the colors of the unit markings are sometimes recorded inaccurately. In these cases, Ted conducts more comprehensive research to develop an accurate, historical presentation. For the last step, Ted brings the illustration to its final form (Bottom). The artwork and squadron markings are painted into position, and highlights and shadows are added to complete the illustration.

That saga is told with great style in *The American Fighter Plane* by Ted and Amy Williams, perhaps the only father/daughter team of aviation authors anywhere. Ted and Amy have combined their individual talents to create a unique perspective on American fighter planes and the great people associated with them.

Amy is the writer on the team and, having earned a master's degree in Scientific and Technical Communication from Bowling Green State University in Bowling Green, Ohio, is well qualified for the task. I had the opportunity to personally benefit from Amy's skills when she edited a series of articles for me in *Skyways, The Journal of the Airplane, 1920–40*. The subject was fairly technical (early French fighter planes) and had been translated (to a degree) from French, so the task was by no means easy.

The very pleasant and rewarding experience in working with Amy certainly extends to the other half of the team as well. As editor of *Skyways*, I have worked closely with Ted for several years as he created many fine aircraft illustrations for our articles, including 3-view drawings, centerfold portraits, and his most recent contribution, a spectacular, full-color, wrap-around cover featuring Curtiss F9C-2 Sparrowhawk fighters and the U.S. Navy rigid airship from which they operated. Ted brings to his portraits a rare combination—the soul of an artist and a love of aviation. An artist will capture the grace, the beauty, the smooth aerodynamic line of a fighter plane; Ted does this as well, but he adds a close-up dimension, rich in detail. In *The American Fighter Plane* we see the airplane not at a distance as we would see it in flight, but close up, as if we had walked up to it on an airfield flight ramp or perhaps in the hangar undergoing maintenance. Ted's 3-view drawings give us an excellent idea of what the fighter looks like from not just one, but many perspectives. Each color portrait depicts an airplane at it appeared in service, complete with service markings, insignia, and camouflage.

Ted's color portraits of 1920s and 30s fighters have a special appeal and give us a new perspective on early American fighters, which, dating from an era before color photography became commonplace, are usually depicted only in black-and-white photographs. Ted brings these classic aircraft to life in full color. And what a colorful lot of fighters they were! We had gotten through the "war to end all wars" and another war was not yet on the horizon. There was no pressing need for planes to be camouflaged to blend in with their surroundings, so many of them sported wonderful color markings—yellow wings and tails; blue fuselages, bands, and stripes; and chevrons of all colors. The advantage of camouflage later became apparent and today's fighters are mostly painted in shades of gray—what a contrast with the colorful biplanes and early monoplane fighters of the 20s and 30s. *The American Fighter Plane* allows us to turn back the hands of time and see the many-hued biplane fighters of yesteryear: the Curtiss P-6E Hawk in the striking "snow owl" paint scheme of the 17th Pursuit

Squadron; the colorful Navy Boeing F4B-4 and Grumman F3F-2 fighters with their yellow wings and multicolored cowlings, tails, and fuselage bands; and the Army Boeing P-26A Peashooter in the very distinctive markings of the 94th Pursuit Squadron.

The early monoplane fighters of the late 1930s were nearly as colorful as their biplane predecessors, and Ted has captured this era with his portraits of the Seversky P-35, Curtiss P-36 Hawk, and Brewster F2A Buffalo. In the early 1940s, as the reality of war loomed, we begin to see the reemergence of camouflage on fighter planes. This is also accurately portrayed by Ted in his illustrations of the Curtiss P-40, Bell P-39 Airacobra, Grumman F4F Wildcat and F6F Hellcat, Vought F4U Corsair, and Republic P-47 Thunderbolt.

Interestingly, toward the end of World War II, as the Allies achieved air superiority, camouflage became unnecessary again, and warplanes began to exhibit a wide variety of colorful markings, as shown in Ted's rendering of the famous North American P-51D Mustang. The jets, too, had their own distinctive markings and are well represented in this book. One can see in this single volume the evolution of American fighter planes in all their colorful glory, from the earliest wood-and-fabric biplanes to the latest stealth jet fighter, the Lockheed F-22 Raptor.

The medium in which Ted works to create the wonderful images in *The American Fighter Plane* is quite remarkable. A talented artist, Ted has executed many airplane portraits in such traditional mediums as pencil, ink, airbrush, watercolors, and oils. In more recent years, however, a new and exciting medium has become available: the computer. Applying his skill and experience as an artist, Ted has perfected the digital techniques necessary to create works of art using a computer. All of his aircraft portraits and 3-view drawings in this book utilize this new medium.

This book also shows the aviation historian side of Ted. With a life-long interest in aviation, Ted has read everything he could get his hands on about airplanes and the people associated with them. He thoroughly researches each of his aircraft portraits, so we see not only an accurate rendering of lines and shapes, but also the correct colors, unit markings, and squadron insignias. Amy's attention to research and detail keeps the subject matter focused and fresh, and combined with Ted's illustrations, her illuminating text leads readers through the rich history of the American fighter plane. In addition, the book is filled with archival photographs that further illustrate the story of these aircraft and the people who designed, flew, and maintained them.

With this volume, Ted and Amy Williams have given us a rich, colorful, and accurate portrait of the fascinating world of the American fighter plane. I hope we'll see more from this talented team.

Dave Ostrowski

Editor, *Skyways, The Journal of the Airplane, 1920–1940.*

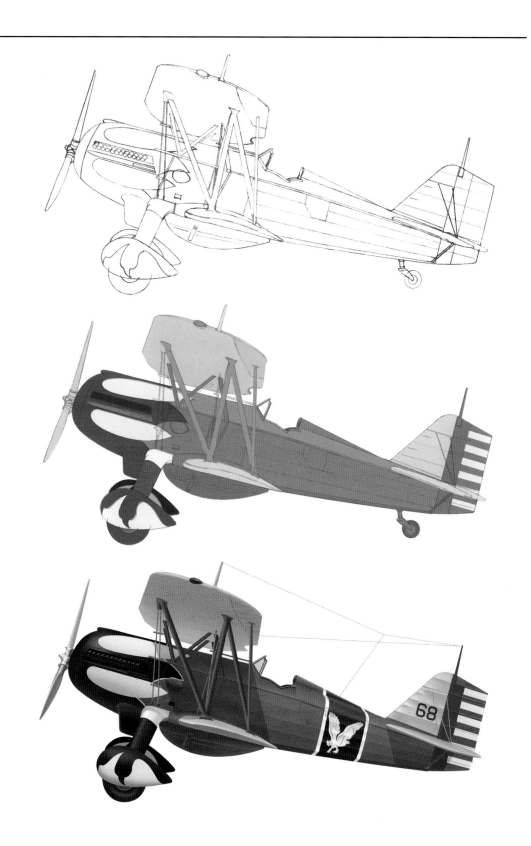

Introduction

No other type of aircraft has as many demands placed upon it as the fighter plane. Engineered to perform a variety of roles in extremely hazardous environments, the fighter plane captures the imagination and inspires awe simply by accomplishing the tasks it is designed to perform.

Who could have predicted that mankind's nearly universal fascination with flight would flourish as it has? Almost a century ago, men like Orville and Wilbur Wright and Glenn Curtiss took to the air in homegrown contraptions that seem almost laughable by modern standards. Yet, while it is difficult to believe that today's robust jets descended from these early delicate fliers, it is even more amazing that the Wright Model A and the McDonnell Douglas F-15 Eagle, although generations apart, are still governed by the same physical principles.

Not surprisingly, once flight became practical, the armed services of the world, including the U.S. Army Signal Corps, adopted the airplane as a communications tool. Recognizing the airplane's promise as a reconnaissance platform, warring armies found they could easily monitor enemy movements and positions on the ground.

Soon, airspace over the battlefields of World War I became crowded with competing observers. It wasn't long before the airplane, already invaluable for communication, developed into its present role as a military weapon as these early aviators came to engage in aerial combat. Planes and pilots went into the air armed, first with handguns and later with mounted machine guns, and within three years air-to-air combat was a deadly reality of war. What had started as a means of deterring reconnaissance pilots from returning to their lines with vital intelligence evolved into an aggressive tactic whereby aircraft equipped with bombs and bullets could determine a battle's outcome by altering the situation on the ground.

Despite its involvement in World War I, the United States did not contribute its own fighter design during the Great War. Instead, it relied on European designs built under license in the United States. It was not until after the Armistice that the fledgling U.S. Army Air Service settled on its own fighter design, the Thomas-Morse MB-3A, manufactured by Boeing.

The quest for air superiority that originated in World War I has taken many developmental twists and turns since the MB-3A took to the air. The first American pursuit aircraft, although not a revolutionary design, was far-reaching in concept. The need to create an airplane with the capability to

ABOVE: In 1909 Wilbur Wright traveled to Europe, where his thrilling flying demonstrations drew crowds at every stop. Here he flies with aviator Paul Tissandier in January of that year at Pau, France.

OPPOSITE: One of five supersonic, stealth Lockheed Martin F-22 Raptors during an evaluation flight over Edwards Air Force Base.

sweep the skies of all enemy aircraft, while denying access to this new valuable "high ground," remains the basis for all military fighting aircraft.

While many books have been dedicated to the fighter plane and the brave pilots who flew them, *The American Fighter Plane* takes a detailed look at the men who designed and built these exceptional aircraft. This book identifies the contributions of the many entrepreneurs, engineers, and designers who literally created an industry. Such men as Leroy Grumman, Kelly Johnson, Alexander Kartveli, and Jack Northrop responded to the needs of the U.S. military by developing new technologies—and by utilizing new materials and engineering theories—to deliver a superior fighter airplane that could perform its specific military mission efficiently and effectively, while increasing the pilot's chances for survival.

The American Fighter Plane traces these engineering developments from the first truly all-American fighter plane to the high-performance jets of today, which are multipurpose airborne reconnaissance and weapons platforms. This technological evolution is part of a rich history, built on the genius of many great engineering minds. Numerous companies—founded by men with names like Boeing, Douglas, Grumman, Lockheed, Northrop, and Vought—all contributed by building successive aircraft that could fly faster, farther, and higher.

From the biplanes, the enduring classics that epitomized the golden era of flight, to the venerated warbirds of World War II, and from the many pioneering designs of the early jet age to today's state-of-the art Advanced Technical fighter, *The American Fighter Plane* chronicles the history of American fighters from their first military function as pursuit planes to today's expanded role as multipurpose air-superiority aircraft. Selected and depicted in astonishing detail by aviation artist Ted Williams, each plane chosen for this volume represents an undeniably historically significant, inventive solution for its day and situation, and is a benchmark in the evolution of the American fighter plane, boasting advancements in aerodynamics, propulsion, construction, avionics, and weapons systems.

As a final note, the data listed in each specification section only details the variant illustrated. A brief overview for each design program appears in the text. Although every aircraft in this book has numerous prototype, evaluation, and production models, the entire variant history is not included with the specifications.

Thomas-Morse MB-3

The MB-3, the first American-designed fighter plane, was also the United States' first, and for some years only, capable frontline fighter plane. Despite its important place in American military aviation history, however, the little fighter with the all-wooden fuselage was actually obsolete from the very beginning.

British-born engineer Benjamin Douglas Thomas, who had worked on many early European plane designs, originally conceived of the MB-3 design. Immigrating to the United States in 1913 to work for Glenn Curtiss, he later joined the Thomas-Morse Aircraft Company in 1915. Thomas (no relation to the founding Thomas Brothers) quickly began work on new designs.

The first MB-3 prototype took flight on February 21, 1919, and it performed well. Even in early trials the MB-3 flew at speeds greater than those of its European counterparts. It was a compact biplane with a one-piece upper wing. The wings had two bays of interplane struts and two distinct lower panels, with inner bays located within each narrow wing to alleviate vibration.

Modeled after the French Spad XIII, the MB-3 first utilized a 300-horsepower Hispano-Suiza engine produced under license. In this incarnation, the "Hisso," as it was known, was a 1,127-cubic-inch, water-cooled V-8—a very powerful engine for its time, though prone to running roughly. In time, a four-bladed propeller was used to further dampen the extreme vibration, which was the result of having built a small airframe around such a strong power plant.

The diminutive fighter was an excellent gun platform. It carried two Browning machine guns mounted in the nose of the aircraft, just above the Hisso. This placement necessitated firing synchronization. To ensure that the bullets would safely pass by the propeller blades, an interrupter gear was assembled to the firing mechanism—an acceptable solution at the time, but one that greatly reduced the guns' rates of fire.

Mounting the twin .30-caliber guns above the engine meant that both the engine housing and the cockpit were cramped. And though the aircraft's fighting effectiveness was improved when the aircraft was refitted with one .30-caliber and one larger .50-caliber Browning machine gun, it made things even tighter for both the mechanics and the pilot. As a result, the MB-3 did not have space for a traditional instrument panel. Instead, gauges were scattered around the cockpit, attached to any available spot. And pilots with larger builds, wearing the appropriate cold weather apparel, were likely to find the cockpit cramped and uncomfortable.

RIGHT: Prized for their skill with fabrics, seamstresses frequently found employment at the early aviation companies of the 1920s. Here, two women rib-stitch a canvas covering to the upper left portion of an MB-3A wing. Their stitches secured the fabric to ribs within the wing, ensuring that it would remain taut and flush with the wood framing while the aircraft was in flight.

OPPOSITE: The Thomas Morse MB-3A packed a big punch for a diminutive fighter. Designed by Thomas-Morse and built by Boeing, this first all-American pursuit ship was modeled after the French Spad XIII. The sheet metal deflector attached to the spent-round ejector chute protected the radiator from damage as the large .50-caliber shell casings were expelled from the aircraft.

Until 1925, aircraft designers were required to turn over the rights to their designs to the federal government, which would then allow multiple manufacturers to bid on the production run. This policy was put into practice to alleviate the quality-control problems—not to mention the deaths and injuries—that stemmed from substandard equipment, such as those that had plagued aircraft during World War I. The Army responded by creating an agency, the War Industries Board, to oversee the manufacturing of big-ticket items like airplanes.

In 1921 Boeing Aircraft, almost unknown in the aviation industry at the time, took advantage of the government's policy and underbid all other manufacturers, including Thomas-Morse, and was awarded the contract to build 200 MB-3s. In another triumph for the Boeing firm, in June 1921 the Army Air Service established an inspection center at Boeing's headquarters in Seattle, Washington, which further helped to develop Boeing's position as a valued supplier to the military.

The Boeing-built MB-3, designated MB-3A, incorporated many enhancements to the Thomas-Morse design. Boeing redesigned the tail for improved stability, relocated and changed the configuration of the single, center-mounted radiator to two radiators—one on each side of the fuselage—and, most indicative of things to come, introduced the idea of a welded steel-tube fuselage.

Ultimately, each Boeing-built MB-3A airframe cost the government $7,240. As was the practice of the day, the government supplied the instrumentation, engines, and armament. After delivery of 200 aircraft to the Army between July and December 1922, the Navy placed an additional order for eleven MB-3s. These planes, including one MB-7 racer, were assigned to the Marine Corps.

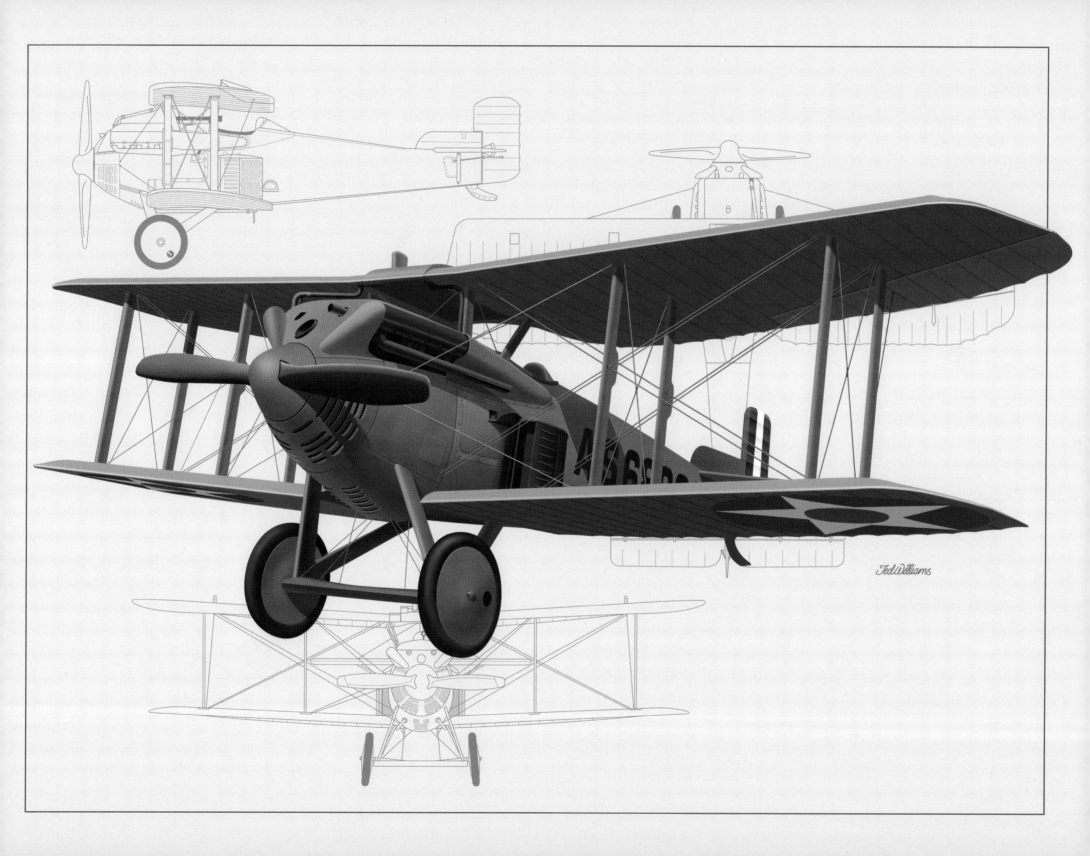

Ted Williams

Thomas Morse MB-3A Specifications

Type: Single-seat fighter

Power plant: One 330-horsepower Wright-Hispano water-cooled engine

Performance: Maximum speed, 141 miles per hour (227kph); service ceiling, 19,500 feet (5,944m)

Endurance: 2.25 hours at 15,000 feet (4,572m)

Weight: Empty, 1,716 pounds (779kg); maximum takeoff weight, 2,539 pounds (1,153kg)

Dimensions: Span, 26 feet (7.9m); length, 20 feet (6.1m); height, 8 feet 1 inch (2.5m); wing area, 229 square feet ($21.1m^2$)

Armament: One .30-caliber and one .50-caliber machine gun

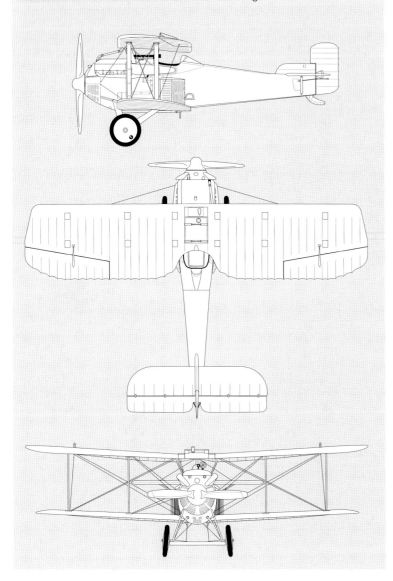

RIGHT: The wood-and-fabric MB-3A had a cramped cockpit, side-mounted radiators, and a cat's cradle of wire bracing between the upper and lower wing.

OPPOSITE: Boeing workers are using specially created tools during the construction of an MB-3A; a device is placed on the topside of the bottom wing to guide in the rigging of the wings. A specific tautness was required in the wire bracing to create the proper dihedral and wing incidence. Without the correct parameters, the aircraft would not fly to its peak performance.

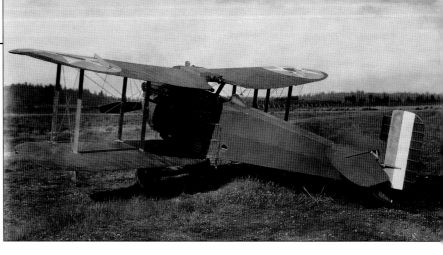

The MB-3A provided the American military with a serviceable pursuit aircraft. It was quick, it could carry heavy armament, and it was comparable to, or possibly even better than, many of the other World War I planes available during the postwar period. Yet the day it hit the production line, it was already behind the times. First, the MB-3 was designed as an all-wood-and-fabric airplane with multiple struts, which induced drag. Engineers were already exploring the tough, resilient, and lightweight application of high-strength steel tubing for airframe construction. Second, the MB-3A's engine had been introduced in 1915—it was old technology by the early 1920s. Finally, the vibration from the hard-mounted engine was a hazard to the structure and the pilot: the airframe could literally vibrate to pieces.

In 1925 the National Advisory Committee for Aeronautics (NACA) selected the MB-3A for a study about pressure distribution over the wings. NACA reported:

> As it was desired to use in this investigation an airplane having a high maximum speed, a new MB-3 pursuit plane was borrowed by the National Advisory Committee for Aeronautics from the Army Air Service. In many ways this airplane was especially suitable for these tests as it was high powered and had good performance; on the other hand, vibration during flight had been observed to be considerable and numerous instances had indicated that this type was structurally weak.

Despite the negatives, the MB-3A rightfully earned its place in American aviation history. A testament to its longevity, no other pursuit plane was ordered in greater quantity until 1939, when the government commissioned 542 Curtiss P-40s.

The MB-3 may have been designed and produced too late to participate in World War I, but it retains its status as the grandfather of all modern American military fighting aircraft. Once its military career was over, the MB-3A design found a new life as a racer. In 1929, the Thomas-Morse Company became part of Consolidated, and by 1934 the Thomas-Morse nameplate had been retired for good.

Boeing PW-9

As a result of receiving the contract to build 200 Thomas-Morse MB-3As, Boeing felt it was well suited to offer the government a new fighter design. As the principal manufacturer of the MB-3A, Boeing had two key advantages: it was in a unique position to know the full extent of the MB-3A's deficiencies and, more importantly, Boeing had the ear of the War Department.

Boeing's first foray into pursuit ship design coincided with its MB-3A production run. In preparation, Boeing's lead engineer, Clairmont L. Egtvedt, toured several European factories. While in Europe, he paid particular attention to the designs coming from the Dutch firm Fokker. Stateside, Egtvedt interviewed Army pilots and McCook Field personnel. This field data was indispensable to the creation of Boeing's new design: the Boeing Model 15.

On April 29, 1923, the first Model 15 was tested and deemed ready for military approval. After a U.S. Army Air Corps fly-off, the Model 15, or PW-9 (Pursuit Water-cooled, ninth design), as it was officially designated, became the first all Boeing-designed pursuit aircraft accepted into the U.S. Army Air Corps. Later, the PW-9 and its variants would supply both the Army and the Navy (where it was designated FB-1) with a serviceable, frontline, single-seat pursuit plane until 1928.

Not to say it wasn't a struggle. When Boeing introduced its new design, the military was convinced that the MB-3A design was sufficient. After all, the MB-3A was new, too. Plus, the military was critical of the Boeing Company and its products. Despite Boeing's involvement with the Thomas-Morse MB-3A, Boeing was still an upstart. In its attempt to get the Model 15 off the ground and into military hangars, Boeing was squaring off against the well-known Curtiss firm. With its PW-8 and a venerable reputation in the aviation industry, Curtiss was a tough adversary.

While Boeing's PW-9 may have incorporated many of the MB-3A's design elements, advancements in airframe technology and engine development are what really made the PW-9 a next-generation pursuit aircraft, and it is clear that Boeing also drew design ideas from the famed Fokker D-VII. After the Armistice, the Fokker D-VII was specifically mentioned in the Treaty of Versailles. As a testament to the excellence of the D-VII design, the treaty mandated that the Fokker D-VII be turned over to the Allies for research and study.

The PW-9 had an arc-welded, steel-tube fuselage. Boeing had invented the arc-welding technique specifically for the construction of this airplane. The

95th Pursuit Squadron

RIGHT: The Boeing PW-9 was the first American pursuit plane to utilize a welded, steel-tube construction for the fuselage and tail. The wings, however, were still built of fabric-covered wood.

OPPOSITE: This PW-9C, with is big, liquid-cooled V-12 Curtiss Conqueror engine, carries the insignia of the "Kicking Mules" of the 95th Pursuit Squadron.

wings, although still built out of fabric-covered wood, were modernized to a sesquiplane configuration (from the Latin *sesqui-*, meaning one and a half). A term still in use today, "sesquiplane" refers to a biplane with a lower wing that is proportionately shorter than its top wing. The wings were also tapered for better aerodynamic performance and unmatched maneuverability, and a single "N" interplane strut on each side of the aircraft braced the wings for torsional strength. The tail assembly, or empennage, although fabric-covered, was metal-framed like the fuselage.

Boeing's original design had called for the same engine used in the MB-3A. The introduction of the new Curtiss D-12, however, curtailed any further developments with the antiquated 300-horsepower Hispano-Suiza. The D-12 liquid-cooled engine offered twelve cylinders, measured 1,150 cubic inches, and yielded 435 horsepower. Not only was it bigger than the V-8s commonly in use, it was also designed specifically for aircraft applications. The dynamics of turning a propeller at a constant rpm while an aircraft is in a dive or a climb are quite different than the operating expectations for an automobile engine. The forces and temperature extremes experienced by an aero engine in flight are much more severe than those encountered by any engine in use on the ground.

To accommodate the D-12's cooling needs, a Boeing-designed tunnel radiator was placed underneath the nose. This radiator proved so effective that it was adopted on the competing Curtiss PW-8A.

The PW-9's top speed in initial testing was 167 miles per hour (267.2kph). This and many other characteristics secured the PW-9's future as a military pursuit plane: with its larger engine, the PW-9's guns could be mounted in a better location than on the MB-3, one that was more convenient and that simplified

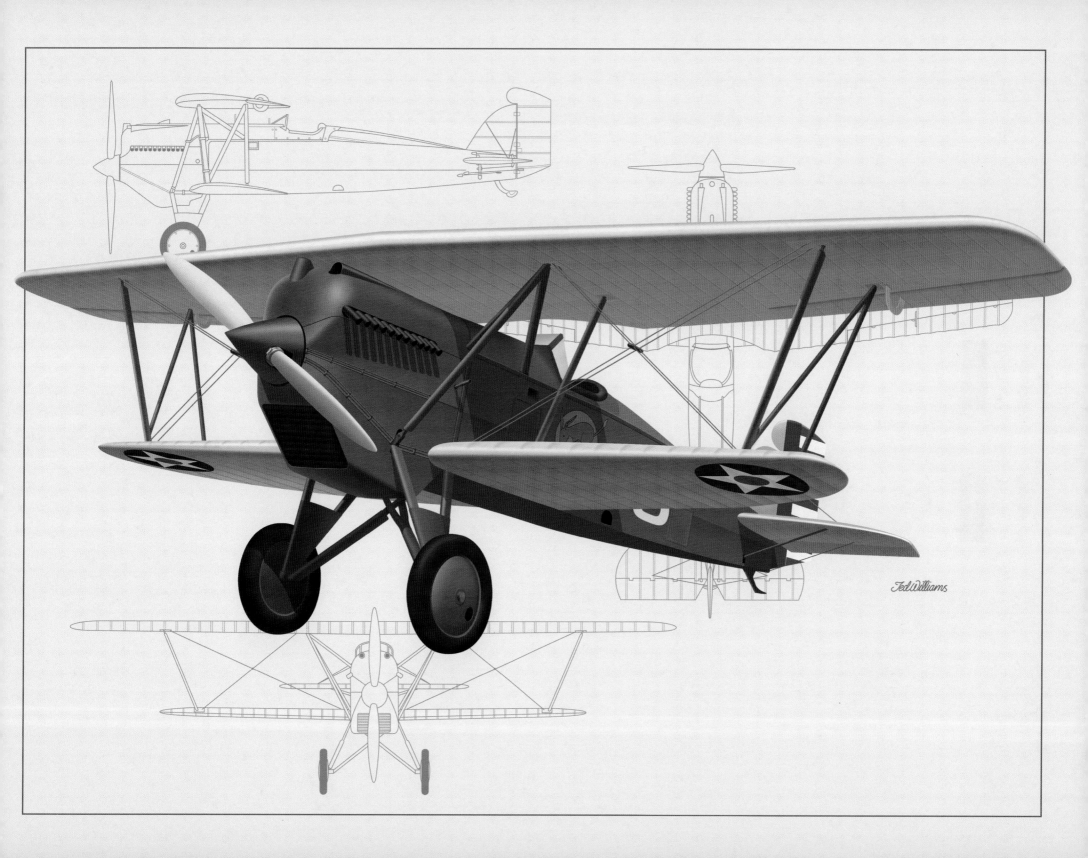

Ted Williams

Boeing PW-9C Specifications

Type: Single-seat fighter
Power plant: One 435-horsepower, Curtiss D-12, water-cooled inline engine
Performance: Maximum speed, 159 miles per hour (256kph); service ceiling, 18,925 feet (5,768m); maximum range, 390 miles (628km)
Weight: Empty, 1,936 pounds (879kg); maximum takeoff weight, 3,120 pounds (1,416kg)
Dimensions: Span, 32 feet (9.8m); length, 23 feet 1 inch (7m); height, 8 feet 8 inches (2.6m); wing area, 260 square feet (23.9m^2)
Armament: One .30-caliber and one .50-caliber machine gun

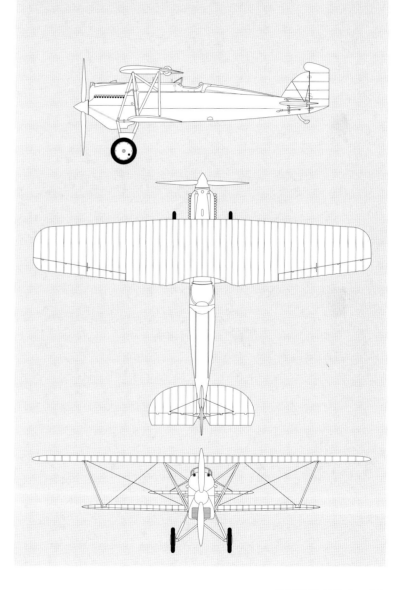

maintenance; it was easier, overall, to maintain mechanically; and the sleek nose dove through the slipstream more aerodynamically than previous pursuit designs. For the most part, it proved to be more maneuverable than its closest competitor, the Curtiss PW-8. There was one drawback with the water-cooled engine, however: locating the radiator underneath the engine and behind the nose, although superior from an engineering standpoint, made the plane vulnerable to ground fire. Radiator placement would continue to be a design challenge through World War II.

The PW-9 carried the standard armament of the day. On it could be mounted two .30-caliber Browning forward-firing machine guns, or the more typical .30-/.50-caliber configuration. It could also carry two 122-pound (55kg) bombs. Like the MB-3A, the PW-9 employed an interrupter gear to ensure that the guns would not fire when a propeller blade was aligned with either muzzle. Although this was an ideal solution to prevent a fighter pilot from shooting his own propeller, it greatly reduced each gun's rate of fire.

The Navy version, the FB program, is most notable for its use in carrier landing testing on the USS *Langley*, the first U.S. aircraft carrier. The FB-2 sported an experimental arresting hook for testing purposes. Later, once proven as a competent carrier aircraft, the FB-5 served on the USS *Lexington*.

Throughout its career, the PW-9 underwent several major design improvements—the A, B, C, D, and an E (which was never produced thanks to a new, more advanced Boeing design). Boeing records indicate that 157 Army PW-9s and Navy FB models, including seven additional Navy training planes, were built between 1923 and 1928—all in all, a successful run for the plane.

Curtiss P-6E Hawk

Although the Curtiss PW-8 is inextricably linked with Boeing's PW-9, Curtiss seized the spotlight with its P-6E Hawk. Ultimately, the Curtiss-Boeing rivalry wouldn't end with the PWs: the two manufacturers would supply the Army and Navy with many frontline pursuit aircraft throughout the years between the world wars, competing intensely at every step of the way for government contracts.

While Boeing's PW-9 outperformed the Curtiss PW-8 militarily, the Curtiss model had it own virtues. To its credit, the PW-8 had flown well in air races, and on June 23, 1924, Lieutenant Russell L. Maughan flew a PW-8 coast to coast in his celebrated "dusk to dawn" flight.

Boeing's initial success with the PW-9 can be attributed to the plane's cleverly tapered wings. At the Army's request, Curtiss redesigned its PW-8 to accommodate tapered wings, similar to the ones already on the PW-9. The modification was successful. In 1925, this new airplane was renamed the Curtiss P-1 Hawk—the grandfather of one of the most famous series of biplane fighters. It was also the first Army pursuit ship to use the designation "P" to indicate *pursuit*, initiating the standard categorical military markings still in use today (though the categories have changed to represent modern specifications).

The Curtiss Hawk airframe was used to test many emerging ideas. After multiple prototypes and variants of the P-1, the P-6E Hawk was completed in 1931. Originally known as Y1P-22, it was redesignated P-6E because of its similarity to the P-6 series of airplanes. The P-6E quickly became the most renowned model in the Curtiss Hawk biplane family, thanks in part to the striking "snow owl" paint job of the 17th Pursuit Squadron, 1st Pursuit Group, based at Selfridge Field in Michigan.

The P-6E was a perfect evolution of design and a case study in technological advancement. It was built around the large Curtiss V-1570 Conqueror engine, the successor to the D-12. It was a powerful, yet hot-running engine with 600 horsepower. Because radiator placement was known to affect aerodynamics, the Army, with the help of Union Carbide, invented Prestone. By using this ethylene glycol mixture, Curtiss was able to design the P-6E with a much smaller radiator, greatly reducing its surface area. Less liquid was needed because Prestone was much more effective at cooling than ordinary water.

Maximum speed was 193 miles per hour (311kph) for the P-6E, although a prototype with a higher-compression engine could fly at more than 200 miles per hour (322kph), reaching a record-breaking 204 miles per hour (328kph).

ABOVE: The Curtiss P-6 fuselage assembly was fitted with two flare tubes just aft of the cockpit. These tubes would be used to launch flares over a ground battle. Flares were used both as a distraction to the enemy and as a rudimentary method of communication, since no form of wireless communication between the pilot and the command unit on the ground was yet available.

OPPOSITE: In the "snow owl" paint scheme of the 17th Pursuit Squadron, the Curtiss P-6E is considered by many aviation enthusiasts as the prettiest of all the Army fighters of the biplane era.

The consensus was that the P-6E was very quick, but not maneuverable enough for combat, which, luckily, the P-6E never saw.

The P-6E included a drop tank. This extra fuel tank could be attached to the underside of the fuselage before long flights to offer the pilot greater range. The tank could be jettisoned, if the immediate need for speed arose, or eliminated (not attached) altogether for short-range flights or if weight was an issue.

The P-6E was outfitted with a dynamic tailwheel that could be steered 30 degrees to the right or left, and it could spin 360 degrees if released—a marked improvement over the tailskid typically used at the time. Plus, the P-6E offered the pilot toe-operated wheel brakes, which soon became standard on all aircraft in use throughout the Army Air Corps.

Another innovation—the drag-resistant, single-strut landing gear—was an outstanding feature on the P-6E; however, the gear employed inadequate oleo hydraulic struts. One key complaint about the P-6E relates directly to these struts. The shock absorption offered by each oleo was insufficient, especially on the uneven surface of a grass landing strip. Low-pressure tires, balloon-like in appearance, were used to provide additional cushioning against the load placed on the oleo struts during landing.

The P-6E was equipped with the standard Army armament, typically carrying two .30-caliber Browning machine guns. A-3 bomb racks could be mounted onto the P-6E for a payload of 244 pounds (111kg). Later, some P-6Es were refitted with two .30-caliber Browning machine guns on the top

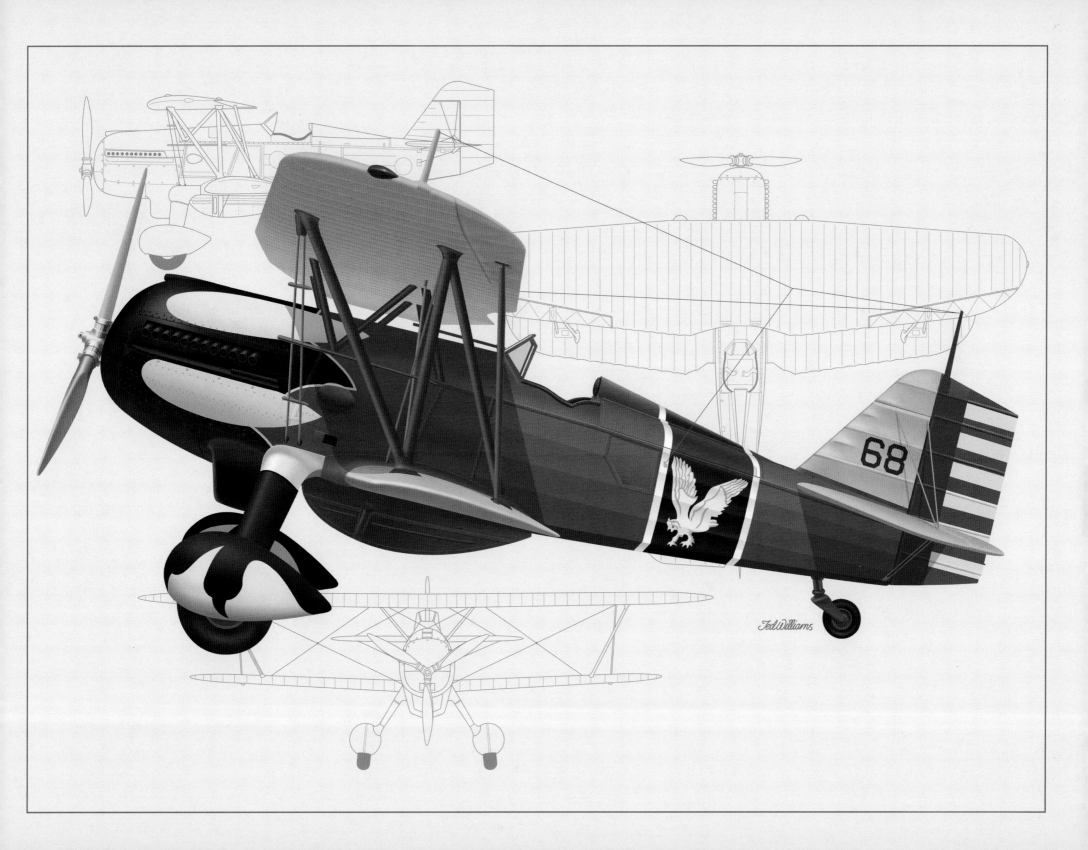

Ted Williams

and bottom wing. All four guns were placed so that their muzzles fired outside the propeller's arc—a logical solution that nonetheless proved inefficient. The new system precluded the need for an interrupting, synchronized firing system, but it required a complex charging apparatus and accuracy was not guaranteed. Still constructed of wood fitted onto a steel-tube airframe, the wings had a tendency to bounce, foiling even the best marksmen.

The P-6E has the distinction of being the last biplane purchased and flown by the Army Air Corps. The monoplane was already taking over the draftsman's table and, soon, the skies. Only forty-six original P-6E Hawks were built. During its five-year service period, from 1932 to 1937, the Depression was at its height and funds were scarce. The P-6Es served with the 1st and 8th Pursuit Groups and were flown by the 17th, 94th, and 33rd Squadrons, located at Selfridge Field, Michigan, and Langley Field, Virginia.

The Curtiss P-6E Hawk had reached the pinnacle of what a fabric-covered biplane should and could be. For many, the Curtis P-6E is a favorite biplane from this era, its pizzazz being the primary attraction. Perhaps because so few were built, the P-6E retains an aura of preciousness. Or, perhaps the Hawk image stands as an enduring symbol of early aviation, when planes were still birdlike, with seemingly fragile, flexible construction. Today, only one original P-6E still exists. It is on display at the U.S. Air Force Museum in Dayton, Ohio.

OPPOSITE: A Curtiss P-6E being fitted with a .50-caliber machine gun. Considerably larger than the .30-caliber, the .50-caliber machine gun is extremely long, measuring nearly six feet (1.8m) from breech plate to muzzle.

BELOW: In an early attempt to reduce the parasite drag that could result from a bulky fuselage placement of the radiator, this prototype XP-6A, with its constant-chord (non-tapered) wing, has brass tube radiators located on the top of the wing surfaces, conforming to the airfoil shape of both wings.

Curtiss P-6E Specifications

Type: Single-seat fighter
Power plant: One 700-horsepower Curtiss V-1570-23 12-cylinder Vee liquid-cooled engine
Performance: Maximum speed, 198 miles per hour (319kph); service ceiling, 24,700 feet (7,529m); maximum range, 285 miles (459km)
Weight: Empty, 2,715 pounds (1,233kg); maximum takeoff weight, 3,436 pounds (1,560kg)
Dimensions: Span, 31 feet 6 inches (9.6m); length, 23 feet 2 inches (7.1m); height, 8 feet 10 inches (2.7m); wing area, 252 square feet (23.2m^2)
Armament: Two .30-caliber machine guns

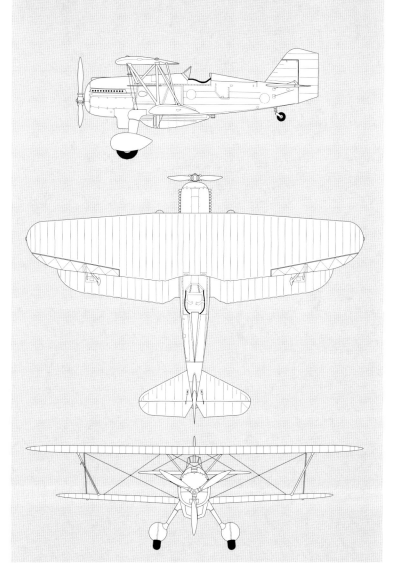

Curtiss F11C

In 1934, the U.S. Navy began operating a fleet of Curtiss F11Cs, specified for multiple purposes. The F11C was the first Curtiss-designed combination fighting and bombing aircraft, and the last Curtiss Hawk to be built for the Navy.

The Curtiss firm had already made significant inroads selling its product to the U.S. Army Air Corps. Glenn Curtiss, the name and force behind the company, had been involved in aviation since 1904. Passionate about the future of manned flight, Curtiss had been just as busy as the Wright brothers trying to develop his own flying machine, often leading to confrontation and legal disputes with the Ohio duo.

Curtiss' early commercial successes with the Golden Flyer and the JN "Jenny" grew into an aviation empire. Although Glenn Curtiss died in 1930, successful business enterprises and mergers organized after his death—including an unlikely alliance with the Wright Aeronautical Corporation—ensured that the acclaimed, pioneering Curtiss and Wright legacies were prolific well into World War II.

For the F11C, the U.S. Navy requested that Curtiss design a Hawk similar to the P-6E, but *navalized*—that is, suitable for the Navy. Since the conclusion of World War I, the Navy had developed its own specific set of aircraft requirements for naval operations. Of primary importance, all Navy airplanes needed to be designed to endure the rigors of carrier landings. Also, unlike the Army Air Corps, the Navy used its fighters as dual fighter-bombers for dive-bombing operations. As a result, the airframe needed to be strengthened to withstand extreme dive forces, and it needed to be fortified to carry external ordnance.

Furthermore, although liquid-cooled engines powered most Army aircraft, the Navy preferred air-cooled engines. This preference led to a precedent that would last until the emergence of the jet age. Army proponents of the liquid-cooled engine touted its inline, streamlined shape, which allowed for a sleek aerodynamic frontal area. While the Navy conceded that it was giving up a degree of performance, the radial offered several features that pleased the Navy. Foremost, radial engines were easier to support than liquid-cooled engines because radial engines have fewer parts, an important consideration when maintenance and supply occurs on a carrier in the middle of the ocean. Plus, the liquid-cooling system, an obstacle for engineers and maintenance crew alike, was eliminated with an air-cooled radial.

VB-3

OPPOSITE: The U.S. Navy required its pursuit ships to perform double duty as fighter/bombers. Because of the nature of fleet operations, naval aircraft required a stronger airframe, tougher landing gear, and a beefed-up fuselage to mount the arresting gear. This F11C carries the markings of Bombing Three (VB-3). The white tail indicates service aboard the USS *Saratoga*.

Curtiss presented the Navy with two single-seat prototypes. These experimental prototypes were designated the XF11C-1 and the XF11C-2. The XF11C-1 had an all-metal airframe, wings, and tail. It was powered by a two-row radial Wright R-1510-98, 600-horsepower engine with a three-bladed propeller. The XF11C-2 had a more traditional, fabric-covered, steel-tube fuselage and wooden wing assembly. It was powered by a slightly bigger engine, a single-row Wright R-1820-78 Cyclone with 700 horsepower and a two-bladed propeller.

After deliberation, the Navy chose the XF11C-2 for production. All twenty-eight of the F11C-2s ordered from Curtiss were ready for duty by May 1933. These F11Cs found their place with the men of the VF-1B fighter squadron, the "High Hat" squadron, stationed on the USS *Saratoga*.

The navalizing of the F11C included the addition of several special design features. Underneath the fuselage, an arresting hook was mounted just aft of the cockpit, with the hook extending to the tailwheel. Since the arresting hook absorbed all the G forces from the typically hostile and jarring carrier landing, the airframe had to be reinforced at the spot where the arresting hook was attached, so as not to unduly stress the airframe. The non-navalized P-6E's airframe, by comparison, could not withstand the rigors of constant carrier-based landing. The F11C also had a reinforced suspension and hard rubber tires, as opposed to the balloon tires on the P-6E. The harder tires were less likely to bounce along the unforgiving carrier deck. Even with its naval modifications, the F11C could still land successfully on grass.

The "Goshawks," as they were named to reflect their Hawk lineage, flew as F11Cs for less than one year. The Navy officially reclassified all F11C Goshawk pursuit planes as attack aircraft in March 1934. These attack aircraft were responsible for both bombing and fighting, but bombing was the higher priority. To authenticate this new function, the F11C was renamed the BFC-2. The majority of the F11C's service life was spent as a BFC-2 (Bombing, Fighting, Curtiss, second model), yet the F11C was the first plane to prove that a fighter could indeed serve as an all-around, first-line, carrier-based attack aircraft. The squadron numbers and associations of the men who flew the BFC-2s would also change to better represent their new attacking, bombing, and fighting assignments.

The F11C, and later BFCs, carried two .30-caliber Browning machine guns. The F11C could carry a 50-gallon (19L) drop tank, which could be

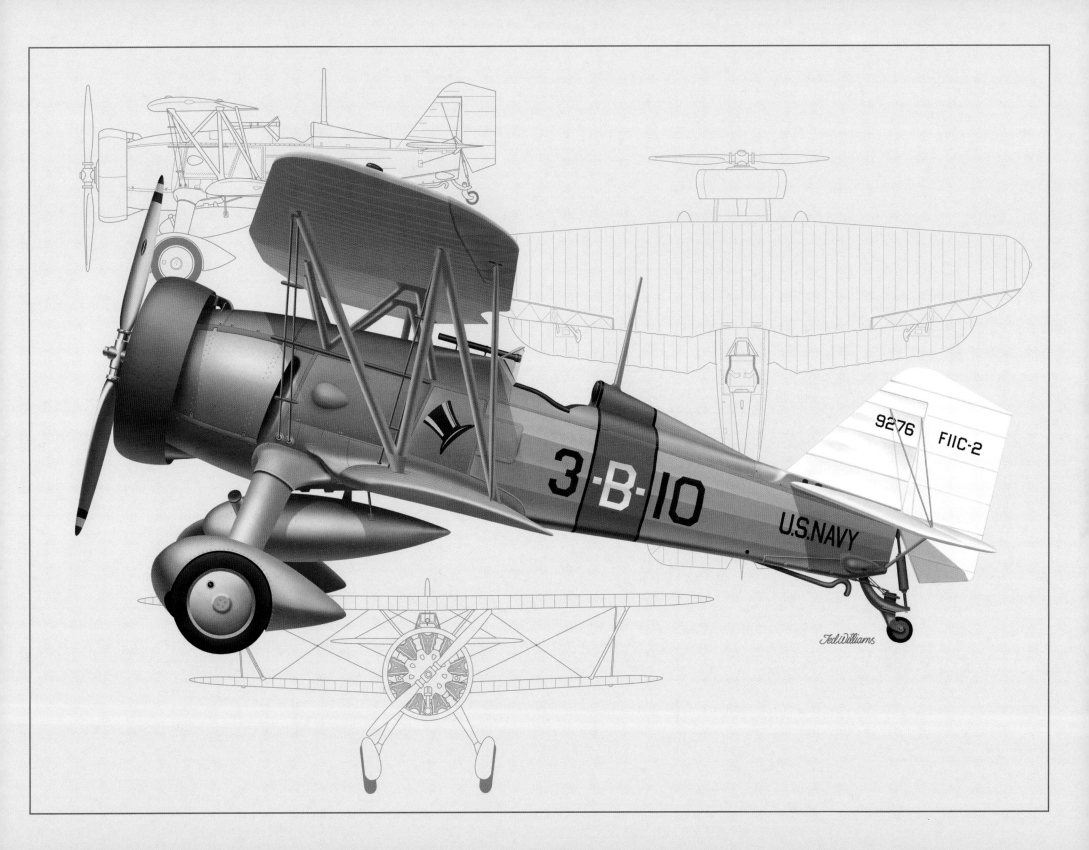

Curtiss F11C-2 Specifications

Type: Single-seat fighter
Power plant: One 600-horsepower Wright R-1510-98 engine
Performance: Maximum speed, 202 miles per hour (325kph); service ceiling 23,800 feet (7,254m)
Weight: Empty, 3,037 pounds (1379kg); maximum takeoff weight, 4,132 pounds (1,876kg)
Dimensions: Span, 31 feet 6 inches (9.6m); length, 23 feet 1 inch (7m); height, 10 feet 6 inches (3.2m); wing area, 262 square feet (24.1m^2)
Armament: Two .30-caliber machine guns

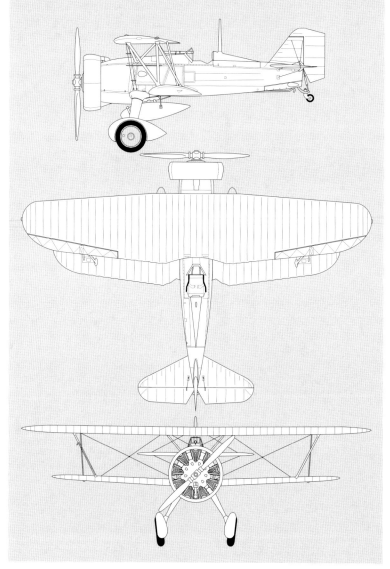

exchanged for a 500-pound (227kg) bomb suitable for dive-bombing, and had a maximum speed of 202 miles per hour (325kph). Improvements to later models increased its speed another twenty miles per hour (32kph). The BF2C-1 featured a manual retractable undercarriage.

In service until 1938, the Goshawk was withdrawn from active status when problems were discovered with the innovative landing gear. Known primarily for its short-lived career during the transitional period from the last biplanes to the first monoplanes, the F11C performed a very important function. It paved the way for developments to the naval carrier–based light attack planes of the future, and it did it in style. The 1930s were colorful years for naval aviation, and the Goshawk was no exception. All Navy aircraft were color-coded: cowls, wings, and tails were painted to identify their squadron and carrier. Many squadrons adopted unique graphics that would capture the imagination of aviation enthusiasts and leave a memorable imprint on history.

ABOVE: This Curtiss F11C-2 has underwing hardpoints for the attachment of bombs. Even as early as the 1920s, the Navy used its pursuit aircraft as both fighters and bombers.

OPPOSITE: A U.S. Navy XF11C-2 for evaluation. During testing its arresting gear placement was deemed unacceptable. Later variants incorporated a redesigned tailwheel that was located further aft, this allowed the hook to snag the deck wire at a better angle during landing. The redesigned wheel also provided better shock absorption.

Boeing P-12

Regarded as a classic in every way, the Boeing P-12 reached the pinnacle of pursuit biplane evolution. Quick, responsive, and a dream to fly, this acclaimed design from Boeing was the crème de la crème of flying machines, favored by the silk-scarf-and-goggles set of the late 1920s and early 1930s.

After establishing itself with the MB3-A, the Boeing Airplane Company was awarded the contract to provide the Army Air Corps with the Boeing-designed PW-9, cementing its relationship with the military as a quality supplier of superior aircraft. Headed by Bill Boeing, a savvy businessman educated at Yale, the Seattle-based company literally grew up alongside the aviation industry. First founded in 1916 as the Pacific Aero Products Company, the company quickly became the Boeing Airplane Company after Boeing's partner, Naval Commander Conrad Westervelt, was assigned to a new post away from Washington State and the company's business dealings in Seattle.

In the early days, Boeing established a toehold in the aviation industry by building and flying aircraft designed for delivering mail, as well as by building seaplanes and trainers for the Navy. However, Boeing truly made its mark in the 1930s when it designed some of the best military fighter aircraft available at the time. And it was while developing these revolutionary fighter designs that Boeing pioneered innovative manufacturing methods and new devices that would eventually change the entire industry.

So it was not unexpected that the U.S. military looked to Boeing to develop the next pursuit fighter for its evolving air fleets. Anticipating the military's needs, Boeing was ready with a concept it had developed as a private venture. Earlier, Boeing had designed the F2B and F3B to Navy specifications for carrier-based use. Boeing tapped into this experience when crafting its new plane. The manufacturer was certain it could develop a new lighter-weight pursuit plane that could top all others being developed by other companies. They were so certain that they could sell this new design, Boeing self-funded the development of two prototypes. Known as Model 83 and Model 89—descendants of the PW-9/FB series—each prototype possessed attributes that would appeal to both the Army and Navy. And with the company's PW-9 production coming to an end, it was smart business for Boeing to have something new ready to demonstrate to the military. This program was to yield the last biplane created by Boeing before the monoplane overtook the aviation industry.

With its last biplane design, the company took the standard biplane layout as far as it could go. While the prototype wings were still constructed out of

6th Pursuit Squadron

OPPOSITE: This Boeing P-12C displays the colorful markings of the 6th Pursuit Squadron. The P-12 may have epitomized the golden age of pursuit aircraft from the 1920s and 30s, but the biplane layout was soon obsolete. The lack of government spending brought on by the Depression, however, allowed the P-12 to serve as a frontline fighter well into the thirties.

fabric-covered wood, the central skeleton was surprisingly modern. Instead of utilizing a welded steel-tube construction throughout, the fuselage framework aft of the cockpit was bolted together. Bolting the fuselage provided additional flexibility and strength. The entire fuselage was still covered in fabric, making it the last of the "rag bags," although that, too, was soon to change.

The ailerons were made of corrugated duralumin sheeting. Like the ailerons, the tail surfaces were covered in a corrugated metal. Advances in alloys were making aluminum a viable material for use in aviation. Metallurgists had developed effective manufacturing processes to blend aluminum with other metals to obtain a malleable yet durable substance for airplane construction and covering. A Pratt & Whitney Wasp radial, R-1340B, powered both models.

Models 83 and 89 were indistinguishable except for their landing gear. Model 83 had a spreader bar landing assembly and an arresting hook, while Model 89 was built with a split-axle landing arrangement to make room for a 500-pound (227kg) bomb. Each of the prototypes could be outfitted with underwing bombs and an auxiliary tank for an additional fifty-five gallons (208L) of fuel.

Armament was situated in the nose. Typical of the dogfighting strategy of the era, the guns were synchronized to fire through the propeller's arc. As usual, either two .30-caliber or one .30- and one .50-caliber machine gun could be mounted.

After successful testing by the Navy in June 1928, both prototypes were purchased. Soon after, the Army also approved the design for future production and acquisition. After removing all unnecessary Navy equipment, the Army dubbed its version the P-12. The Army's quick decision to adopt the P-12 was quite astounding, considering its preference for liquid-cooled engines.

Once designated P-12, the Army's version developed independently from the Navy's program. The P-12 went through several variants to correct minor flaws and incorporate new technology. The most noteworthy variant is the P-12C. The P-12C covered its new, more powerful Pratt & Whitney R-1340-9 with a NACA-inspired Townend cowl to more efficiently cool the radial engine and offer better aerodynamic performance. The P-12 also pioneered the use of frise ailerons to minimize drag along the wing.

The P-12 evolved into a B, C, D, E, and F variant. Over the course of this unique dual program, Boeing produced 365 P-12s for the Army.

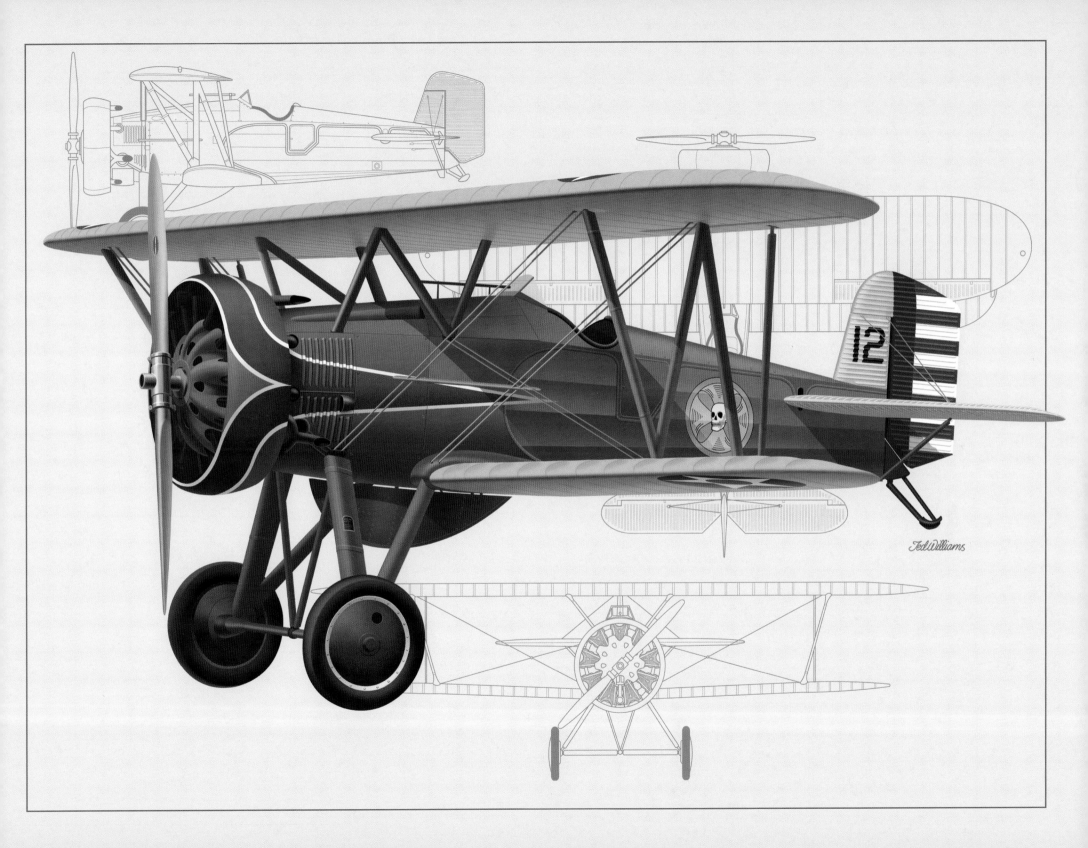

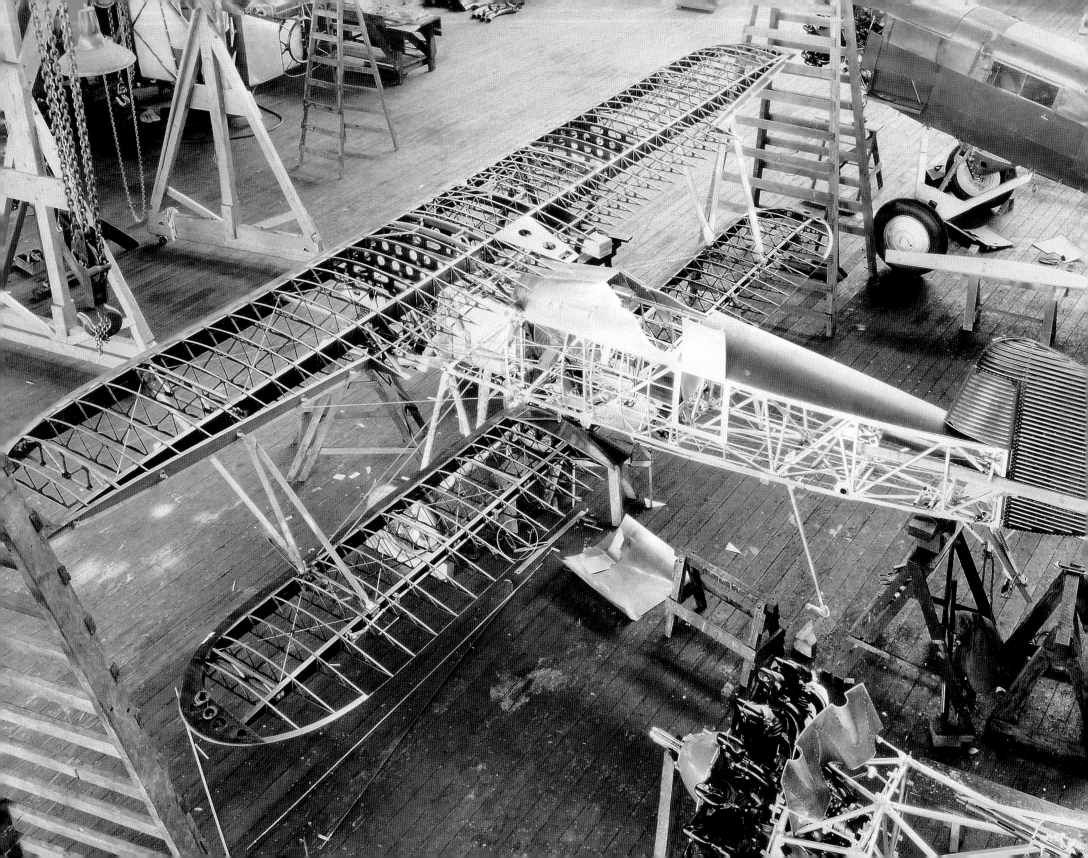

OPPOSITE: Note the construction details of this prototype for the P-12/F4B series, such as the corrugated metal covering on the empennage. A Boeing Model 40 short-range mail and passenger transport fuselage sits next to the bare bones of the fighter.

LEFT TOP: This P-12D has its guns installed. The opening of the ejection chute for the spent round casings is located in the side of the fuselage.

LEFT BOTTOM: Compared to today's modern jets, the P-12's instrument panel was quite spartan. On the pilot's left is a fuel tank selector. This switch could be manually dialed to activate the desired fuel source; in this case, either the main, auxiliary, or reserve tank.

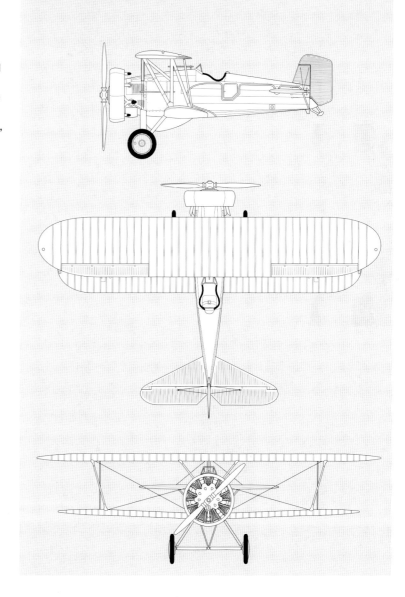

Boeing P-12C Specifications

Type: Single-seat fighter
Power plant: One 450-horsepower Pratt & Whitney R-1340-9 air-cooled radial engine
Performance: Maximum speed, 178 miles per hour (286kph) at 8,000 feet (2,438m); service ceiling, 26,200 feet (7,986m); maximum range, 675 miles (1,086km)
Weight: Empty, 1,941 pounds (881kg); maximum takeoff weight, 2,690 pounds (1,221kg)
Dimensions: Span, 30 feet (9.1m); length, 20 feet 1 inch (6.1m); height, 9 feet 9 inches (3m); wing area, 227.5 square feet (20.9m^2)
Armament: Two .30-caliber machine guns

Boeing F4B

After initial development and design evaluation, the Naval companion to the Army's P-12, the F4B, evolved into an entirely navalized aircraft, becoming one of the most notable Navy aircraft of the interwar era.

The F4B, a single-seat biplane, was a successful naval carrier aircraft for multiple reasons. For one, it offered good visibility. Because of the way the front fuselage tapered toward the engine, the cockpit provided the pilot with a clear line of sight, which was crucial for carrier landings. Accounting for naval preferences, the F4B had provisions for an optical gun sight. Furthermore, the demands of carrier operations dictated the F4B's development and construction: an arresting hook and a structurally reinforced undercarriage distinguish a Navy F4B from an Army P-12.

The first production model, the F4B-1, flew in May 1929. Developed from the original self-funded Boeing prototypes, twenty-seven models were ordered with a split landing gear, like the kind used on the Model 89. The landing gear configuration was split so it could accommodate a bomb between the aircraft's wheels—an important design distinction, since the Navy used its fighting aircraft for pursuit and dive-bombing. The first F4B-1s served on board the USS *Lexington* and the USS *Langley*, two of the Navy's first aircraft carriers. Later, existing F4B-1s were modified with innovations from later variants and served as Navy trainers.

The next modification, the F4B-2, favored the Model 83's pivoting cross-axle landing gear with "V" struts and bracing. This version incorporated a swiveling tailwheel and provisions for flotation, two beneficial features for a carrier-based aircraft. In all, forty-six F4B-2s were built and delivered by May 1931. This F4B closely resembled the P-12C, but the Navy's F4B-2 was built as a fighter-bomber. Unlike the P-12C, the F4B-2 had the capacity to carry 116 pounds (53kg) of external stores.

Having already modified the F4B twice, Boeing came to a design cross-roads. The company decided not to cover the next F4B variants with fabric. Instead, a semimonocoque covering made of duralumin paneling was used to significantly enhance aerodynamic performance and lengthen the service and maintenance life of each aircraft. Duralumin was already used to cover the control surfaces; using the material more extensively was a logical evolutionary progression. At first, engineers were concerned about the additional weight involved in replacing fabric with metal, but the all-metal F4Bs did not experience performance degradation as compared to their older fabric-covered

VF-6B

models. Other enhancements and design evolutions kept pace with airframe improvements, thereby negating any weight issues.

The F4B-3 served on the USS *Saratoga* before being reassigned to the Marine Corps. Besides the semimonocoque fuselage, it featured a turtledeck fairing aft of the cockpit. Twenty-one were built in all. The P-12E most closely followed the modifications made to the F4B-3.

Lastly, the F4B-4 ended the program. Sporting several modern innovations—like the all-metal fuselage, stronger wings, and a redesigned tail for increased stability—the F4B-4 became the flagship of the program. With ninety-two built, not only was the F4B-4 the most-produced variant in the program, it also came to embody the quality design and innovative spirit of 1930s pursuit aircraft design.

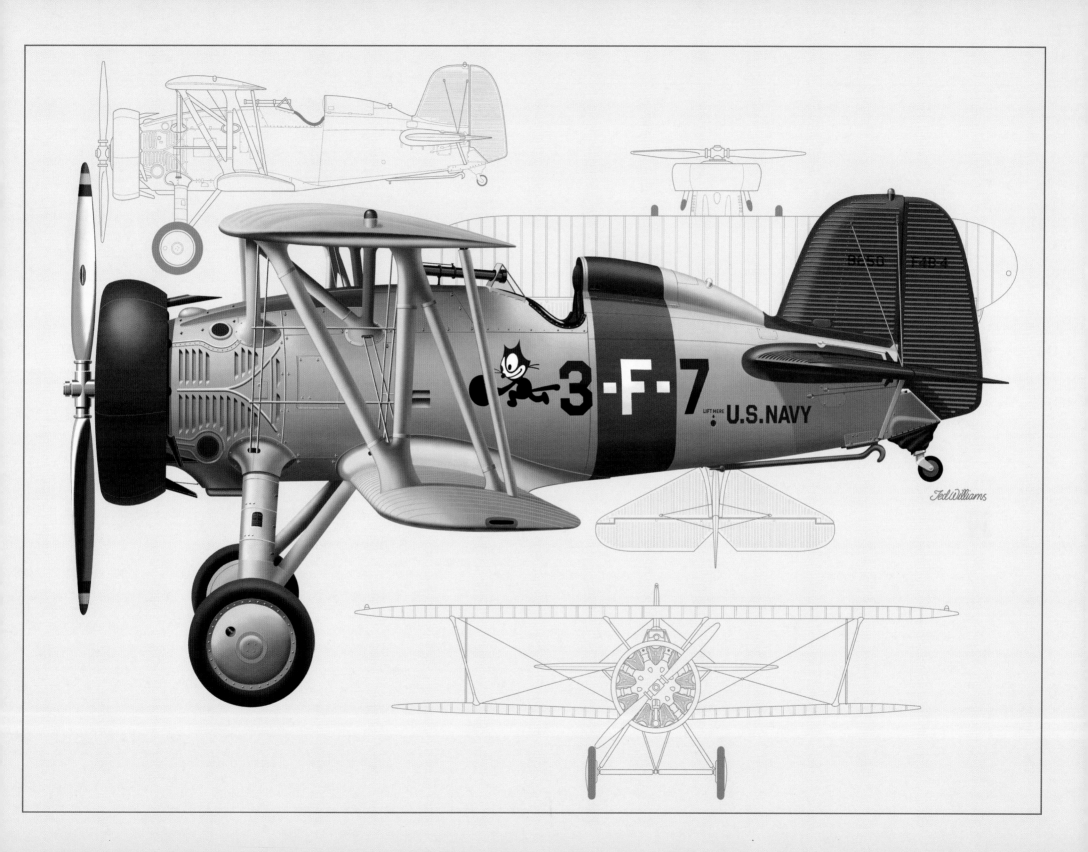

LEFT: An F4B-4 perches on a flight deck extension. These extensions were operated with a pulley system. Keeping the rear of the aircraft off the flight deck created more room on the deck, allowing flight operations to continue without the interference of parked aircraft.

RIGHT TOP: A corrugated tail assembly was used on all Boeing fighters of the time. The clean lines of this F4B-4's all-metal fuselage distinguish it from earlier fabric-covered P-12 and F4B variants.

RIGHT BOTTOM: Onlookers watch as a pilot performs his preflight walk-around. This Marine Corps Boeing F4B-3 is from Bombing Four. The vertical stabilizer bears the squadron's insignia, a flying red devil in a white diamond.

OPPOSITE: The cockpit of the F4B-4 was roomy compared to other aircraft of its day. This view of its interior clearly shows the simplicity of the biplane "stick and rudder" era.

Overall, Boeing produced 187 F4Bs for the Navy. Along with the P-12s made for the Army, 586 aircraft were produced before the program ended; the last F4B left the production line on the last day of February 1933.

The F4B and the P-12 had an amazingly long service life. F4Bs were still serving on American naval carriers as late as 1938, and in 1941, at the start of World War II, existing F4Bs and P-12s were used as radio-controlled drones. Boeing even exported aircraft based on this design to other nations—an uncommon practice at the time, since European-designed aircraft typically had the developmental edge.

The F4B and P-12 evolved from fabric covering and wooden wings to an all-metal semimonocoque construction. Boeing used smart marketing to analyze its buyers' needs, competently developing both a Navy and an Army version from the same basic airframe. It was only a matter of time before those same forward-looking engineers would overcome the inherent flaws built into every biplane design and perfect the monoplane. Soon, newer aircraft, like the Boeing P-26 Peashooter and other monoplanes, would take over the frontline duties, replacing the F4B and P-12 workhorses of the thirties. Sooner still, the warbirds of World War II would take to the skies to test the principles first put into practice by pioneering fighter aircraft like the F4B and P-12.

Boeing F4B-4 Specifications

Type: Single-seat fighter

Power plant: One 550-horsepower Pratt & Whitney R-1340-16 radial air-cooled engine

Performance: Maximum speed, 187 miles per hour (301kph) at 6,000 feet (1,829m); service ceiling, 27,500 feet (8,382m); maximum range, 734 miles (224km)

Weight: Empty, 2,185 pounds (992kg); maximum takeoff weight, 3,611 pounds (1,639kg)

Dimensions: Span, 30 feet (9.1m); length, 20 feet 1 inch (6.1m); height, 9 feet 4 inches (2.8m); wing area, 227.5 square feet (20.9m^2)

Armament: One .30-caliber and one .50-caliber machine gun plus a 232-pound (105.3kg) bomb load

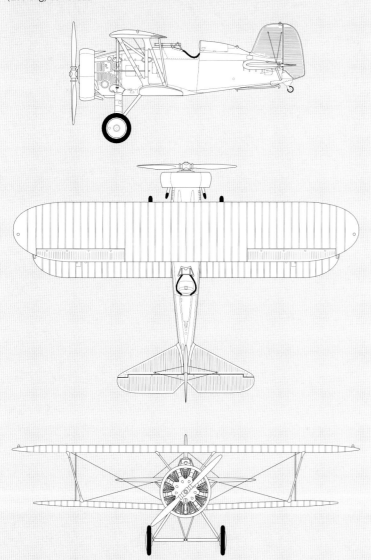

Grumman F3F

Supplying both the Army and Navy with most of the prominent pursuit aircraft designs of the interwar years, the Boeing and Curtiss companies, through their competition, had masterminded the evolutionary development of the American pursuit plane. And then came Leroy Grumman.

Shortly after the stock market crash of 1929, Leroy Grumman, known as Roy, gathered all his assets and the resources of several other financial backers to form the Grumman Aircraft Engineering Corporation of Long Island, New York. His dogged determination and genius would remain central to the spirit of a dynamic organization, one that would, in the future, develop designs for NASA and the U.S. space program.

Trained as a machinist by the military during World War I and educated as a mechanical engineer at Cornell University, Grumman gained practical business experience during his stint with the Loening Aircraft and Engineering Company. At the onset of his Grumman venture, several former Loening employees joined his new team. Leon "Jake" Swirbul, another Loening expatriate, was a perfect administrative foil to Grumman's keen creativity. Together they made Grumman a respected name in aviation.

Working, even growing, through the Depression, the Grumman company began its career building floats for the Navy and subcontracting assemblies for other airframe manufacturers. The first fighter design from the Grumman factory was the FF. Accepted by the Navy in 1931, the FF was soon followed by the F2F. In time, these designs became the basis for the paradoxical Grumman F3F—one of the most forward-looking, yet atavistic designs of the 1930s.

The Grumman F3F was an all-metal biplane with fabric-covered wooden wings. The fuselage's metal covering was flush-riveted to the metal formers. Inauspiciously, the first two F3F prototypes crashed, killing one test pilot and forcing another to "hit the silk." A third prototype flew without complications and was accepted by the Navy with only minor alterations—quite surprising, considering the prototypes' dismal track record.

Delivered to the Navy for carrier-based use in 1936, the F3F's wingspan and fuselage were slightly longer than those of the F2F, a modification that suppressed the spin tendencies exhibited by the first two ill-fated F3F prototypes. A massive 850-horsepower radial Wright engine, the XR-1820-22, powered the F3F-2. This monster power plant required a three-bladed propeller to distribute its torque. Coupled with the new breed of high-octane fuel, the F3F-2's maximum speed was an astounding 260 miles per hour (418kph).

6th Pursuit Squadron

RIGHT: A crew chief poses proudly with his "baby": a Grumman F3F-2 assigned for duty with a Marine Corps fighter squadron.

OPPOSITE: It's easy to see why the F3F acquired the nickname "Flying Barrel." With its last pursuit biplane design, Grumman introduced an all-metal monocoque construction. This new manufacturing method created an exceptionally strong, yet lightweight, fuselage, and its streamlined silhouette, in conjunction with retractable landing gear and an enclosed canopy, was a glimpse of innovations to come. The F3F-2 was the last biplane fighter purchased by the U.S. Navy. This aircraft, from Fighting Six (VF-6), was deployed aboard the USS *Enterprise*.

Further testing in the NACA wind tunnel at Langley Field helped Grumman engineers improve the airframe's aerodynamics, thereby increasing its overall performance. This testing led to a revised F3F-3.

As far back as 1931, Grumman had introduced its revolutionary enclosed cockpit and manually retractable landing gear, both firsts of their kind. Perfected in the F3F, the enclosed cockpit did more than protect the pilot from wind and weather. The sleek aerodynamic line of the fuselage aided performance. Moreover, when the pilot hand-cranked the landing gear into the hollowed-out scoops just behind the engine, the fuselage in flight became a slick, rounded shape.

Much like the radiator placement dilemma faced by the designer of any airframe powered by a liquid-cooled engine, the radial engine cowling had been a point of consternation for Grumman's aerodynamic engineers. The new pudgy shape created by the flush cowl design earned the planes from this series of Grumman fighters the nickname "Flying Barrels." In addition, the F3Fs fuselage was sealed. This meant that the aircraft could float, should it wind up in the water, a handy feature for a carrier-based airplane.

By 1939, all U.S. Navy and Marine Corps combat squadrons flew Grumman designs exclusively. All variants were equipped with the standard U.S. military armament: one .30-caliber and one .50-caliber Browning machine gun. These synchronized firing guns were mounted in the cowl. Two 116-pound (53kg) bombs completed the armament capabilities.

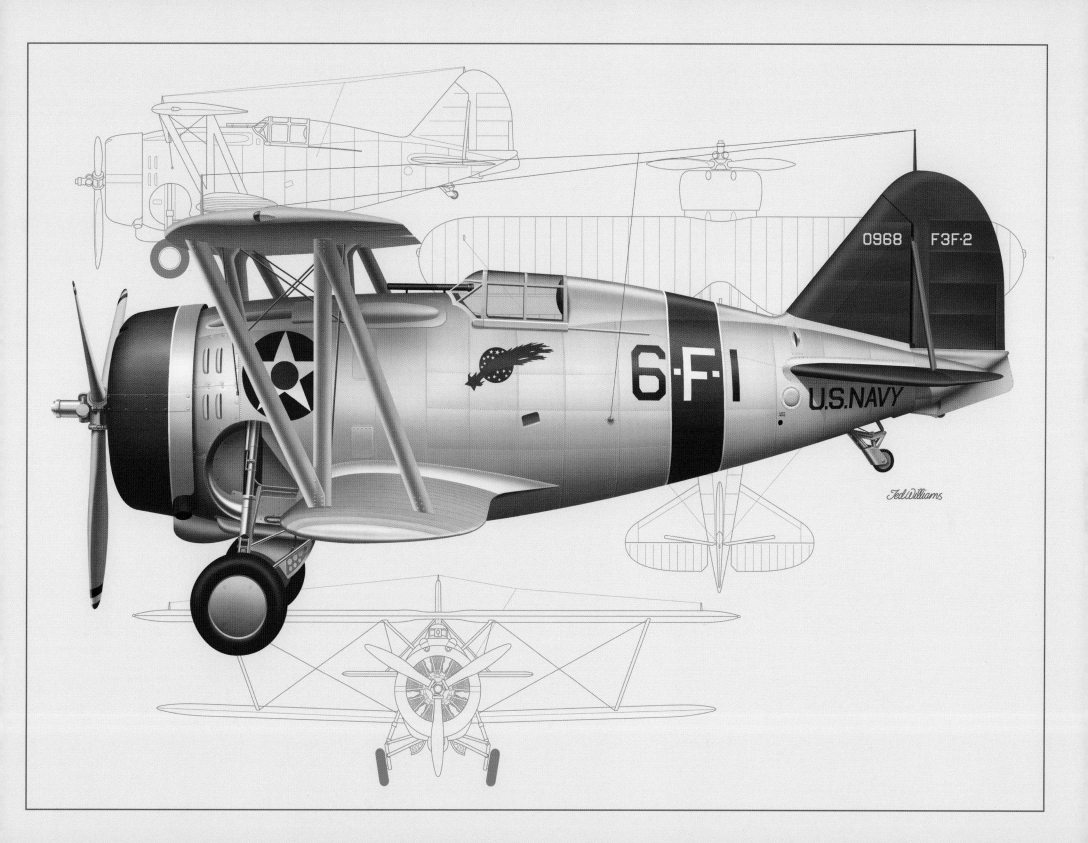

Grumman F3F-2 Specifications

Type: Single-seat fighter

Power plant: One 850-horsepower Pratt & Whitney R-1820-22 radial air-cooled engine

Performance: Maximum speed, 260 miles per hour (418kph) at 17,250 feet (5,258km); service ceiling, 32,000 feet (9,754m); maximum range, 975 miles (1,569km)

Weight: Empty, 3,254 pounds (1,477kg); maximum takeoff weight, 4,750 pounds (2,157kg)

Dimensions: Span, 32 feet (9.8m); length, 23 feet (7m); height, 9 feet 4 inches (2.8m); wing area, 260 square feet (23.9m^2)

Armament: Two .30-caliber machine guns

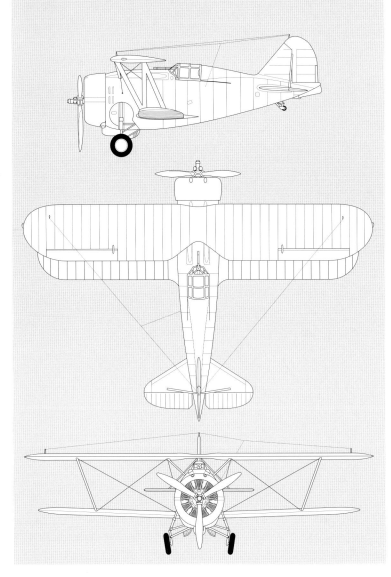

Three civilian planes were built from the F3F design. Two were built for the Gulf Refining Company, appropriately named Gulfhawks. One, the G-22 Gulfhawk, was flown by an aerobatic Navy pilot, Alford Williams, at air shows in the United States and abroad. A third, with two seats, was developed for use by the Grumman company.

The F3F was the last new biplane design assigned to active frontline duty with the Navy. Over the course of the program, 166 F3Fs were built. While it exhibited many new design ideas and handled better than all other in-service fighter aircraft available at the time, the F3F was still a biplane with fabric-covered wooden wings. The biplane structure was sturdy, stable, and a pilot's familiar friend, but emerging technologies and monoplane designs were eliminating the drag caused by the second wing and its bracing.

Despite the inevitability of the monoplane, the Navy continued to fly F3Fs until the advent of the F4F Wildcat, an all-metal monoplane representing another groundbreaking design from Grumman. The last of the Navy F3Fs were removed from active service in late 1943. World War II had brought American pilots face to face against the Japanese in the very effective, and modern, Zero. It was a case of progress or perish for American pursuit planes.

BELOW: Grumman F3F-1s line up in front of the Bendix pylon at the National Air Races in Cleveland, Ohio. These aircraft, which were designed for the Navy, are powered by the 650-horsepower Pratt & Whitney R-1535-84 engine.

OPPOSITE: F3F-2s await delivery to the Marine Corps inside the "Ironworks," the Grumman facility in Bethpage, Long Island.

Boeing P-26 Peashooter

With the Army's encouragement, Boeing developed its first pursuit mono-plane prototypes as self-funded projects, since it was the midst of the Depression and government spending was highly scrutinized. This pioneering strategy had proved successful with the Boeing P-12 and F4B, and, luckily, it would serve the company well again with the P-26 Peashooter. Between 1932 and 1934, the Army Air Corps purchased all the Boeing-developed P-26 proto-types (originally designated XP-936), and ordered a production run of 136 P-26A Peashooters. This was largest single order Boeing had received since the MB-3A in 1921.

The first XP-936 prototype was ready for testing on March 20, 1932. Two others soon followed. After a thorough assessment of all three prototypes, the Army Air Corps placed its significant order for the A variant, with slight modi-fications. The monoplane had arrived.

Named "Peashooter" because of the long, thin gun sight mounted atop the forward fuselage, the P-26's fuselage was semimonocoque, with partitions for strength and shape throughout its internal structure. Duralumin, an aluminum alloy, covered both the fuselage and the wings. This aluminum "skin" was flush-riveted to reduce surface drag. Also, as a precaution, the fittings were fashioned out of high-stress alloy steel. In addition, the low placement of the two-spar wings did not impair the pilot's visibility. This was an important distinction for the P-26, for poor visibility had been a common pilot complaint with earlier monoplane designs.

But not all of the P-26's design was so innovative. Boeing, sensitive to the Army's conservatism, retained several longstanding design elements. To appease the Army's fear of the unknown, the P-26 was intentionally designed without retractable landing gear or an enclosed canopy. And, because the Army did not yet trust cantilever wing technology, the mono-wing was designed to employ external wire bracing that was very similar to biplane construction. These decisions may have led to the P-26's quick adoption and prestigious position as the first all-metal pursuit monoplane, but, in the end, they shortened the spunky single-seater's service time and hastened its obsolescence.

Despite these inherent limitations, the P-26's performance was strong. It maneuvered as well as any biplane, reaching speeds of 234 miles per hour (504kph), much faster than the Boeing P-12. The Peashooter was also more cost-effective than the P-12. Unit cost per plane, not including the standard government-furnished equipment (radio, engine, and armament), was consider-

94th Pursuit Squadron

RIGHT: This Boeing P-26 has a gun camera installed on the wing. The black item mounted to the side of the fuselage, above the camera, is the vacuum tube for the instruments, and the pole-like object is the radio antenna. The P-26 was named the Peashooter because of its long, thin tubular gun sight (the circular rod mounted in front of the windshield). To improve marksmanship, pilots would sight along the tube, lining the target up with the end of the rod.

OPPOSITE: The P-26 Peashooter was the Army's first all-metal monoplane fighter, but it still incorporated a number of design elements from the older biplanes, such as an open cockpit, fixed gear, and external wing bracing. This colorful example bears the markings of the 94th Pursuit Squadron, 1st Pursuit Group.

ably less than the P-12. Furthermore, the P-26 would boast the best mainte-nance record of any Army Air Corps aircraft.

The P-26 Peashooter was powered by a 600-horsepower Pratt & Whitney R-1340-27 Wasp engine. A later model, the P-26B, gained additional power from fuel injection.

The P-26 design was flawed, however. Its main deficiency, discovered during prototype testing, was its narrow landing gear, which had a tendency to make the aircraft ground-loop and flip over on its back. Without a top wing, the pilot was left vulnerable. Numerous tragic accidents can be attributed to this flaw, and one in particular killed the pilot. As a result, a higher headrest was introduced to protect the pilot in a turnover situation. This tripod headrest prevented the pilot from being crushed by the weight of the airplane.

Also, the P-26's landing speed was quite fast at nearly 82 miles per hour (132kph). At the Army's request, Boeing added flaps to slow the final approach to a more manageable speed, approximately 73 miles per hour (117kph). These manually hand-cranked, underwing flaps were fitted on all P-26s.

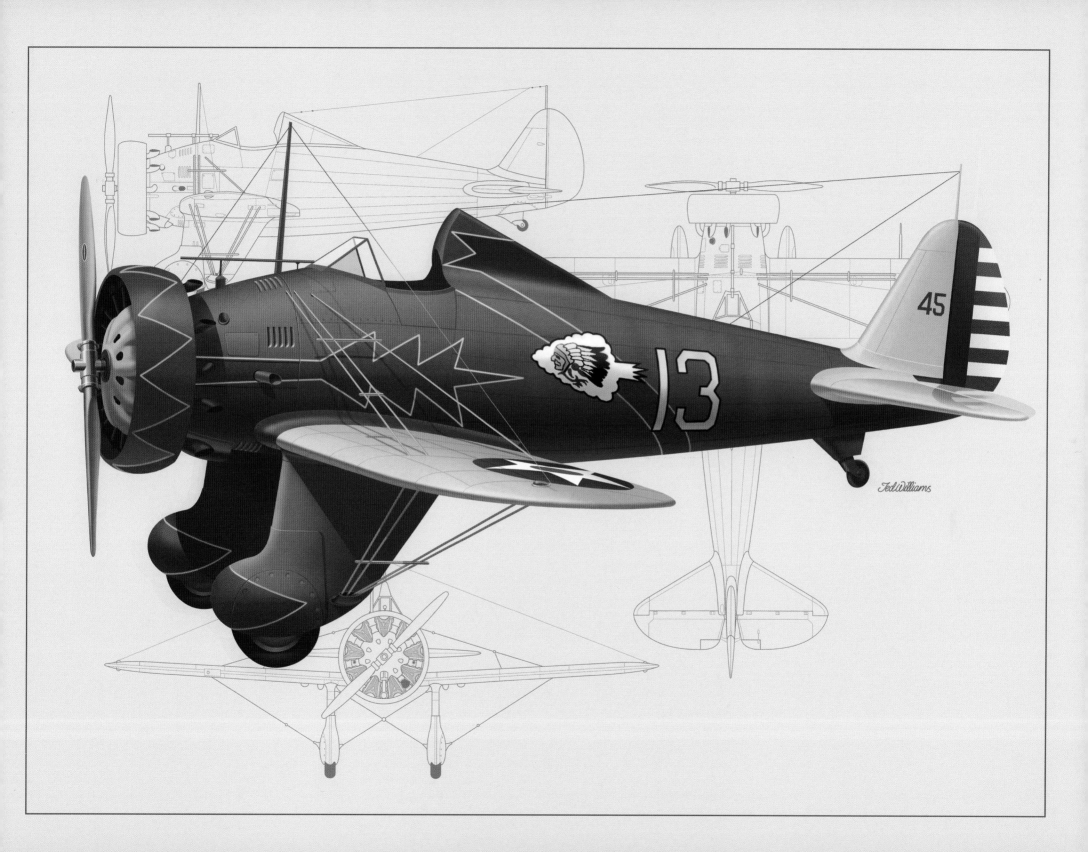

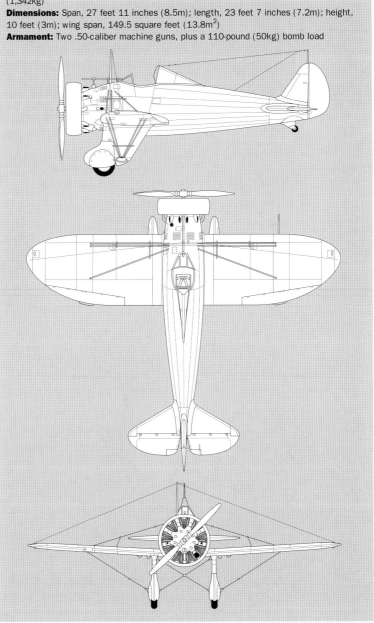

Boeing P-26A Peashooter Specifications

Type: Single-seat fighter

Power plant: One 600-horsepower Pratt & Whitney R-1340-27 radial air-cooled engine

Performance: Maximum speed, 235 miles per hour (378kph) at 7,500 feet (2,286m); service ceiling, 27,400 feet (8,352m); maximum range, 620 miles (998km)

Weight: Empty, 2,197 pounds (997kg); maximum takeoff weight, 2,955 pounds (1,342kg)

Dimensions: Span, 27 feet 11 inches (8.5m); length, 23 feet 7 inches (7.2m); height, 10 feet (3m); wing span, 149.5 square feet (13.8m^2)

Armament: Two .50-caliber machine guns, plus a 110-pound (50kg) bomb load

The P-26 was armed with either two forward-firing .30-caliber machine guns or one .30- and one .50-caliber gun, which were still equipped to fire through the propeller disc. The P-26 could accommodate two 120-pound (54kg) bombs or five 30-pound (14kg) practice bombs on a bomb rack mounted between the landing gear.

Model 281 was the export equivalent of the P-26. Ten 281s were purchased by China and one went to Spain. Although the domestic P-26 and its A, B, and C variants were in frontline service for five years, the exported versions were the only Peashooters used in combat. Ultimately pulled from service in 1940, the Peashooter was replaced by such newer planes as the Seversky P-35 and the Curtiss P-36. The Navy never purchased P-26s from Boeing and, in fact, did not adopt a monoplane design until the Brewster Buffalo in 1938.

With the reality of another war looming, fighter aircraft evolution picked up speed. The pursuit planes of World War II, seemingly lifetimes more advanced, can attribute much of their development to the Boeing P-26 Peashooter. With its many design firsts, most notably its mono-wing, the Peashooter is also an important last. It is the last Boeing-designed military pursuit plane of the twentieth century.

OPPOSITE: P-26 Peashooter fuselages in the process of being assembled at the Boeing facility.

RIGHT: One of the last surviving P-26As, owned by the "Planes of Fame" Air Museum in Chino, California, carries the markings of the 34th Pursuit Squadron. This former Guatemalan Air Force Peashooter was restored to flying condition by the Autonetics Division of North American Aviation in 1962.

BELOW: Five Air Corps pilots hold a last-minute briefing before climbing into their Peashooters for air-to-air publicity photos.

Consolidated PB-2A

The inspiration for change can come from the most unlikely places. In this case, parallel bomber plane development helped nudge the pursuit plane's evolutionary progression. Innovative new monoplane bombers like the Martin B-10 were capable of higher air speeds than any of the American fighter aircraft already in service with the military.

To "get up to speed," the Army circulated a request throughout the airplane manufacturing community. The Army specified its immediate need for a fast, all-metal, monoplane pursuit aircraft, explicitly stipulating a two-seat model. This unusual request led to the Army's endorsement of the Consolidated PB-2—the wrong airplane, but a quick fix at the right time.

Consolidated was founded in 1923 by the former vice president of Gallaudet Aircraft Corporation. Consolidated would earn its reputation building large flying boats in its modern facility in Buffalo, New York. The Thomas-Morse Aircraft Corporation, designers of the first American pursuit airplane, merged with Consolidated in 1929. Other mergers and acquisitions followed. Consolidated joined with the Hall Aluminum Aircraft Corporation in 1940 and Vultee Aircraft Incorporated in 1943 to form Consolidated Vultee Aircraft.

The PB-2 was Consolidated's only pursuit plane developed for the U.S. Army Air Corps. The company's talents were best put to use with large, multi-engined World War II bombers like the B-24 Liberator. Over the course of World War II, more than 21,000 B-24 designs were produced, making it the most-produced design of the entire war.

The PB-2's lineage takes many twists and turns. Its story starts at Lockheed. In 1931, Robert Wood, a prominent engineer with the Lockheed-Detroit Company, was actively designing a two-seat monoplane with cantilevered wings for military pursuit. It was based on the company's successful two-seater transport, the Altair, which had already received military attention because of its many inventive features. The Army bought the Wood-designed prototype for evaluation, designating it YP-24, but the contract to build more planes could not be fulfilled by the Lockheed-Detroit Company; it had gone bankrupt in the Depression.

Consolidated rescued what was to become the PB-2 by hiring Robert Wood. While employed by Consolidated, Wood developed the Y1P-25, the next generation of his YP-24. In 1933, Wood's Y1P-25 was still the only available fighter with speeds comparable to the Martin B-10. Unlike its Lockheed

36th Pursuit Squadron

predecessor, the Y1P-25 was constructed entirely of metal. This modification made the aircraft heavier, but the Y1P-25's top speed was an astounding 247 miles per hour (395.2kph), thanks to a 600-horsepower V-1570-27, 12-cylinder, liquid-cooled, Curtiss Conqueror engine and a specially mounted General Electric F-3 turbo-supercharger.

Still enamored with the idea of a two-seat monoplane, the Army purchased four Y1P-25s for further evaluation, while four additional models were ordered without superchargers. This second set was tested for viability as attack aircraft. Now designated P-30, Wood's two-seat pursuit ship with a cantilevered mono-wing was finally a reality, but by this point Wood was no longer employed by Consolidated. The P-30 was built in Consolidated's new West Coast factory. Sensing opportunity in western New York, Wood had chosen to remain in Buffalo, where he co-founded Bell Aircraft.

The P-30, now powered by an even more powerful 675-horsepower V-1710-57 Curtiss Conqueror, notably featured retractable, hand-cranked landing gear and an enclosed, partially heated cockpit. With a ceiling of 28,000 feet (8,534m), the enclosed cockpit was a necessity for the pilot and rear gunner. A rudimentary oxygen setup also supplied the crew with supplementary oxygen, required for any high-altitude operation.

The P-30 and its ancestors were designed around a cantilevered wing. The physically superior cantilevered wing design did not require any external bracing, thus instantly surpassed the Boeing P-26 Peashooter and its drag-inducing external supports.

In June 1934, the Army approved the purchase of fifty modified P-30As. The P-30A engine, a 700-horsepower V-1710-61 Curtiss, was even bigger, but it was still a satisfactory match with the originally intended GE turbo-supercharger. An electric, controllable-pitch Curtiss propeller replaced the fixed-pitch propellers on earlier models.

The P-30A was armed with two forward-firing .30-caliber machine guns, which were operated by the pilot. The rear gunner had a flexible .30-caliber machine gun. The two forward guns were governed by an antiquated World War I synchronized firing mechanism; the rear gun had an interrupter gear to prevent damage to the tail. Bomb capacity was one 170-pound (77kg) bomb.

The Army redesignated the P-30 and P-30A as PB-2 and PB-2A (Pursuit, Bi-place, second design) shortly after receiving its final shipment from Consolidated. Subsequently, the PB-2 series was the only bi-place (two-seat),

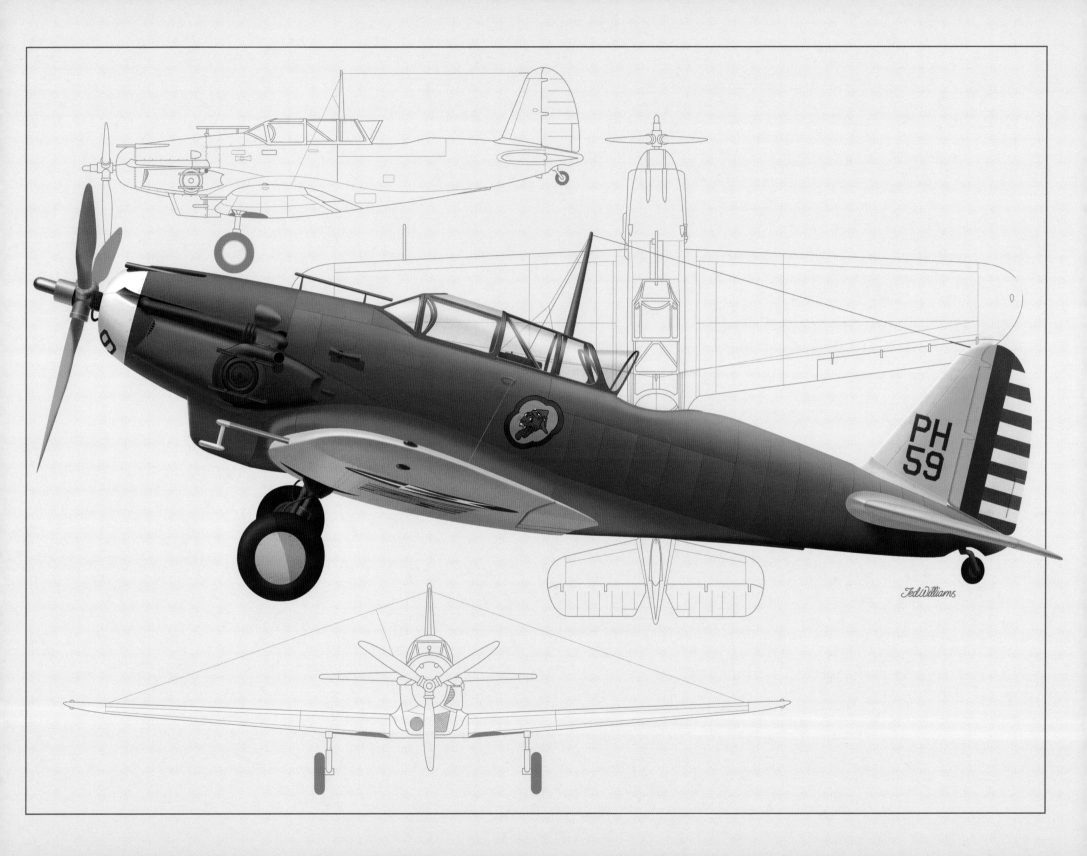

Ted Williams

LEFT: A ground crew outfitted in cold weather gear changes the engine on a PB-2A. Fighter aircraft maintenance was done outdoors year-round, in all weather conditions.

BELOW: A U.S. Army Consolidated PB-2A performs maneuvers over Muroc Dry Lake, California. The turbo-supercharger on the side of the fuselage required a large air intake, which was positioned under the nose.

single-engine pursuit monoplane series operated by the Army Air Corps. Yet despite its many niceties, the PB-2 possessed serious design flaws.

First, the rear gunner spent most of his time in the air blacked-out or nauseated. His location behind the aircraft's center of gravity, facing the tail, guaranteed unconsciousness during maneuvers exceeding five Gs. Adding insult to injury, when opened to operate the machine gun, the rear cockpit drew in noxious exhaust fumes.

In addition to all this discomfort, the added weight of the rear gunner and his machine gun caused the PB-2 and PB-2As to climb more slowly. Maneuverability was stunted as well. A special, single-seat model was developed in 1936, but met with a lukewarm reception. It failed to offer an appreciable performance gain and, in vying to replace the P-26, it was woefully unsuccessful.

Despite more than enough government dollars and numerous design modifications, the PB-2 was never truly a feasible pursuit aircraft for the Army Air Corps. The rear gunner's unpredictable lapses into unconsciousness were certainly unacceptable, especially in the kinds of combat situations for which the aircraft was designed. The Air Corps was finally forced to recognize the inherent ineffectiveness of its two-place pursuit ship ideal, a holdover from World War I thinking.

Consolidated PB-2A Specifications

Type: Two-seat fighter
Power plant: One 700-horsepower Curtiss V-1570-61 with GE F-3 turbo engine
Performance: Maximum speed, 214 miles per hour (344kph) at 15,000 feet (4,572m); service ceiling, 28,000 feet (8,534m); maximum range, 508 miles (817km)
Weight: Empty, 4,306 pounds (1,955kg); maximum takeoff weight, 5,643 pounds (2,562kg)
Dimensions: Span, 43 feet 11 inches (13.4m); length, 30 feet (9.14m); 297 square feet (27.3m^2)
Armament: Three .30-caliber machine guns

BELOW: The rear view of a Consolidated PB-2A, formally designated P-30, with its distinctive rear-facing cockpit for the second crewmember. The PB-2A had an incredibly long wingspan: its tapered, cantilevered wings were almost 44 feet (13.4m) long.

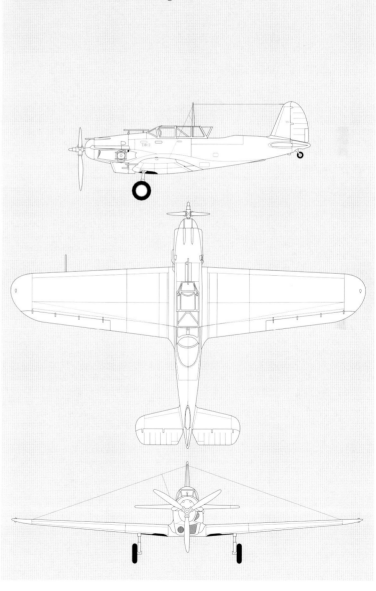

Seversky P-35

In 1935, the U.S. Army Air Corps held an aviation competition at Wright Field in Dayton, Ohio, to determine which American manufacturer had the best fighter prototype that year. The much-anticipated competition was a disappointment for newcomer Seversky Aircraft Corporation and the design team of Alexander de Seversky and Alexander Kartveli. The Seversky entrant, the SEV-2XP, was damaged en route to the competition.

Given a chance to repair their prototype, Seversky and Kartveli returned to Wright Field just a few weeks later with a revised design—much to the chagrin of their fellow competitors, who thought Seversky had received preferential treatment. Having had the opportunity to see the Curtiss and Vought prototypes, the Seversky team used the reprieve to redesign their original entry from a two-seat model into a more desirable single-seat model. With performance in mind, a streamlined hydraulic landing mechanism now retracted the front wheels and tailwheel. Plus, the inclusion of an 850-horsepower Wright R-1820-65 9-cylinder Cyclone was sure to help their design exceed the Army's required speed of 300 miles per hour (483kph).

This SEV-1XP, as it was renamed, flew favorably and demonstrated several positive characteristics, but it failed to reach 300 miles per hour (483kph). The Army granted Seversky yet another modification period. This time the designers chose to power their machine with a Pratt & Whitney R-1830-9 Twin Wasp. Still, the airplane could not attain 300 miles per hour (483kph). Nonetheless, even with such lackluster speed performance, the Army Air Corps liked other elements of the design well enough to draw up a contract for the purchase of seventy-seven aircraft, which were designated P-35.

The P-35 is recognized as the Army's first modern fighter aircraft. It was the first all-metal (except for the control surfaces), single-seat, low-wing monoplane design, with full instrumentation, an enclosed cockpit, and hydraulic, retractable landing gear. These key design attributes are still the basis for contemporary fighter jets.

Extraordinarily, this first modern fighter plane's airframe was interchangeable with an earlier amphibious cousin. Alexander de Seversky and Alexander Kartveli shared a core design principle: one uniform airframe could be used as the foundation for multiple military aircraft. While this manufacturing mantra did not appeal to the Army at the time, as only a limited number of aircraft types based on the P-35 airframe saw service, this thinking was later applied with many different military aircraft types, such as trainers, fighters, and attack ships.

27th Pursuit Squadron

RIGHT: A row of P-35 fuselage assemblies at a Seversky plant. The lack of activity is a far cry from the aircraft factory's assembly lines of the World War II years.

OPPOSITE: With an all-metal monocoque construction, cantilevered low-wing, retractable gear, and enclosed canopy, this Kartveli design from Seversky Aircraft is considered America's first modern fighter. Fast for its time and an excellent gun platform that packed the firepower of .50-caliber machine guns, the P-35 created a sensation when it was introduced. The P-35A shown here has the markings of the 27th Pursuit Squadron stationed at Selfridge Field, Michigan.

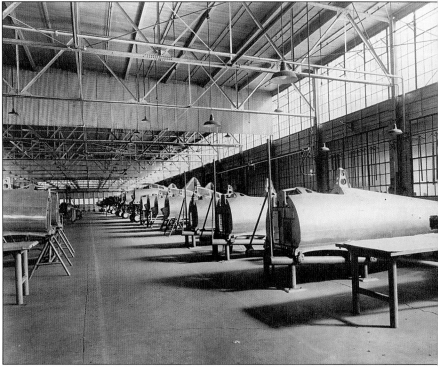

Alexander de Seversky, the founder of the Seversky Aircraft Corporation, was a Russian World War I pilot. On his first air combat mission, Seversky lost a leg, but he never lost his zeal. Seversky returned to combat with a prosthetic limb, quickly becoming one of his country's top aces. After the war, he was sent to the United States on official military business. The communist uprising in his homeland discouraged the young airman from returning. Instead, he remained in the United States, and eventually became an American a citizen in 1927.

Seversky met Alexander Kartveli, also a Russian immigrant, in 1931. An engineering genius, Kartveli was the mastermind behind the P-35, the esteemed P-47 Thunderbolt, and many early jets. In 1939, when Seversky was ousted from the company by its board of directors, Kartveli would remain to become vice president and technical director of Seversky Aircraft Corporation, which was renamed Republic Aircraft Corporation.

The P-35 entered service in 1937. The first few models exhibited aerobatic instability, so a slight dihedral was added to the cantilevered low-wing. The wide cowling around the Pratt & Whitney engine had a very modern shape, portending the future look of pursuit aircraft. One .50-caliber and one .30-caliber machine gun were located within the cowling, and the wings could support up to 300 pounds (136kg) of external ordnance.

LEFT: A Seversky employee uses a pneumatic riveting gun to assemble the one-piece cantilevered wing of a P-35. The wing is mounted in a jig.

ABOVE: This P-35 in flight shows its family resemblance to the famous P-47 Thunderbolt—another successful Alexander Kartveli–inspired design of the World War II era.

Seversky P-35A Specifications

Type: Single-seat fighter

Power plant: One 1,050-horsepower Pratt & Whitney R-1830-45 Twin Wasp radial air-cooled engine

Performance: Maximum speed, 310 miles per hour (499kph) at 14,300 feet (4,359m); service ceiling, 31,400 feet (9,571m); maximum range, 950 miles (1,529km)

Weight: Empty, 4,575 pounds (2,077kg); maximum takeoff weight, 6,723 pounds (3,052kg)

Dimensions: Span, 36 feet (10.97m); length, 26 feet 10 inches (8.2m); height, 9 feet 9 inches (3m); wing area, 220 square feet (20.2m^2)

Armament: Two .30-caliber and two .50-caliber machine guns, plus a 350-pound (159kg) bomb load

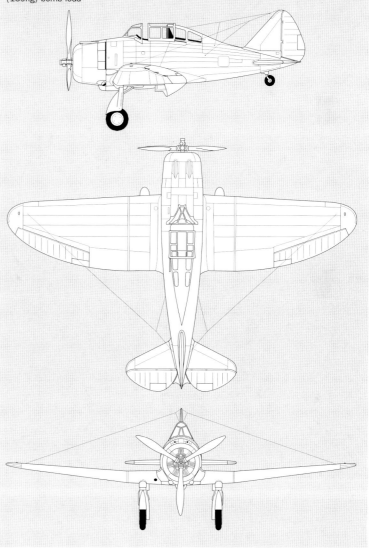

The SEV-S2, a civilian version of the Seversky P-35 built for air racing, was flown to victory in many competitions. Flying the SEV-S2, pilots won the coveted Bendix Trophy twice: Jacqueline Cochran in 1938, then Frank Fuller, Jr., in 1939. The Bendix route was a grueling 2,043-mile (3,287km) flight from Burbank, California, to Cleveland, Ohio.

Like many of it predecessors, the P-35 was obsolete before its first oil change. Its armament was light compared to contemporary European fighters. Lacking self-sealing fuel tanks and protective armor plating, all remaining P-35s were retired by 1941. During its short life cycle, more P-35s were sold for export than were used in service with the Army Air Corps.

With war approaching, the performance needs of the Army Air Corps grew rapidly and the P-35 was no longer adequate. Although an evolutionary step up from the Boeing P-26 Peashooter, it was not a serviceable pursuit aircraft for combat against faster and more heavily armed opponents.

ABOVE: Workers at Seversky Aircraft build the wing spars for the P-35. The finished spars will be sent to the wing shop where they will be mounted in jigs so the final one-piece wing can be constructed. The dihedral in the spars is clearly visible.

Curtiss P-36 Hawk

Although the Curtiss company was displeased by the events of the 1935 and 1936 Army Air Corps pursuit aircraft competitions—and in particular, by the resulting Seversky contract to build seventy-seven P-35s—Curtiss would have his day with the P-36 Hawk. In 1937 Curtiss sold 210 of its P-36s to the Army Air Corps, the largest single order to date for the aircraft manufacturer since World War I. Plus, another 753 were exported, with an additional twenty-five built under license in foreign factories.

Prior to the 1935 competition, Curtiss and Boeing had been two of the primary companies supplying pursuit aircraft to the Army and Navy. After Boeing won the contract in 1933 to build the P-26 Peashooter, the first military monoplane, Curtiss was anxious to claim the next lucrative Army contract. With this goal in mind, Donovan R. Berlin was hired as Curtiss' chief engineer. His assignment was to design the next big thing, an airplane called Model 75.

Berlin had learned his trade well at the Douglas and Northrop companies. The Hawk 75 he designed for Curtiss was maneuverable and pleasing to fly. When it was first flown in May 1935, it was designated P-36. Like its primary opponent, the Seversky P-35, the P-36 had modern innovations such as an all-metal stressed skin, retractable landing gear, flaps, an enclosed cockpit, and other equipment that is now standard on all modern military aircraft. Originally, its power was generated by a 900-horsepower Wright air-cooled radial engine, but when the Army finally placed a sizable order, the model agreed upon was modified to carry a more powerful engine, and was renamed P-36A.

The P-36A was identical to the original P-36, except for its larger Pratt & Whitney R-1830-17 Twin Wasp radial engine, engine cowl flaps for increased air intake, and its Curtiss electric, constant-speed propeller. Consequently, the P-36 was quick. It could easily exceed 300 miles per hour (483kph), a feat never accomplished by its Seversky rival.

The basic airframe was a duralumin monocoque fuselage (movable control surfaces were still fabric-covered) with a cantilevered low-wing incorporating slotted flaps on the trailing edge to lower the speed of landing approaches. The wingtips were easily detachable to facilitate the repair of ground-loop damage, a common field accident. A NACA-designed and wind tunnel–tested cowl covered the engine. The P-36's retractable landing gear was based on Boeing's patented technique. The gear could rotate 90 degrees as it was lifted hydraulically, neatly folding the wheels into the underside of the

55th Pursuit Squadron

OPPOSITE: The P-36 was Curtiss' first modern, all-metal, low-wing fighter. Although it had nothing in common with previous Curtiss biplane designs, the company still called its new creation "Hawk"— the name attached to a long line of famous fighters that gained legendary standing. This P-36A carries the markings of the 55th Pursuit Squadron.

wing. Like the Seversky P-35, the cockpit was fully enclosed, now a necessity to ensure pilot safety because of the faster speeds and higher altitudes required by the Army.

The P-36's sturdy wing structure and perfectly proportioned control surfaces made the Hawk take to flight like its namesake, but the aircraft was not destined to have a long service life. The P-36 was designed to carry the standard government-provided equipment of one .30-caliber and one .50-caliber forward-firing, synchronized machine gun: not enough firepower to be a contender, considering that its contemporaries—for instance, the British Supermarine Spitfire—had eight machine guns mounted in the wings. And none of the P-36's three fuel tanks was self-sealing, a compulsory safety feature for all World War II American pursuit aircraft. These World War I–era design limitations, coupled with production slowdowns and in-service structural corrections, plagued the P-36 program. Yet, Curtiss enjoyed a successful overseas career with its export version, the Curtiss Hawk 75. Many models and variants were developed for France, England, and Thailand.

By 1941, the P-36 was obsolete and most remaining models were transferred to training units around the United States and in Panama as newer P-40s and Bell P-39 Airacobras took to the frontline squadrons. The day the Japanese attacked Pearl Harbor, December 7, 1941, the Army's air defense consisted of fourteen P-26As, thirty-nine P-36As, and ninety-nine P-40s at Hickam Field. Although the airfield was targeted for destruction, four P-36As were able to get off the ground during the surprise attack, shooting down two incoming Nakajima B5N1 torpedo bombers. This would be the P-36's last—and only—hurrah.

Throughout the late 1930s, as the world readied itself for war, fighter aircraft designs evolved swiftly. New requirements, technological demands, and wartime procurement displaced the Curtiss P-36 Hawk. European advancements and the liquid-cooled V-12, which came back into favor as a viable aero engine because of advancements in cooling, defined the next generation of American pursuit aircraft.

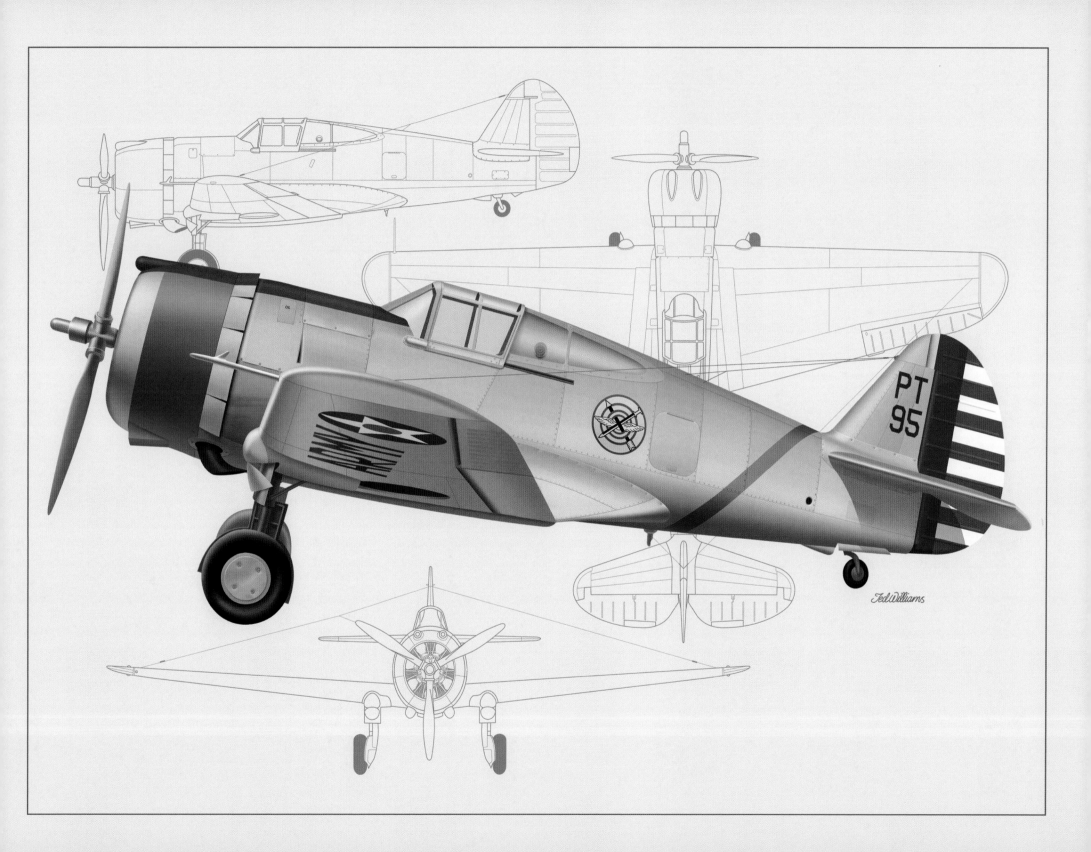

OPPOSITE: This P-36 from the 27th Pursuit Squadron carries the colorful camouflage paint scheme created especially for its appearance at the 1939 National Air Races at Cleveland, Ohio.

LEFT TOP: Curtiss P-36Cs were fitted with wing guns. Rectangular fairings underneath the wings act as retainer boxes, which were added to collect the spent .30-caliber cartridges.

LEFT BOTTOM: A P-36A from the First Pursuit Group stationed at Selfridge Field, Michigan, is viewed from above. The dark paint on the forward fuselage in front of the windshield prevents sunlight from reflecting off the bright aluminum surfaces. All unpainted aluminum fighter aircraft require an anti-glare panel so reflections will not interfere with pilot visibility.

Curtiss P-36C Hawk Specifications

Type: Single-seat fighter

Power plant: One 1,200-horsepower Pratt & Whitney R-1830-17 Twin Wasp 14-cylinder radial air-cooled engine

Performance: Maximum speed, 311 miles per hour (500kph) at 10,000 feet (3,048m); service ceiling, 33,700 feet (10,272m); maximum range, 820 miles (1,319km)

Weight: Empty, 4,619 pounds (2,097kg); maximum takeoff weight, 6,150 pounds (2,792kg)

Dimensions: Span, 37 feet 4 inches (11.4m); length, 28 feet 6 inches (8.7m); height, 8 feet 5 inches (2.6m); wing area, 236 square feet (21.7m^2)

Armament: Three .30-caliber and one .50-caliber machine guns

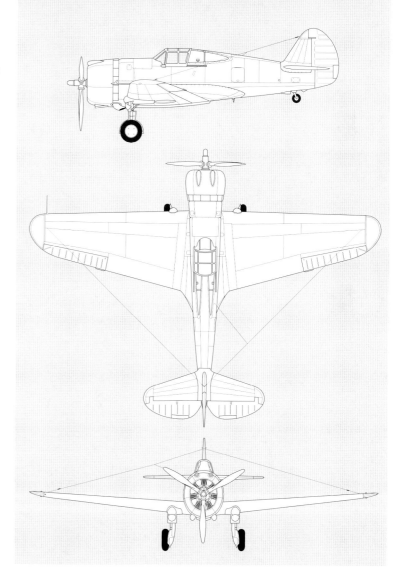

Brewster F2A Buffalo

As late as 1931, the Navy was not only flying biplanes for pursuit, it was also contracting with manufacturers like Boeing and Grumman to build even more biplanes. The Navy, aware that the Army Air Corps had made the switch to the low-wing pursuit monoplane exclusively, knew it was time to issue a specification for a navalized monoplane design capable of carrier-based service.

In 1936, Seversky, Grumman, and Brewster presented the Navy with designs in response to the latest naval specifications. Seversky offered a navalized version of its P-35, while Grumman, reticent to give up on its biplane designs, submitted a biplane model that would evolve into the famed F4F Wildcat. But Brewster had the edge. Brewster's XF2A-1 (Model B139) swept the naval competitions with its highly original design.

Although Brewster had already developed a monoplane dive-bomber, the XSBA-1, the 1938 contract to build fifty-four F2A-1s (after a significant prototype trial period, which included wind-tunnel testing to correct and modify structural inadequacies) came as an added relief to the Brewster establishment.

The Brewster Aeronautical Corporation had only recently shifted its focus to aircraft engineering and manufacturing. Although the manufacturing firm got its start in 1810 building coaches, beginning in 1932, aviation was its new charter.

Like all first-generation monoplane aircraft, the F2A-1 had an all-metal monocoque fuselage with metal-frame, fabric-covered control surfaces. The single-seat fighter's mid-wing construction contributed to the Brewster F2A's impressive maneuverability and fun-to-fly rating. Power was delivered by a 940-horsepower Wright R-1820-34 engine, generating a maximum speed of 301 miles per hour (484kph). Like many other planes of its day, it was engineered with a retractable undercarriage.

The Brewster F2A-1 was the first monoplane to enter service with the U.S. Navy, but of the original fifty-four F2A-1s, only eleven flew for the Navy. The remaining forty-three were sold as surplus to Finland's air force for use against Russia, while the Navy purchased forty-three F2A-2s in their place. The F2A-2 variant switched to a Wright 950-horsepower R-1820-40 Cyclone and used an electric propeller, which replaced the original hydraulic propeller. A carburetion system was added, as well as armor plating for pilot protection and self-sealing gas tanks, increasing the airplane's weight considerably.

VF-2 Fighting Two

RIGHT: This XF2A-2 was used in eighty-eight test flights conducted from July to November 1939 at Anacostia Naval Air Station. The tests were performed to evaluate the -2 variant of the Brewster Buffalo and to determine its suitability for naval operations.

OPPOSITE: The Brewster Buffalo was the Navy's first operational all-metal monoplane. Early versions of the Buffalo performed well, but the additional equipment added to meet modern fighter requirements deteriorated its performance and maneuverability. This F2A-2 served with Fighting Two (VF-2). Its insignia is a Chief Petty Officer chevron indicating that its pilots were all enlisted men. They served aboard the USS *Lexington*.

Armament included four 0.5-inch (1.27cm) Colt machine guns. Two of the guns still employed synchronization because of their location in the cowl. Popular opinion held that the guns should be mounted on the forward fuselage, level with the pilot's chest, to ensure maximum marksmanship. In reality, it was the cowl-mounted guns' reduced rate of fire that was the prohibiting factor when it came to accuracy, not the guns' proximity to the pilot. The military changed its thinking when it realized that more guns could be mounted in the wings, outside of the propeller's arc, once more accurate gun sights had been developed. This would dramatically increase the firepower of the single-seat fighter plane.

In 1939, Brewster received international orders for a land-based version of its F2A-1. By 1940, the British had acquired 170 aircraft, designated B-339 for export, which they called Buffalo. Belgium, Finland, and the Netherlands also placed orders for the Brewster Buffalo. Like its domestic counterpart, the exported Buffalo also suffered from added weight. The Wright GR-1820-G105A engine used in the Buffalo was unable to compensate for the loss of performance and maneuverability because of the increased weight. As a potential remedy, the heavier Colts were replaced by four 0.303-inch (.77cm) Brownings. Each plane also carried fewer rounds and less fuel.

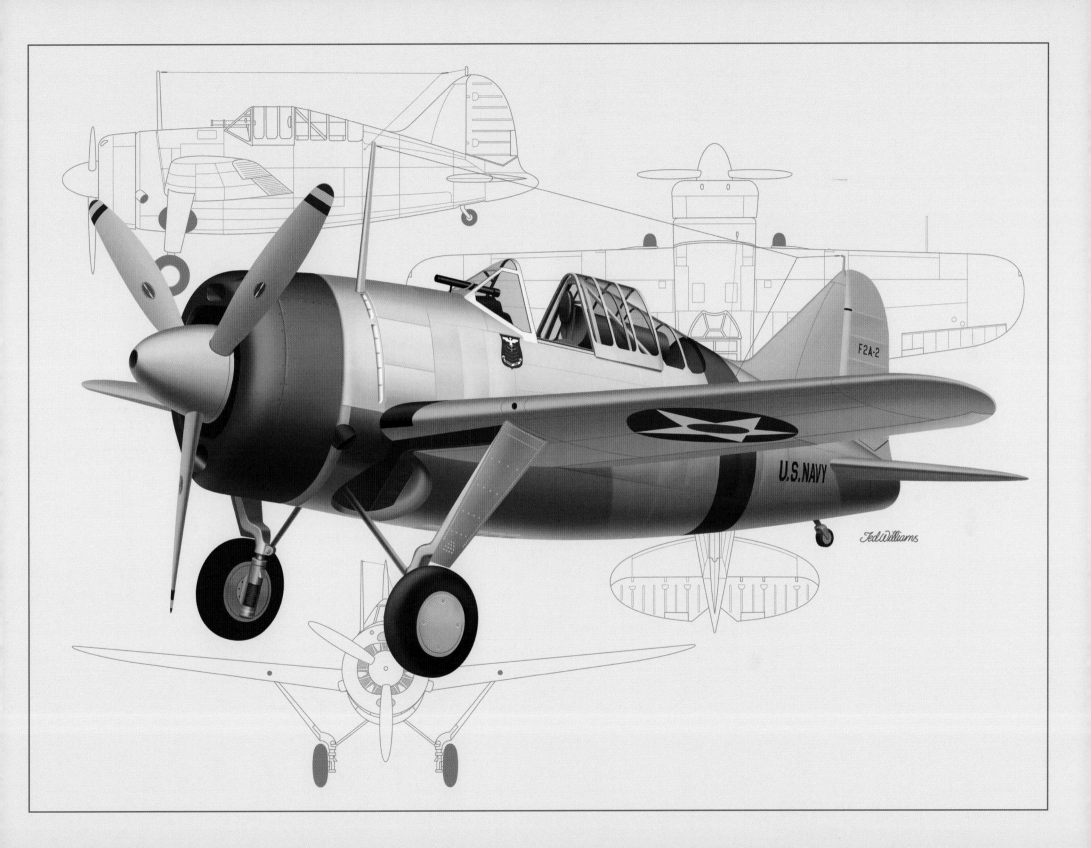

F2A-2

U.S.NAVY

Ted Williams

Brewster F2A-2 Buffalo Specifications

Type: Single-seat, carrier-based fighter

Power plant: One 1,200-horsepower Wright R-1820-40 Cyclone 9-cylinder air-cooled radial engine

Performance: Maximum speed, 321 miles per hour (502kph) at 16,500 feet (5,029m); service ceiling, 33,200 feet (10,119m); maximum range, 965 miles (1,553km)

Weight: Empty, 4,732 pounds (2,148kg); maximum takeoff weight, 7,159 pounds (3,250kg)

Dimensions: Span, 35 feet (10.7m); length, 26 feet 4 inches (8m); height, 12 feet 1 inch (3.7m); wing area, 209 square feet (19.2m^2)

Armament: Four .50-caliber machine guns

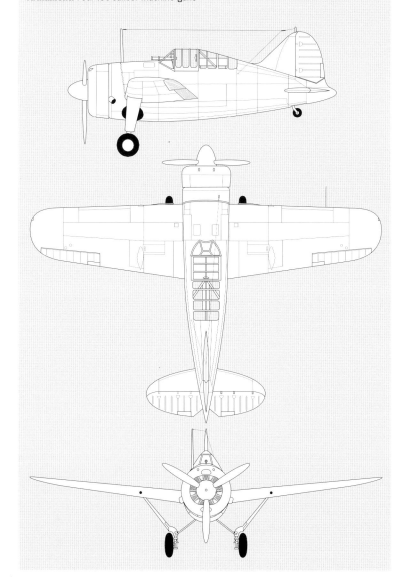

RIGHT TOP: F2A-1 wing panels are being assembled in the wing shop of Brewster's factory in Long Island, New York.

RIGHT BOTTOM: A British export Buffalo mounted on assembly horses has final adjustments made to its retractable landing gear.

OPPOSITE: A rare glimpse at the underside of the Brewster Buffalo shows the installation of the nine-cylinder Wright Cyclone engine. Evident in this photograph is the high quality of craftsmanship used in the assembly of these fighters.

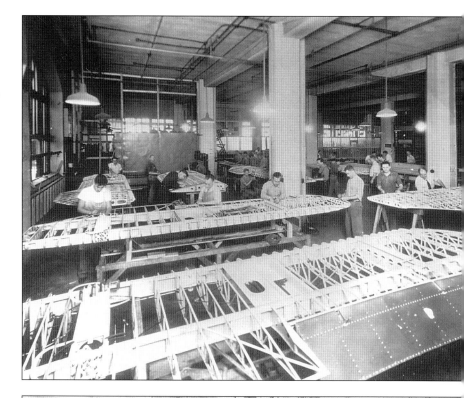

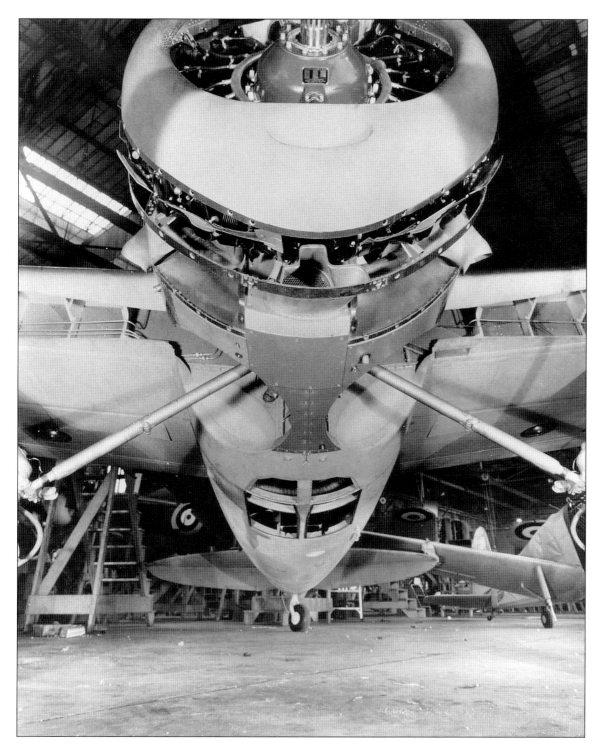

Back on American soil, the Navy commissioned an F2A-3, but this plane was heavier still. The Navy's request for larger fuel tanks and increased armor overwhelmed the little plane. Nor did the F2A stand up well to carrier service. Its inherently weak undercarriage was predisposed to collapsing on carrier landings, which are much more stressful than grass-field landings. Plus, the Wright Cyclone's single-row engine performed poorly. Normally, another more powerful engine would have been substituted, but the F2A was designed to accommodate only the Cyclone engine. A complete redesign was needed to fit any other engine, in particular the Pratt & Whitney XR-1830-76 that Grumman was using successfully in its prototypes. The Pratt & Whitney engine may have helped the F2A, but the Navy decided that the aircraft was not a suitable candidate for modification since it could not handle the stresses of carrier life. Instead, the Navy contracted with Grumman to build the F4F Wildcat, which had improved greatly since its 1936 prototype.

By 1942, the Navy ceased all production of the F2As. Despite its tumultuous history, the Brewster Buffalo will always have the distinction of being the first monoplane stationed on a U.S. Navy carrier. Unfortunately, the Brewster F2A is most remembered for a devastating loss of American life. A squadron of F2As flown by Marine Corps pilots squared off against Japanese Zeros at the Battle of Midway, losing thirteen planes and their pilots.

The F2A was the last pursuit aircraft to come out of the Brewster Aeronautical Corporation. Manufacturing problems with some of the later-model F2As worried pilots, and factory slowdowns were deemed unacceptable. By 1944 the Brewster Aeronautical Corporation of Long Island, New York, was no longer in business.

Grumman F4F Wildcat

Although the Navy ultimately selected the Brewster F2A monoplane after a series of Navy Bureau of Aeronautics design competitions in the late 1930s, it never turned a blind eye to the Grumman prototype. Originally presenting a biplane design in 1936, Grumman soon realized it would need to develop a monoplane, so it requested and received Navy clearance to commence with a monoplane design. Grumman followed through with the XF4F-2.

The XF4F-2 prototype looked like a Grumman. It closely resembled its forefather, the F3F, because of its familiar squat, rotund shape and its trademark Grumman-style retractable landing gear and its cantilevered mid-wing and semimonocoque fuselage, featuring a mill-riveted metal skin, foreshadowed Grumman designs to come.

The XF4F-2's undercarriage manually retracted into the fuselage. To nestle the gear into a precise niche under the wing's leading edge, the pilot had to turn a crank inside the cockpit nearly thirty times. The arresting hook was retracted during this process as well, but not the tailwheel, which was a fixed feature on the airframe. The pilot needed to be especially mindful while cranking. Hand cranking was not an optimal solution; it was strenuous, time-consuming, and could cause injury.

Behind its three-bladed propeller, the XF4F-2 prototype had a 900-horsepower Pratt & Whitney R-1830-66 Twin Wasp 14-cylinder double-row engine with a supercharger. By 1937, the XF4F-2 was ready to confront the Brewster F2A once again in a fly-off; each had undergone many performance modifications since the 1936 competition. Both pursuit ships were put through the motions only to discover engine problems and in-flight instability issues with the XF4F-2. Not surprisingly, Brewster won the contract.

Testing after the 1937 fly-off demonstrated the value of continued modification to the XF4F-2, however. In 1939 an XF4F-3 was presented to the Navy. It had a bigger engine (a 1,200-horsepower Pratt & Whitney XR-1830-76 with a two-stage supercharger) for more power, a greater wingspan (38 feet [11.6m], 4 feet [1.2m] longer than the XF4F-2), and increased wing area (260 square feet [23.9m^2]) for an improved center of gravity and better stability. The F4F-3 also introduced squared wingtips, which became a Grumman exclusive. The XF4F-3 was faster than both the XF4F-2 and the Brewster F2A. In 1939, the Navy ordered seventy-nine F4F-3s for testing, replacing the Brewster program.

The F4F-3 design matured into the F4F-4, the variant most revered because it earned the series the name "Wildcat." The F4F-4 featured six

machine guns in the wings. It was one of the first Navy planes with manually rear-folding wings for space economy on carrier decks, and it came standard with such safety features as protective armor and self-sealing fuel tanks. The F4F-4 also included two additional 50-gallon (189L) drop tanks. Overall, 1,169 F4F-4 Wildcats were produced and another 1,060 were built by General Motors (these models were designated FM-1). These figures do not count the variants and the models being produced for export to American allies.

The Wildcat and its later variants were active through 1943, when the Grumman F6F replaced all remaining F4F Wildcats. The Wildcat's contribution to the early years in the Pacific theater is legendary. For the first year and a half of the U.S. involvement in World War II, the F4F was the Navy's only pursuit aircraft available in quantity. Although the Japanese Zero, with its superior rate of climb and speed and its awesome performance, was a significant foe, the F4F held its own. Evaluation performed on a downed Japanese Zero concluded that the F4F, with its heavy armament, sturdy structure, and safety innovations (including self-sealing fuel tanks, bulletproof windshields, and armor plate), could best the faster, more nimble Zeros when in the hands of a well-trained, cunning Navy airman employing wily tactics.

One such tactic was the Thach Weave, developed by Lieutenant Commander John S. Thach. Navy and Marine pilots were trained to fly and fight in tandem. Each pilot provided cover for his wingman so multiple F4F pilots could exploit the aircraft's firepower potential while protecting each other from their faster, more nimble opponents. To this day, operating in pairs or teams remains the basis of modern fighter tactics. The first Navy ace from World War II, Edward Henry "Butch" O'Hare, the namesake of Chicago's O'Hare International Airport, flew an F4F Wildcat.

Originally designed with two guns in the cowl, the first F4F-3s were outfitted with four .50-caliber machine guns in the wings. This was soon increased to six wing guns in the F4F-4. Surprisingly, at the start of World War I, the World War I–era Browning machine gun was still one of the most effective armaments available for aircraft use; even today some modern tanks still use the Browning. It is a high-velocity weapon that can dispense 750 to 850 rounds per minute. With six Brownings, the F4F-4 was one of the most heavily armed aircraft in the sky.

The F4F Wildcat was invaluable to American naval operations during the early days of the war in the Pacific. A large contingent of F4F Wildcats was

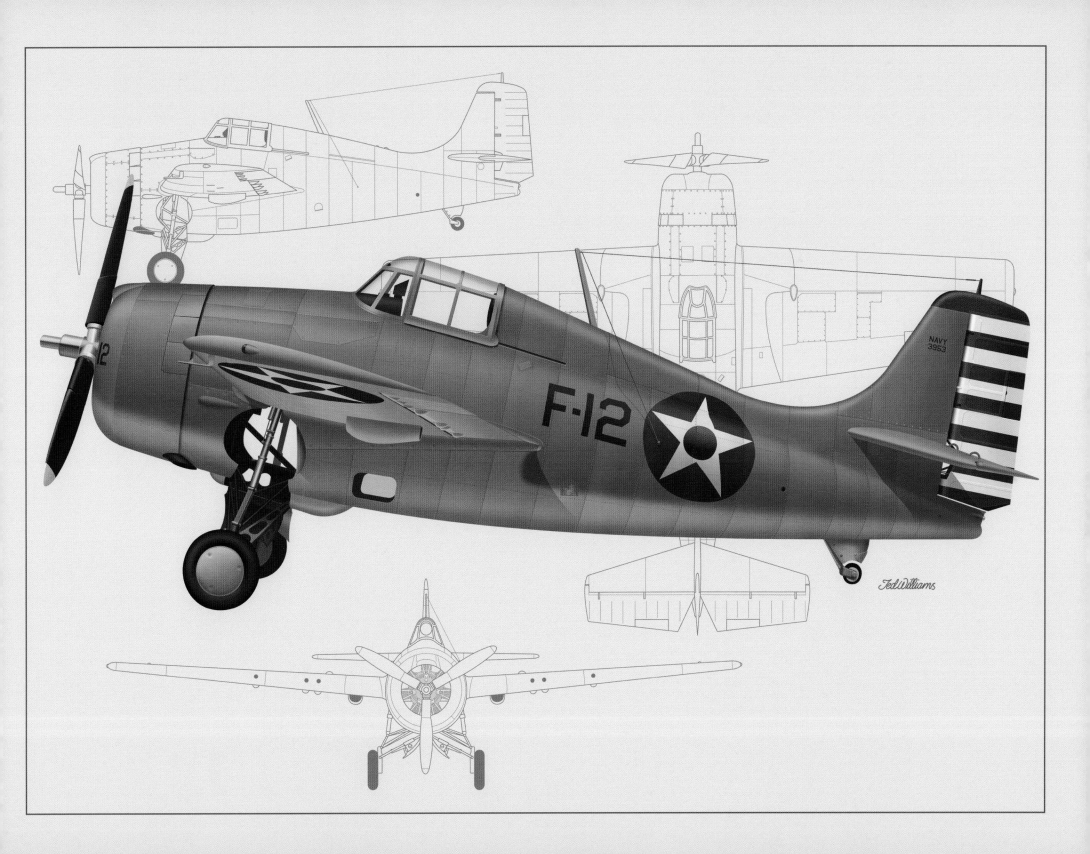

LEFT TOP: A propeller spinner was added to this early F4F-3 to streamline the large frontal area created by the radial engine. Grumman engineers discovered, however, that the spinner reduced the airflow to the engine, causing it to over-heat. This aircraft also has a telescopic gun sight, which was replaced by a more modern sight in later -3 production models.

LEFT BOTTOM: Lt. Commander John S. Thach and his wingman Lt. Edward H. "Butch" O'Hare, two of the most famous Navy pilots of the early-war period, pose for an air-to-air photo in their Grumman F4F-3 Wildcats. Thach (foreground) originated the Thach Weave and was the commanding officer of VF-3. O'Hare, the first naval aviator to receive the Congressional Medal of Honor, downed five Japanese Mitsubishi G4M "Betty" bombers in defense of the USS *Lexington* on February 20, 1942.

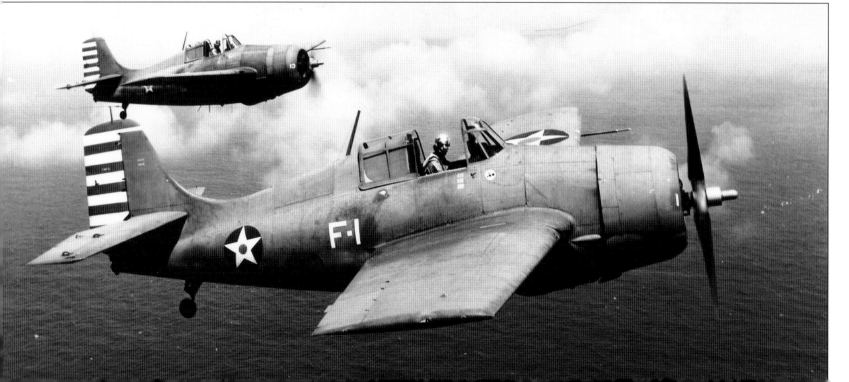

involved in the Battle of the Coral Sea, the first exclusively carrier-versus-carrier sea battle, and in the Battle of Midway.

The Wildcat ended its tenure with nearly a seven-to-one victory ratio: for every one Wildcat lost, the Japanese lost seven aircraft. It was sturdy and easy to fly; it could survive extreme dive speeds; it recovered well from spins and stalls; it could tolerate hard landings; and, most importantly, it could bring a pilot back to the carrier even when heavily damaged. While it may not have been the most graceful steed in the stable, the Wildcat was a workhorse and a lifesaver.

BELOW: An F4F Wildcat is moved into position on the flight deck of the USS *Santee* (ACV-29) in November 1942.

Grumman F4F-4 Wildcat Specifications

Type: Single-seat, carrier-based fighter
Power plant: One 1,200-horsepower Pratt & Whitney R-1830 Twin Wasp 14-cylinder air-cooled radial engine
Performance: Maximum speed, 318 miles per hour (512kph) at 19,400 feet (5,913m); service ceiling, 34,900 feet (10,638m); maximum range, 770 miles (1,239km)
Weight: Empty, 5,785 pounds (2,626kg); maximum takeoff weight, 7,952 pounds (3,610kg)
Dimensions: Span, 38 feet (11.6m); length, 28 feet 9 inches (8.8m); height, 11 feet 10 inches (3.6m); wing area, 260 square feet (23.9m^2)
Armament: Six .50-caliber machine guns

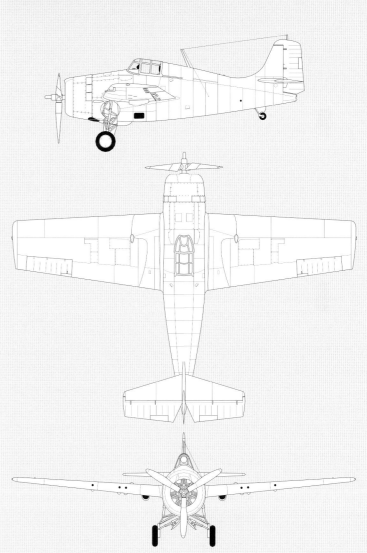

Lockheed P-38 Lightning

Just like the Navy, the Army Air Corps was looking for a new pursuit design in 1937. Despite the United States' isolationist stance toward events occurring outside its borders, a world war was imminent. The Army Air Corps put out a specification for a pursuit aircraft that could demonstrate unsurpassed speed and performance. The Army expected this aircraft to excel at high altitudes: to be capable of making a six-minute climb to 20,000 feet (6,096m) and to achieve a top speed of 360 miles per hour (579kph) at that elevation.

In one of the most ingenious engineering solutions in the evolution of military pursuit aircraft, designers Hall L. Hibbard and Clarence L. "Kelly" Johnson of the Lockheed Aircraft Company decided that the only way to get the kind of speed and power the Army required was to design an airframe around two engines. The team developed six possible dual-engine designs, eventually choosing what would become the famous silhouette of the P-38 Lightning, or *Der Gabelschwanz Teufel*, ("the fork-tailed devil," as the Germans would dub the twin-tailed aircraft).

Its distinctive shape came from a twin-tail boom with two turbo-supercharged 1,150-horsepower V-1710-27/29 Allison engines, one in each boom. The cockpit pod had an assortment of deadly firepower in the nose: one 37mm cannon and two .03-caliber and two .50-caliber machine guns. Their placement in the nose, without obstruction by the propellers, allowed the pilot greater accuracy and a full rate of fire. Contra-rotating propellers negated the effect of the torque from the powerful V-12 engines.

A prototype of Hibbard and Johnson's design, designated XP-38, was ordered on June 23, 1937, beating out designs by Consolidated, Curtiss, Douglas, and Vultee. The prototype's maiden flight took place on January 27, 1939, at March Field in California. From there, the XP-38 was to arrive at Wright Field in Ohio. Instead, Lt. Benjamin S. Kelsey, who had piloted the XP-38 on its first flight, took off in California and headed to Mitchell Field on Long Island, New York, in an attempt to beat the coast-to-coast record set by Howard Hughes in 1937.

Even though he hit speeds of 420 miles per hour (676kph), Kelsey was seventeen minutes short of Hughes' record. In addition, the aircraft was destroyed upon landing, though the pilot himself was unharmed. Despite all that, the Army was impressed with the plane's performance and ordered thirteen additional prototypes. This order was quickly followed up with an order for sixty-six P-38s, and another order for 410 more. Simultaneously, the British

RIGHT: A Lockheed inspector uses a flashlight to examine an access hatch in the right engine nacelle of a P-38 Lightning. In her left hand she holds a mirror that allows her to peer into tight places. During World War II, increased production demands and the lack of manpower required that women fill jobs traditionally performed by men.

OPPOSITE: The twin-boom design of the P-38 Lightning was the result of thinking beyond the bounds of conventional wisdom. This way of thinking became the philosophy of the Lockheed Aircraft design team and the foundation of the legendary "Skunk Works." The highest scoring American ace, Major Richard Bong, flew the P-38 through his full tour of duty in the Pacific during World War II.

ordered 674, all without superchargers. This order was canceled for various reasons, and the United States acquired most of these aircraft.

Eighteen variants were developed from the XP-38 prototype, each with design tweaks and performance gains and losses. The P-38D was the first version to go into service during World War II, while the P-38L was the final variant. The RAF would name it "Lightning."

The Lightning set new standards for pursuit aircraft performance. However, because of such spectacular performance, the P-38 revealed a new problem for aviation engineers: compressibility. Compressibility is a condition that occurs at high speeds. At transonic speed, approximately 425 miles per hour (684kph), the turbulence created by the air as it moves over an aircraft's aerodynamic structure generates a force that can lock the control surfaces in a vice-like grip, making it impossible for the pilot to control the aircraft. With its unique design, the P-38 was highly susceptible to this phenomenon. A dive brake was added to the P-38 to augment drag should the pilot sense the onset of compressibility. While the dive brake was an acceptable interim fix, it was not a solution. Compressibility would continue to stymie engineers for a while, especially once the jet engine took over.

The Lightning was one of the most versatile aircraft of World War II. Across all theaters, P-38s were employed as high- and low-altitude fighters.

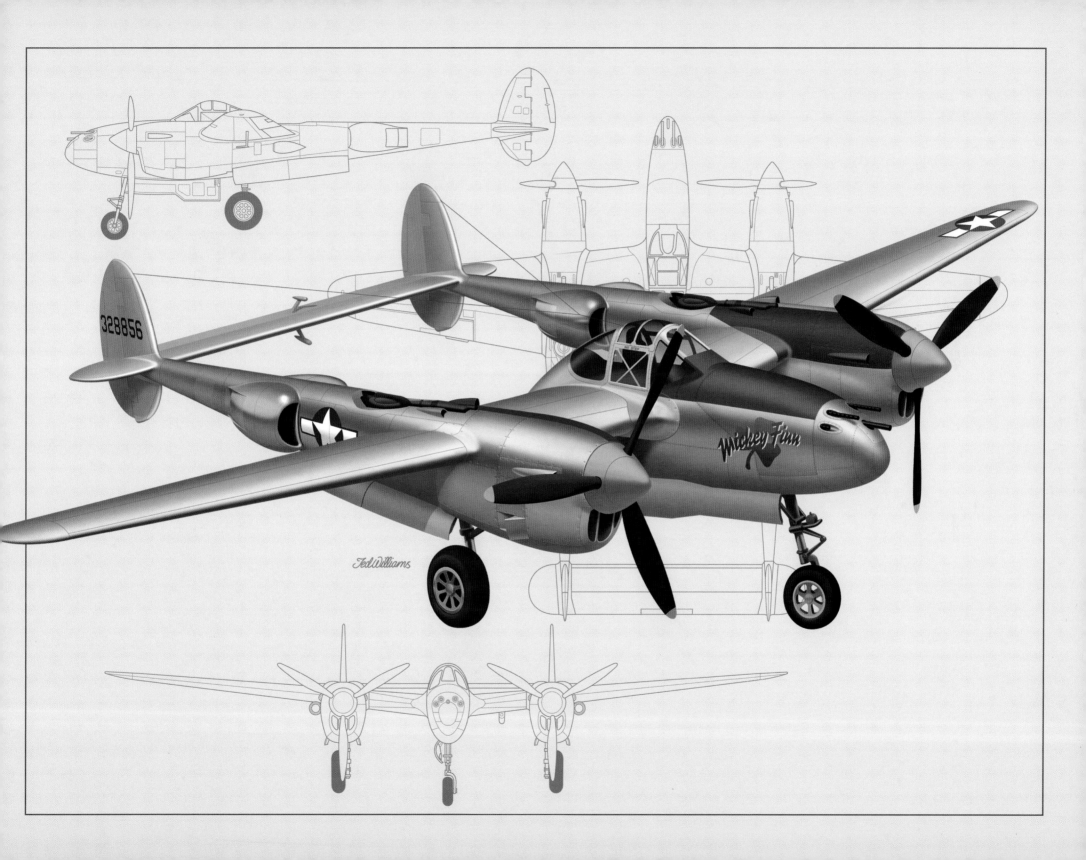

Lockheed P-38J Lightning Specifications

Type: Single-seat, long-range fighter
Power plant: Two 1,225-horsepower Allison V-1710 12-cylinder Vee liquid-cooled engines
Performance: Maximum speed, 414 miles per hour (666kph) at 25,000 feet (7,620m); service ceiling, 44,000 feet (13,411m); maximum range, 2,260 miles (3,636km)
Weight: Empty, 12,800 pounds (5,811kg); maximum takeoff weight, 21,600 pounds (9,806kg)
Dimensions: Span, 52 feet (15.8m); length, 37 feet 10 inches (11.5m); height, 9 feet 10 inches (3m); wing area, 327 square feet (30.1m^2)
Armament: Four .50-caliber machine guns, one 20mm cannon, and a 3,200-pound (1,453kg) bomb load

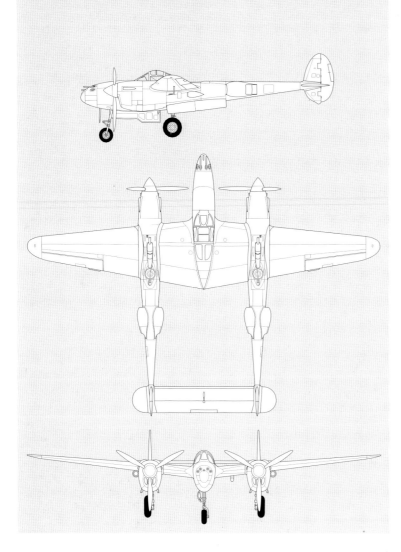

They also provided escort, dispensed bombs and rockets in a ground attack role, and performed aerial reconnaissance.

Not only was its varied service record impressive, Lockheed's twin-tailed creation was also responsible for numerous noteworthy achievements. The first twin-engine twin-boom accepted into service by the U.S. Army, the P-38 was also the first pursuit aircraft with the range to fly directly from the United States (via Greenland) to Europe, rather than having to be transported. Once in Europe, it was the first fighter to shoot down a German aircraft and it was the first U.S. fighter aircraft to escort U.S. bombers to Berlin. In the Pacific theater, P-38s downed more Japanese aircraft than any other Allied aircraft.

Perhaps most telling, the P-38 Lightning was in production on the first and last day of the war. In 1939, the Lockheed Aircraft Company had 332 employees; by 1943 that number had grown to 90,853. Between 1941 and 1944, Lockheed produced 19,077 aircraft of various types for the war effort. Lockheed certainly did its part, both with its revolutionary designs like the P-38 and its timely mass production ramp-up.

Lockheed's design creativity and its experiences with the P-38 readied the company and its principal engineers as the world prepared to leap from World War II technology into the emerging jet age.

BELOW: A bird's eye view of the Lockheed production facility at Burbank, California, where many P-38s are in various stages of assembly.

ABOVE: Unlike most fighter planes of World War II, the Lockheed P-38 Lightning had a steering wheel–like control yoke, similar to those used on bombers and multiengine transports.

RIGHT: Finished P-38s wait for delivery to USAAF units. Aircraft were either disassembled into sections and crated for shipment, or, when possible, flown to their destinations. As fighter planes with greater range were developed, they could be flown directly to their theater of operations. Between 1942 and 1944 it was the job of the Women's Airforce Service Pilots (WASP) to ferry military aircraft.

Curtiss P-40

I n 1937, the Army was looking for a platform to test the 1,150-horsepower, Allison V-1710-11 V-12, liquid-cooled engine with turbo-supercharger. The Army Air Corps still believed that the key to pursuit aircraft performance was the small frontal area of an inline engine. Curtiss complied by producing its XP-37. The XP-37 was developed from the successful P-36 airframe, with design modifications that allowed it to carry an inline engine instead of a radial. The Army commissioned thirteen XP-37 prototypes, but subsequent evaluation determined that the XP-37 was insufficient for military requirements. It had too many mechanical problems, especially with the turbo-supercharger. And visibility was nil. To make room for the longer inline engine, the cockpit was too far aft for the pilot to see past the engine at takeoff.

Not satisfied with the XP-37, another competition was held to find a military pursuit plane that could support an inline, liquid-cooled, Allison engine. In 1939 Donovan Berlin, designer of the ill-fated XP-37, won with another design based on the Curtiss P-36 airframe. This adaptation would become the P-40.

The P-40 was a modern monoplane fighter with an enclosed cockpit and retractable landing gear. It had a single seat and a cantilevered low-wing without external bracing, and a monocoque fuselage. Covering its metal wing was an aluminum alloy laminate called Alclad, which was attached by a series of milled rivets. It gained extra power from an engine-driven supercharger, a more stable solution than the supercharging unit on the XP-37. Control surfaces were still fabric-covered, though, a vulnerability left over from the P-36 Hawk's 1934 airframe design.

The first production P-40s flew with a 1,040-horsepower, V-1710-33, liquid-cooled, Allison engine. After testing and modification, the radiator found a home just under the engine, near the nose. This became the trademark P-40 snout, best remembered as bearing the shark-tooth scowl of the American Volunteer Group's Flying Tigers.

The P-40 was initially armed with two .50-caliber machine guns in the fuselage and four .30-calibers in the wings. The wings could be rigged to carry six twenty-pound (9kg) bombs or a ventral drop tank.

The Army's first order for P-40s was for 524, at this time, the largest one-time order since World War I. Over its service life, from 1939 to 1944, close to 14,000 P-40s were built by Curtiss. Only Republic's P-47 and North American's P-51 Mustangs were made in greater quantity. At one point during the height of war preparation, Curtiss could complete sixty new P-40s a day.

33rd Pursuit Squadron

RIGHT: This P-40 Kittyhawk carries the famous "Flying Tigers" markings of the American Volunteer Group (AVG). Formed in 1941 by Clair Chennault to aid the Nationalist Chinese forces against the invading Japanese, the AVG operated from airstrips in Burma and China. The AVG participated in numerous air battles and is credited with 297 victories during a thirty-week period.

OPPOSITE: The P-40, although not the best fighter ever designed, became a legend and one of the most important fighters in the United States' arsenal. Known as the "Warhawk" by the Americans and the "Kittyhawk" by the British, it was built in unprecedented numbers, fought in every theater of World War II, and acquitted itself well in combat. The USAAC example rendered here carries the markings of the 33rd Pursuit Squadron stationed at Pearl Harbor in 1941.

Despite the sheer numbers of Curtiss P-40s produced, its capabilities were greatly limited. In fact, all early P-40s were obsolete by 1941. Generally, the P-40 was not as fast or as maneuverable as its Japanese and German counterparts, or even as its American sister pursuit aircraft. The Lockheed P-38, for example, exhibited better overall performance than the P-40, but the P-40 did have its strong points. Its impressive range was twice that of European pursuit aircraft and it was made of strong stock. Also, the P-40 was less expensive to build and easier to maintain than the P-38. Perhaps most importantly at the time, the Curtiss organization was geared up to quickly produce the high volume of aircraft that the government needed to make its entry into the war.

Many P-40 variants, A through N, were produced throughout World War II. Modifications included additional armor plate, a bulletproof windshield, self-sealing fuel tanks, repositioned armament, and bigger engines. All P-40s, except the P-40F and the P-40L, which had a Packard/Rolls Royce Merlin, used the Allison engine. (Allison was a division of General Motors.) All these modifications may have protected the pilot one way or another, but they added weight, and thus decreased performance. Incidentally, the P-40E was the variant that earned the Warhawk handle. The E was the first P-40 to have six .50-caliber machine guns in the wing.

The last production model, the P-40N, was produced in the largest quantity. One P-40Q variant was also developed. With a top speed of 422 miles per hour (679kph), it was the fastest P-40, but newer pursuit aircraft like the P-51 Mustang and the P-47 were better performers. The P-40Q never went into production.

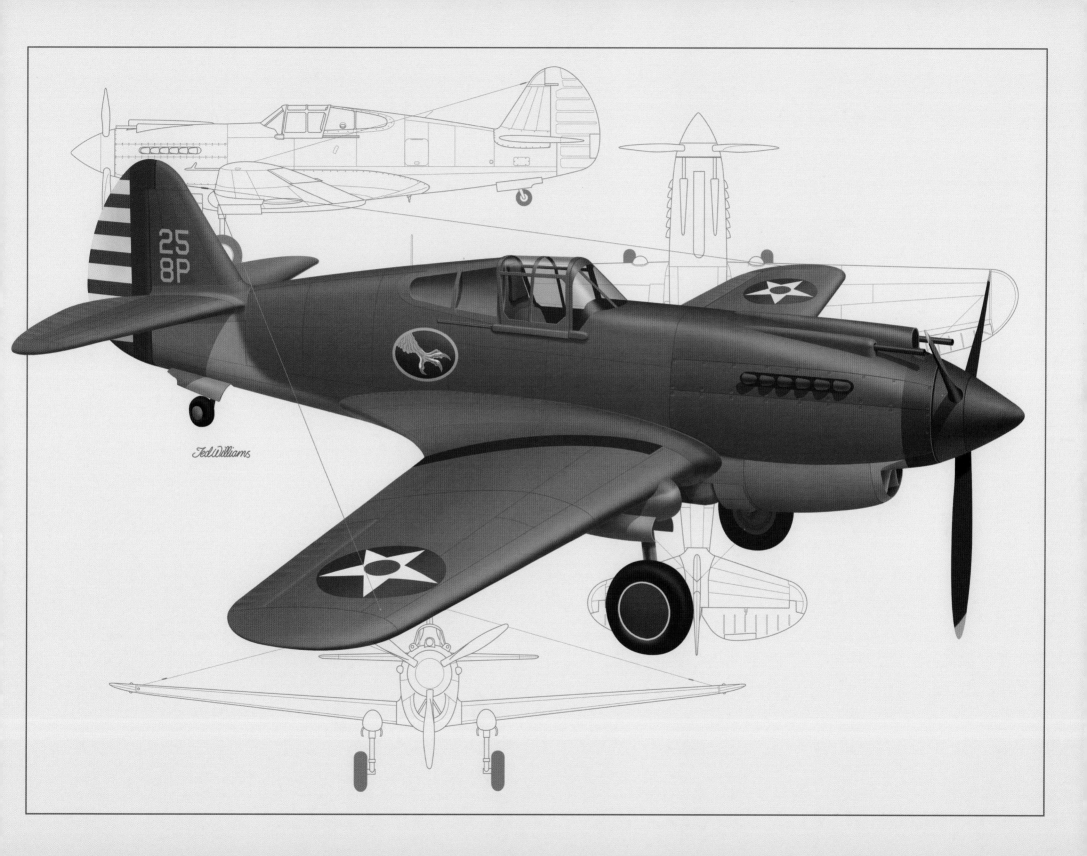

25
8P

Ted Williams

Curtiss P-40B Specifications

Type: Single-seat fighter

Power plant: One 1,040-horsepower Allison V-1710-33 V-12 liquid-cooled engine

Performance: Maximum speed, 352 miles per hour (566kph) at 15,000 feet (4,572m); service ceiling, 32,400 feet (9,876m); maximum range, 940 miles (1,512km)

Weight: Empty, 6,000 pounds (2,724kg); maximum takeoff weight, 7,600 pounds (3,450kg)

Dimensions: Span, 37 feet 4 inches (11.4m); length, 31 feet 9 inches (9.7m); height, 10 feet 7 inches (3.2m); wing area, 236 square feet (21.7m²)

Armament: Four .50-caliber machine guns

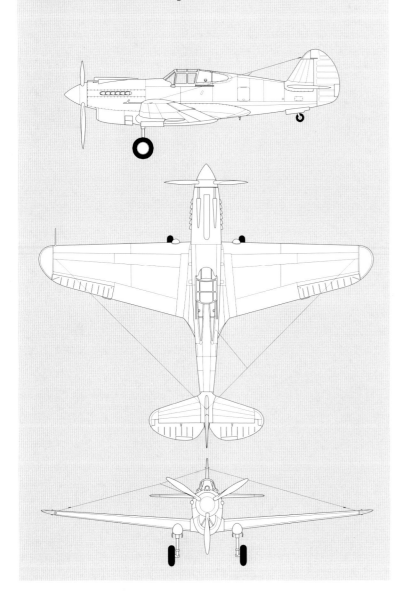

BELOW: Curtiss employees calibrate this P-40E's compass. The compass reference painted on the tarmac is aligned with true north.

OPPOSITE: A P-40E Kittyhawk is held stationary against a wooden frame as Curtiss employees boresight the six wing-mounted guns. Aircraft factories worked twenty-four hours a day to meet the wartime production needs of the armed services.

The P-40 was built for export to many Allied nations. The RAF purchased the P-40, calling it the Tomahawk. Later, the RAF dubbed the P-40D and the P-40E Kittyhawks. Australia, New Zealand, Canada, China, Brazil, France, South Africa, and the Soviet Union all flew P-40s.

Even with its less-than-stellar performance as compared to its contemporaries, the P-40 participated in combat in nearly every World War II theater of operations. The P-40 pilots learned to work within the aircraft's limits. It was a rugged plane, known for its dependability, and, most importantly, it could bring its pilot back to base even when it was riddled with bullet holes.

Bell P-39 Airacobra

The first pursuit aircraft built around its armament, the Bell P-39 Airacobra represented an evolutionary leap forward in pursuit aircraft thinking. In a time when most pursuit aircraft were developed from the airframe out, with the guns added later at the military's request, the P-39's airframe was merely a means of carrying a 37mm cannon. Essentially, the P-39 was designed to be an efficient, airborne way to deliver heavy fire to the enemy.

The Bell Aircraft Corporation was founded in 1935. After the Consolidated Aircraft Corporation relocated to California, several key employees remained in Buffalo, New York, to start their own aircraft firm. Named for Lawrence D. Bell, former vice president of Consolidated, Bell was joined by Robert Wood, designer of the Consolidated PB-2A.

The P-39 was the fledgling firm's second original aircraft submitted to the military. It was designed by Robert Wood as a close support aircraft based on the Army Air Corps requirements in 1937. The Army approved the design and ordered a prototype that same year, designated XP-39, which was ready to fly at Wright Field by April 1938.

The prototype was an aerodynamic marvel. Its semimonocoque fuselage included a metal trapezoidal wing with a curved leading edge for increased ease in cutting through the slipstream. The flaps and empennage were not covered in fabric, but in a metal laminate. For continued performance at higher altitudes, an Allison V-1710-17 liquid-cooled engine with a turbo-supercharger powered the XP-39.

The Allison liquid-cooled engine was not a surprising choice considering the Army's preference for Allisons at the time, but its placement behind the pilot was. Wood designed the Airacobra around two key principles: armament and pilot visibility. In 1935, Wood attended a munitions competition held jointly by the Army Ordnance Corps and the Army Air Corps. At that event, Wood witnessed a 37mm Oldsmobile cannon seriously damage a demonstration aircraft. This sight influenced him to create an airframe capable of carrying the mighty 37mm cannon.

To make room for the large, 106-pound (48kg) cannon, the engine was mounted in the middle of the aircraft, at its center of gravity. A gearbox in the nose, attached to the engine by a ten-foot (3m) extension shaft, turned the XP-39's three-bladed propeller. This mid-engine design addressed many space issues. Now the nose could hold an unprecedented amount of deadly forward-firing, unobstructed firepower. Furthermore, the XP-39 featured an advanced

39th Pursuit Squadron

RIGHT: A USAAF overhaul line at McClellan Field in Sacramento, California, where a line of Bell P-39 Airacobras receive attention from civilian workers employed by the Air Service Command. Lockheed P-38s are also getting overhauls at this facility.

OPPOSITE: The P-39 never met its designer's expectations; yet, with its engine located amidships, turning a driveshaft connected to the propeller's gearbox, it was an innovative design for its time. Ultimately, the U.S. Army authorized P-39 sales to the Russians, who rapidly turned it into a very effective ground attack ship and tank buster. This P-39, painted in wartime olive drab and gray, is from the 39th Pursuit Squadron.

Bell P-39D Airacobra Specifications

Type: Single-seat fighter

Power plant: One 1,150-horsepower Allison V-1710-35 12-cylinder liquid-cooled engine

Performance: Maximum speed, 376 miles per hour (605kph) at 15,000 feet (4,572m); service ceiling, 31,900 feet (9,723m); maximum range, 800 miles (1,287km)

Weight: Empty, 5,462 pounds (2,480kg); maximum takeoff weight, 8,200 pounds (3,723kg)

Dimensions: Span, 34 feet (10.4m); length, 30 feet 2 inches (9.2m); height, 11 feet 10 inches (3.6m); wing area, 213 square feet (19.6m^2)

Armament: Four .30-caliber and two .50-caliber machine guns, plus one 37mm M4 cannon

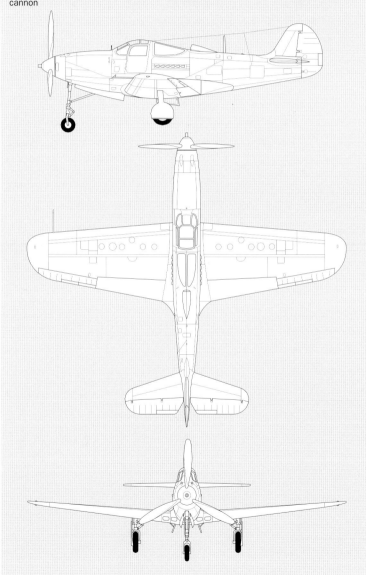

tricycle configuration for its landing gear. The front wheel could easily retract into the space made available by the placement of the engine. Plus, the pilot's forward visibility was completely unobstructed.

Early performance was outstanding. The XP-39 could climb to 20,000 feet (6,096m) in five minutes with speeds close to 400 miles per hour (644kph)—stats comparable to the XP-38.

The Army and NACA tested the XP-39, and the resulting modifications eliminated the super-turbocharger; incorporated a different Allison (the V-1710-39 with 1,090 horsepower at 13,300 feet [4,054m]); repositioned air intakes, ducting, and other surface drag inducers; and reconfigured a longer fuselage with a shorter wing. Though no longer a high-altitude charger, the plane still pleased the Army with the low-altitude performance it gained from

these modifications; it was designated the XP-39B. An evaluation model that followed incorporated additional modifications for increased armor plate and armament. In 1941, the Army placed its first full-scale order. This was followed by another order with provisions for self-sealing fuel tanks, four .30-caliber machine guns that were added in the wings, and an undercarriage rigging for bombs or a seventy-five-gallon (284L) drop tank.

In total, 9,558 Airacobra variants with minute design distinctions and various Allison engines were produced from 1941 to 1944. Nearly half that total was sent to the Soviet Union under the new Lend-Lease Act. After March 1941, this act authorized the U.S. military to purchase aircraft to lend to its Allies. Russian pilots had success with the P-39 and its ground support and antitank capabilities, keeping some models in service until the mid-1960s. British and French pilots also flew the P-39.

Like the P-40, the P-39 was readily available at the start of the war. In its day, frontline P-39s were fast, capable of top speeds of 376 miles per hour (605kph) at 15,000 feet (4,572m). The P-39's serious firepower was ideally suited for strafing missions, and its many innovations—such as disc brakes—

OPPOSITE : A Bell supervisor looks on as an Allison 1710 is lowered into a P-39 fuselage. The Airacobra was designed with the engine aft of the cockpit—primarily so it could carry a 37mm Oldsmobile cannon in the nose. This unorthodox engine placement complicated engine installation and maintenance.

ABOVE: Bell P-39 Airacobras on display. Note such distinguishing features as the long, front nosewheel strut of the tricycle landing gear, the unconventional automobile-like door, and the opening in the propeller spinner to accommodate the barrel of the nose-mounted 37mm cannon.

led the way for future aircraft designs. Typical of an American-built pursuit aircraft, it could take a considerable amount of combat damage and still meet its objectives.

On the flip side, the P-39's weight increased with each successive modification, though its power remained the same. Maneuverability, rate of climb, and speed were compromised as a result. Mistakenly, the United States assumed that air combat would occur at lower altitudes. The Army's decision to remove the super-turbocharger to increase the aerodynamic lines of the fuselage proved imprudent. Moreover, it was the smallest pursuit aircraft of World War II, restricting all P-39 pilots to a height of five feet ten inches (1.8m). And the 37mm cannon was inclined to jam, topping the list of in-service complaints.

Although not a great performer, the Airacobra still carried out its combat duties around the world. Perhaps its greatest victory was its selection in 1937. The Army's willingness to accept an unconventional solution was quite promising. Sadly, the military-approved modifications limited the P-39's effectiveness against worldwide competition.

Vought F4U Corsair

The Vought name has been a part of aviation history almost as long as Boeing and Curtiss. Dynamic aviation pioneer Chance Milton Vought and the company he founded in 1917 were involved in several fruitful aviation partnerships until his sudden death in 1930. Most notably, his company built one of the most successful carrier-based pursuit aircraft of World War II, the F4U Corsair.

Rex B. Beisel, chief engineer of the Vought-Sikorsky Company, designed the F4U-1 around the most powerful radial engine available. Much like the Allison inline, liquid-cooled engine developments in the mid-1930s, which had been spurred on by the Army, the Navy's preference for radial power plants encouraged Pratt & Whitney to develop the most phenomenal radial engine possible at the time. Beisel was determined to incorporate this new Pratt & Whitney 2,000-horsepower Twin Wasp R-2800 double-row radial engine into a pursuit airframe for the Navy.

The R-2800 Twin Wasp was a massive engine, assisted by a two-stage, two-speed supercharger. To power the supercharger, the aircraft's exhaust was diverted into turbines that compressed the air through high-speed revolutions. This compressed air was then mixed with fuel and forced into the carburetor to provide the engine with the same amount of air it received at sea level at all elevations. However, just like the R-2800, the supercharging unit was big. In terms of size, it was akin to that of a typical modern household washing machine.

And the propeller was huge, too. The R-2800 was so large and powerful that it required a 13-foot (4m), three-bladed propeller, the largest diameter propeller used on any World War II–era fighter. To compensate for all the bulk in the nose, Beisel knew that the plane's airframe would have to be as small as possible if it were to have any chance performing as a fighter.

The F4U was Vought's sixth attempt to produce a pursuit aircraft for the Navy. In 1938, Vought offered the Navy two designs, one with and one without the R-2800. The Navy chose the prototype with the R-2800 engine.

The prototype's most intriguing characteristic was its inverted gull wing. Not intended as an aerodynamic feature, it was designed to minimize the length of the landing gear struts. If it had been designed with a straight-wing configuration, the landing gear struts would have had to be long and spindly to enable the spinning propeller to clear the ground, resulting in struts too fragile for carrier landings.

RIGHT: A F4U-1 Corsair under construction, with its complex ductwork for the coolers and supercharger still exposed. As on a carrier's hangar deck, space on the factory floor is limited. Vought employees took advantage of the Corsair's folding wing feature for maximum space efficiency.

OPPOSITE: The Vought F4U Corsair was known by many nicknames: "old hog nose" by it pilots; "the bent-wing bird" by its ground crews; "the angel of Okinawa" by Marines on the ground; and even as "whistling death" by the Japanese. Its forward-looking design harnessed the awesome power of the Pratt & Whitney R-2800 radial engine. First flown in 1940, it became the first fighter to reach and sustain 400 miles per hour (644kph). It is shown here in the three-color camouflage paint scheme used in the Pacific until April 1945.

Its semimonocoque metal skin was spot-welded and flush-riveted to eliminate drag on the surface of the fuselage. This type of assembly was a new process devised by Vought and the Navy. Supercharger air intakes were neatly nestled in the area created by the inverted gull wing. The landing gear rotated 90 degrees to lie flat behind recessed doors, and the tailwheel and hook also retracted. In 1941, after modification for additional armor, self-sealing fuel tanks, increased wing-mounted firepower, and simplified manufacturing procedures, the Navy ordered its first installment of 585 planes, designated F4U-1.

In total, almost 5,000 F4U-1 Corsairs were produced by Vought for the war effort. Later variants did exist, but the only one produced in quantity was the F4U-4. The F4U-4 featured the R-2800-18W with a water-injecting system for added horsepower, a four-bladed propeller, and a cockpit with a different design. Goodyear built another 3,808 Corsairs under license from Vought. Designated FG-1D, they were nearly identical to the F4U-1 except the wings did not fold. The Goodyear model was intended for ground base use only. Brewster was also a supplier; however, the company was unable to complete its contract and supplied few aircraft.

Although designed for carrier-based use, the Corsair did not perform well in initial carrier testing. The huge nose—it measured an amazing fourteen feet (4.3m) from the cockpit—blocked pilot visibility on takeoff and landing. Plus, the pilot's seat was quite low in the cockpit, obscuring the pilot's line of sight. The Corsair's landing gear also caused problems. The landing oleo mechanism did not respond well to the jarring carrier landing. These factors relegated all Corsairs to land-based Marine Corps units until they were remedied by modifications to the cockpit and landing struts. Unfortunately, these corrections took

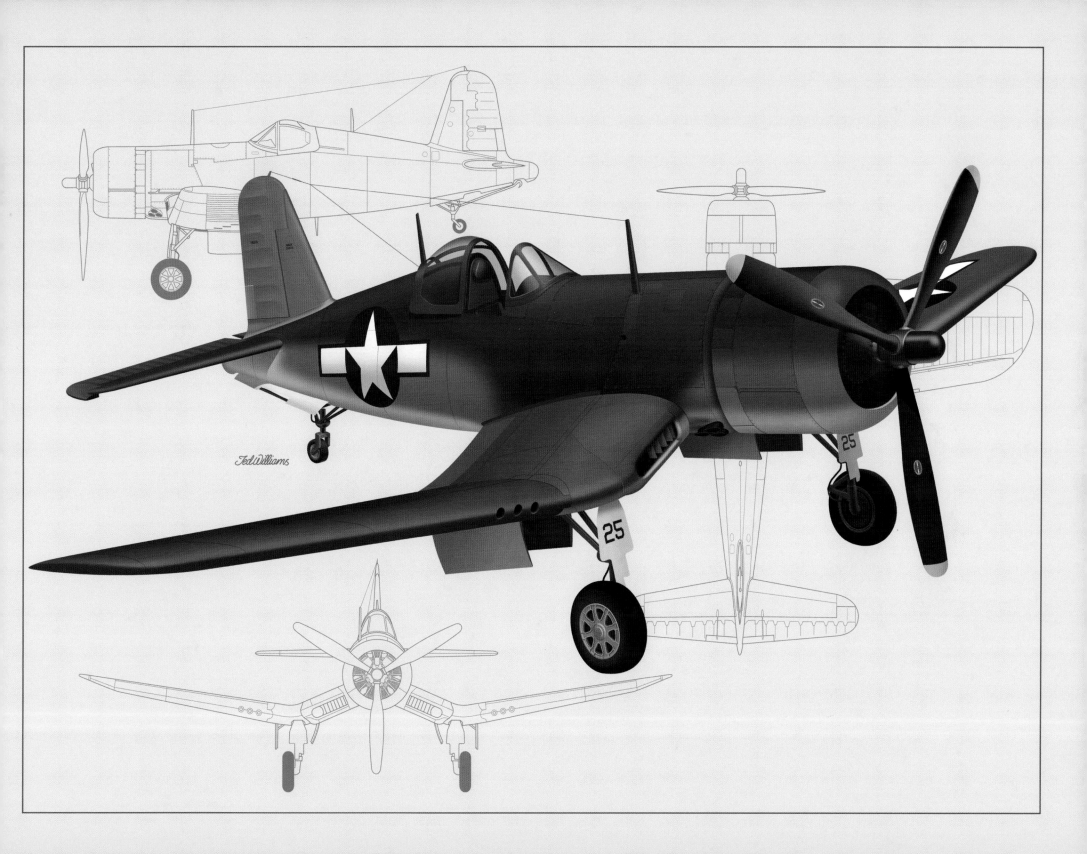

OPPOSITE: One Vought Aircraft employee works near the extended tail gear of a F4U-1 Corsair, while other workers assemble and test instrumentation in the cockpit. It is 1942 and the Corsair line at the Vought facility is going full tilt.

LEFT: While on patrol in Korean waters, armorers aboard the USS *Boxer* arm the four 250-pound (114kg) bombs mounted to the folded wing of an F4U Corsair.

Vought F4U-4 Corsair Specifications

Type: Single-seat, carrier-based fighter

Power plant: One 2,000-horsepower R-2800-8 Pratt & Whitney Double Wasp air-cooled radial engine

Performance: Maximum speed, 446 miles per hour (718kph) at 20,000 feet (6,096m); service ceiling, 36,900 feet (11,247m); maximum range, 1,015 miles (1,633km)

Weight: Empty, 9,205 pounds (4,179kg); maximum takeoff weight, 13,120 pounds (5,956kg)

Dimensions: Span, 41 feet (12.5m); length, 33 feet 8 inches (10.3m); height, 14 feet 9 inches (4.5m); wing area, 314 square feet (28.9m^2)

Armament: Six .50-caliber machine guns

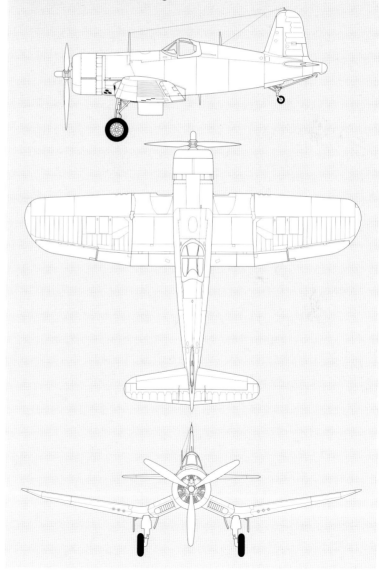

two years. In the meantime, the Marines carried the war to many of the islands throughout the Pacific theater in the land-based F4U.

The Corsair's maneuverability, however, was outstanding. It could perform all the necessary air combat maneuvers with ease. For a big airplane, it was remarkably agile and very fast, and it was the first pursuit aircraft capable of flying 400 miles per hour (644kph). Consequently, the F4U was one of the first military aircraft built to parameters beyond the capacity of its pilot. The aircraft could withstand forces that would incapacitate its human pilot.

The Corsair was twice the size of the Zero, but its size was in proportion, allowing for a confident grace and an eleven-to-one victory ratio over the Japanese. Armament included six .50-caliber machine guns in the wings. The wing could support a significant payload of 500 pounds (227kg), and later variants were upped to 1,000 pounds (454kg). Some carried under-wing rockets.

The British acquired Corsairs through the lend-lease program. The Corsair also saw service in the Korean War. It was removed from frontline service in December 1954.

The Corsair served the Navy and the Marines well. With its inverted gull wings, the F4U had one of the most distinctive pursuit silhouettes in the sky, and it had the muscle it needed to vanquish its opponents.

Republic P-47 Thunderbolt

The P-47 Thunderbolt was the largest single-seat, single-engine pursuit aircraft of World War II. Designed by Alexander Kartveli, designer of the Seversky P-35, the P-47 weighed an astounding seven to ten tons (6,356–9,080kg), depending on the variant, fuel, and payload. When asked about the behemoth he had created, Kartveli responded, "It will be a dinosaur, but a dinosaur with good proportions."

The P-47 was originally intended to be a light attack plane with an inline, liquid-cooled engine. In 1939, Kartveli and the Seversky Aircraft Corporation submitted their design, the AP-10, to the Army Air Corps. Accepted by the Army as XP-47, it was powered by a 1,150-horsepower Allison V-1717-39. Only a few months later, the Army ordered another prototype of the same design, but it was now 1940. News of the terrifying capabilities of the German aircraft demanded more from the U.S. air fleet. Just six months later, Kartveli submitted an all-new design to the U.S. Army Air Force. It was one of the first designs influenced by actual modern combat.

The new design didn't resemble the original XP-47 except for its clean lines, a Kartveli trademark. It was powered by the 2,000-horsepower Pratt & Whitney R-2800 air-cooled Double Wasp engine, an 18-cylinder beast with a turbo-supercharger. Armament was increased from two to eight .50-caliber machine guns mounted in the wings, four to a side. Self-sealing fuel tanks and extensive armor plate were used throughout the aircraft. As a result, the plane was twice as heavy as the one that preceded it.

In September 1940, the Army purchased P-47 prototypes from Republic, as the Seversky firm was now called. The new, patriotic name reflected the company's direction after the forced expulsion of Alexander de Seversky by the company's board of directors. Soon an order for 170 P-47Bs and 602 P-47Cs went into production. In October 1941, the P-47D was ordered. The D became the most widely produced variant. Over the course of the Thunderbolt program, 12,600 D models were produced for shipment to the frontlines. The Curtiss-Wright Corporation also supplied the Army Air Force with P-47Gs from its Buffalo plant. Overall, more than 15,600 P-47 Thunderbolts were produced for the war effort—the greatest quantity of any World War II pursuit aircraft.

The P-47 was a single-seat monoplane with all-metal construction. Nicknamed the "Jug" because it resembled a milk jug, it was built to defy extensive damage. As with the Corsair, many design challenges had been

RIGHT: Inside a Republic manufacturing facility, a female employee works on an aft section of a P-47 Thunderbolt fuselage.

OPPOSITE: The Republic P-47 Thunderbolt was one of the best fighters of World War II. It could dive with blinding speed and turn on a dime. Add to this performance a gun platform that mounted eight Browning .50-caliber machine guns, and you have an incredibly effective fighter plane. It could also absorb unbelievable punishment and still remain airborne: many a crippled Thunderbolt managed to get its pilot home safely. This P-47D from the 365th Fighter Group has black-and-white D-day invasion stripes applied over its olive drab and gray paint scheme.

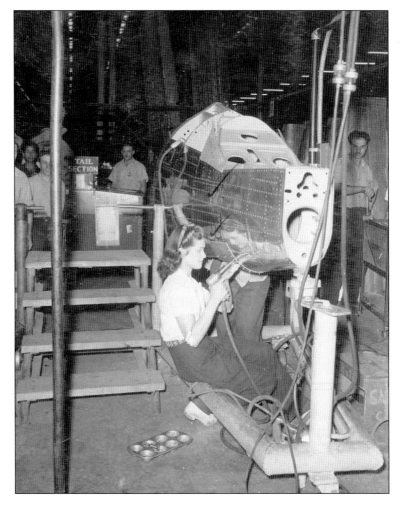

overcome to incorporate the large R-2800. Each designer approached the inclusion of the R-2800 and its bulky supercharger in a different way. Kartveli chose to design the P-47 around the extensive ductwork necessitated by his decision to place the supercharger aft of the cockpit.

With its R-2800, the Thunderbolt could reach speeds of close to 400 miles per hour (644kph). By supplying sufficient oxygen to the fuel mixture, the supercharger helped the P-47 climb to 40,000 feet (12,192m), the highest ceiling yet to be seen in a pursuit aircraft.

Propeller clearance was a design consideration, as it had been with the Corsair. The P-47's twelve-foot (3.7m), four-bladed propeller was enormous, yet a necessity with the R-2800. Republic pioneered a landing gear strut that could "telescope" nine inches (23cm) as needed. When extended, the gear provided propeller clearance for ground activity. Conversely, the gear could

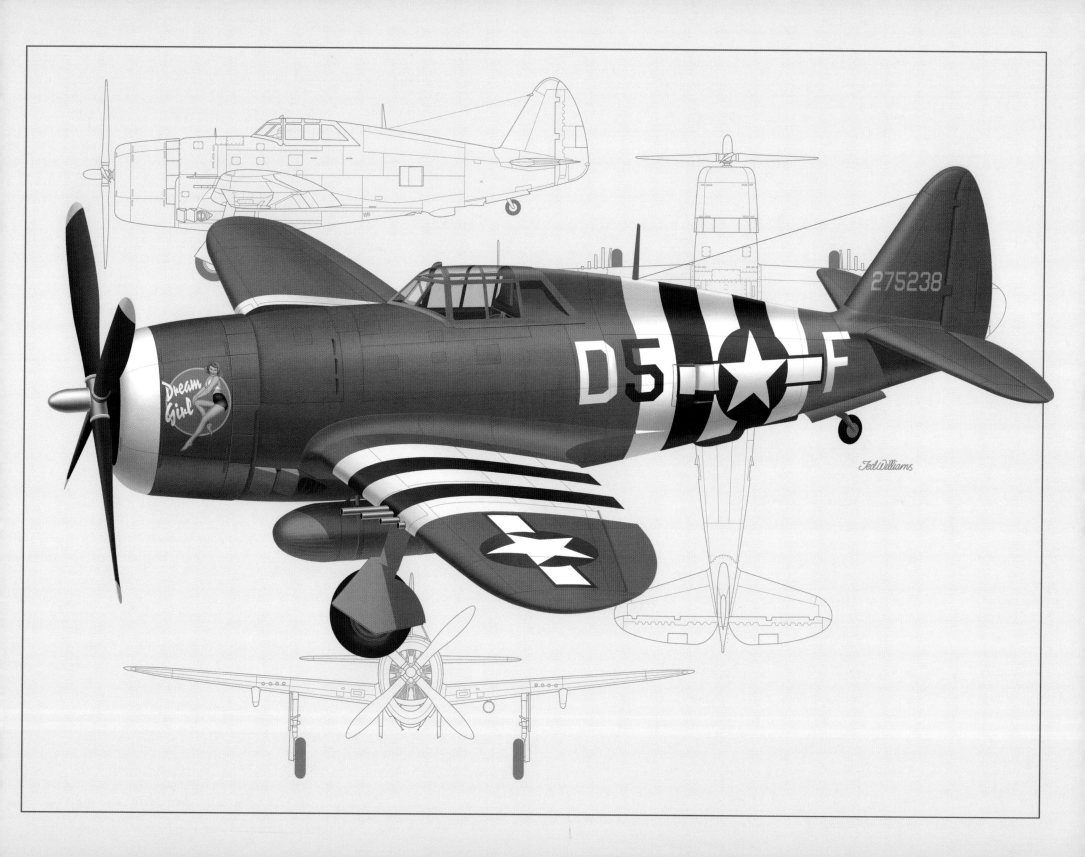

compress for compact storage, leaving ample room in the elliptical wings to mount the machine guns and space for the ammunition.

Later variants were modified to incorporate the new bubble canopy, an improvement over the earlier sliding canopy cover. This improvement eliminated a rearward blind spot that had frustrated and endangered dogfighting P-47 pilots. To compensate for the bubble shape, a dorsal fin was added to maintain the aircraft's lateral stability in flight. The final Thunderbolt variant, the P-47N, was updated with longer wings for additional internal fuel-storage capacity that allowed for the range needed for escort missions in the Pacific theater. It also featured a more powerful Pratt & Whitney R-2800-57 with water injection. This engine was also used in the M variant, which was

ABOVE LEFT: "Lady Ruth," a P-47D of the 19th Fighter Squadron, 318th Fighter Group, is being rearmed at an airfield on Saipan, one of the Mariana Islands, in 1944.

ABOVE RIGHT: Sergeants John A. Koval and Joe Di Franza load Lt. Col. Francis S. Gabreski's P-47 with .50-caliber machine gun rounds. Special care must be used when placing the ammunition belts into the wings. If done incorrectly the guns could easily jam, putting the pilot at risk.

developed in limited quantity—only 130—for low-altitude operations in the European theater. Weighing in at more than 21,000 pounds (9,534kg) and with a maximum range of more than 2,000 miles (3,218km), the N variant could carry 3,000 pounds (1,362kg) of external ordnance, consisting of either bombs or rockets. A total of 1,816 were produced in the N configuration.

The Thunderbolt was an incredibly tough aircraft. P-47 folklore has it that many pilots returning from combat with a damaged Thunderbolt walked away from a wheels-up landing that would have annihilated a lesser aircraft. On a normal approach, the Thunderbolt was easy to land, and it was difficult to ground loop.

The P-47 greatly contributed to the United States' efforts in World War II. It participated in every active theater of war, flying more than 500,000 missions during which many Thunderbolt pilots earned ace status, including Francis S. Gabreski, USAAF, who was lauded for his twenty-eight victories. Allied pilots also operated the Thunderbolt. The French, Russian, British, Mexican, and Brazilian air forces received P-47s from the United States through the Lend-Lease Act.

After the war, the P-47 Thunderbolt went into reserve service. While some went to Central and South American air forces, others were shipped to Portugal, Italy, Chile, and other countries. In the United States, Thunderbolts were still active in the National Guard as late as 1950.

Kartveli's handiwork and the proud Republic heritage continued well into the jet age in a series of big fighting planes, all named for thunder, just like this one.

BELOW: Republic workers install a self-sealing tank into the belly of a P-47 Thunderbolt. All World War II–era American fighter planes were built with self-sealing tanks for fuel and oil. This feature minimized the chance of fire or explosion aboard an aircraft struck by enemy fire.

Republic P-47D Thunderbolt Specifications

Type: Single-seat, long-range fighter

Power plant: One 2,000-horsepower Pratt & Whitney R-2800 18-cylinder radial air-cooled engine

Performance: Maximum speed, 433 miles per hour (697kph) at 30,000 feet (9,144m); service ceiling, 42,000 feet (12,802m); maximum range, 550 miles (885km)

Weight: Empty, 9,900 pounds (4,495kg); maximum takeoff weight, 14,925 pounds (6,776kg)

Dimensions: Span, 40 feet 9 inches (12.4m); length, 36 feet 1 inch (11m); height, 14 feet 2 inches (4.3m); wing area, 300 square feet (27.6m^2)

Armament: Eight .50-caliber machine guns, plus up to a 500-pound (227kg) bomb load

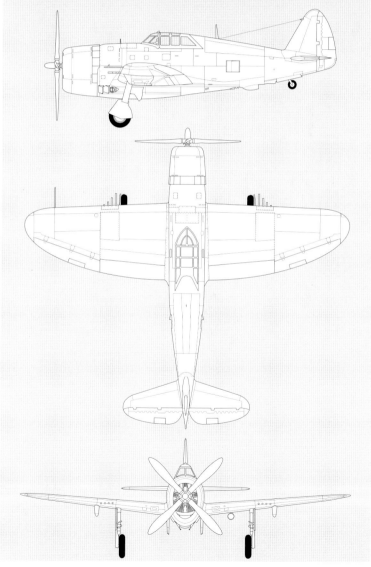

Grumman F6F Hellcat

The F6F Hellcat was Grumman's answer to a call for an improved F4F Wildcat. The F6F was larger, faster, and heavier than its predecessor. Indeed, the Hellcat was the second largest single-engine World War II fighter aircraft, only slightly smaller than the Republic P-47 Thunderbolt. It was designed to overpower and defeat Japanese Zeros, which it did with a staggering nineteen-to-one victory ratio.

To create the Hellcat, Leroy Grumman, William T. Schwendler, and their design team studied the Zero's performance in minute detail. With Japanese successes in mind, the team put considerable thought into not only how the aircraft should fly, but also how it would be manufactured and maintained in the field. Grumman executives were keenly aware that the majority of its manufacturing staff, as well as the enlisted people who would repair and fly the F6F, were not skilled tradesmen or experienced aviators.

In 1942, the first Hellcat design was built around the Wright 1,700-horsepower XR-2600-16 Cyclone, but the XF6F-1 prototype, powered by the Wright engine, didn't meet Navy speed or climb requirements. Soon after, on July 30, 1942, another prototype, the XF6F-3, was flown. It was powered by the larger Pratt & Whitney 2,000-horsepower R-2800-10 Double Wasp. By October 1942, the F6F-3 was available for frontline duty. (Interestingly, the F4U Corsair, which also employed the R-2800 Double Wasp and was designed before the F6F, had not yet been accepted for carrier use.) The timing was good, as the existing Wildcat and Airacobra fleet had become outmoded as far as the conflict in the Pacific was concerned, and the Navy needed the Hellcat quickly. Grumman complied, completing the entire project, from concept to delivery, in record time—only one year from request to prototype.

This rapid turnaround, as well as Grumman's growing reputation as the "Ironworks" (a nickname given to Grumman Aviation by the pilots who flew and appreciated the company's strong planes), helped cement Grumman's reputation with the Navy. Above all else, Leroy Grumman was concerned with pilot safety. The Grumman philosophy was to build strong aircraft that could get the pilot back alive.

To that end, the Hellcat was outfitted with a strong all-metal, semimonocoque fuselage and fabric-covered control surfaces. Unlike the Wildcat, which had a mid-wing design, the Hellcat had a low-wing, with the largest wing area of all the single-seat, single-engine pursuit fighters of World War II. The large wing reduced wing loading to allow the F6F to attain the kinds of speeds needed

RIGHT: A Grumman F6F-5 Hellcat from VF-29 (Air Group 29) prepares for launching from the USS *Cabot* (CVL-28) in October 1944.

OPPOSITE: A big plane with a big engine, the Grumman F6F Hellcat was capable of countering the Japanese Zero's air dominance. The Hellcat was designed to duke it out with the Zero by delivering awesome firepower from its six wing-mounted .50-caliber machine guns and its pilots were responsible for destroying more than 5,000 enemy aircraft with a loss ratio of 19 to 1. This F6F-5 bears the markings of VF-84, which served aboard the USS *Bunker Hill* in the fall of 1944.

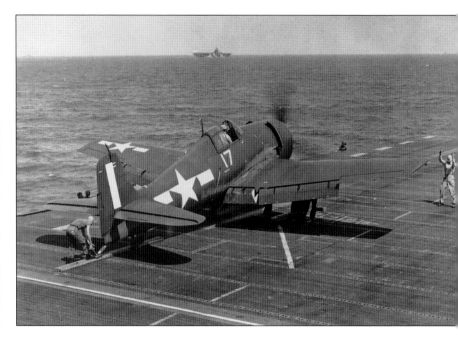

for carrier landings and takeoffs. The tapered wing bore the Grumman trademark square tips.

Unlike the Wildcat undercarriage, which took the wheels up into the fuselage, the Hellcat's landing gear retracted into the wings. In addition, the Hellcats undercarriage, including the tailwheel and arresting hook, was operated hydraulically. Designed specifically for carrier service, the Hellcat's wings twisted rearward to lie lengthwise along the fuselage, maximizing the efficiency with which the plane could be stored on a carrier deck.

Between October 1942 and November 1945, two variants went into mass production: 4,403 F6F-3s were produced and 7,870 F6F-5s followed. The F6F-5 incorporated only slight modifications, including some that were outfitted with radar for night fighting, spring tab ailerons that favorably increased the rate of roll, a stronger windshield and canopy, a stronger tail assembly, and a redesigned cowl. Once the production lines were rolling, Grumman could supply the Navy with 500 Hellcats a month.

The Hellcat literally swept the skies of Japanese carrier aircraft in the Pacific. With 250 gallons (946L) of fuel held in self-sealing tanks in the fuselage and wings and a 150-gallon (568L) drop tank, it had excellent range, despite the weight of all that fuel.

The Hellcat's ammunition also added weight, but provided the necessary firepower for success. With six machine guns mounted in the wings, the plane held 2,400 rounds with an armament sequence of fire that included incendiary and armor-piercing rounds in its mix; in addition, the machine guns were

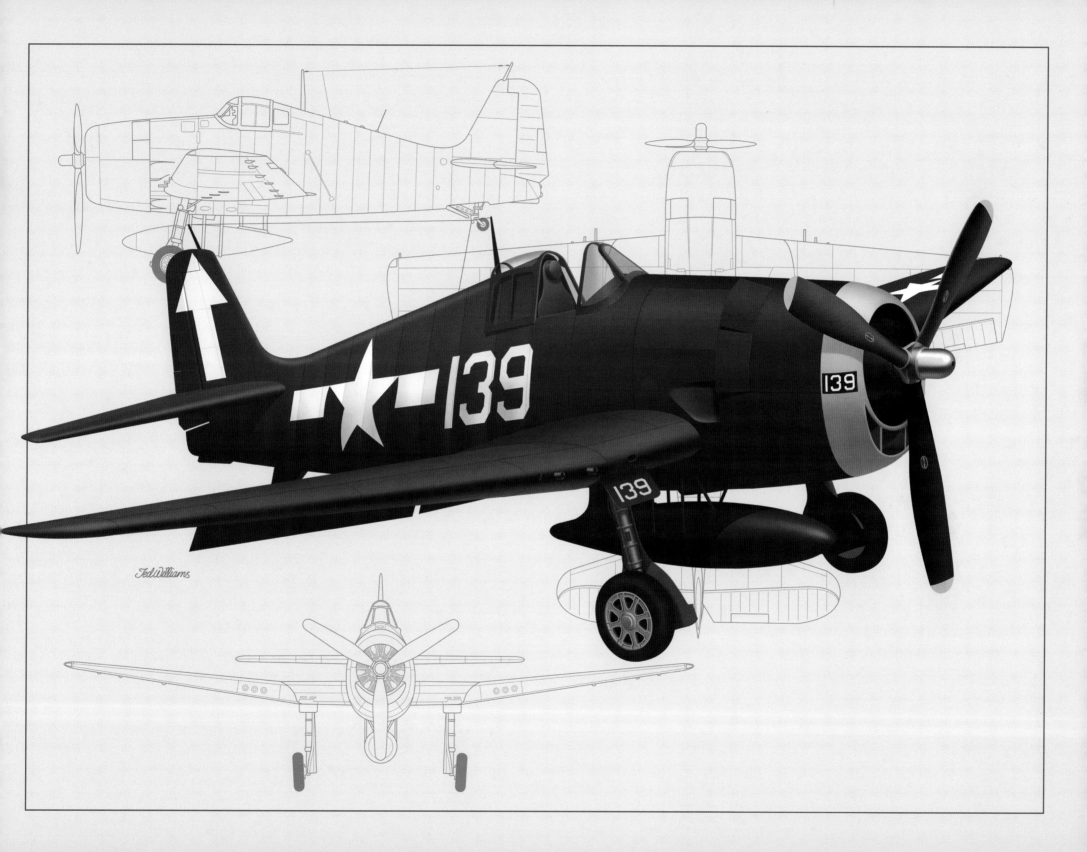

Ted Williams

Grumman F6F-5 Hellcat Specifications

Type: Single-seat, carrier-based fighter
Power plant: One 2,000-horsepower Pratt & Whitney R-2800-10W Double Wasp 18-cylinder air-cooled radial engine
Performance: Maximum speed, 380 miles per hour (611kph) at 23,400 feet (7,132m); service ceiling, 37,300 feet (11,369m); maximum range, 945 miles (1,521km)
Weight: Empty, 9,238 pounds (4,194kg); maximum takeoff weight, 15,413 pounds (6,998kg)
Dimensions: Span, 42 feet 10 inches (13.1m); length, 33 feet 7 inches (10.2m); height, 13 feet 1 inch (4m); wing area, 334 square feet (30.7m^2)
Armament: Six .50-caliber machine guns, plus a 3,000-pound (1,362kg) bomb load

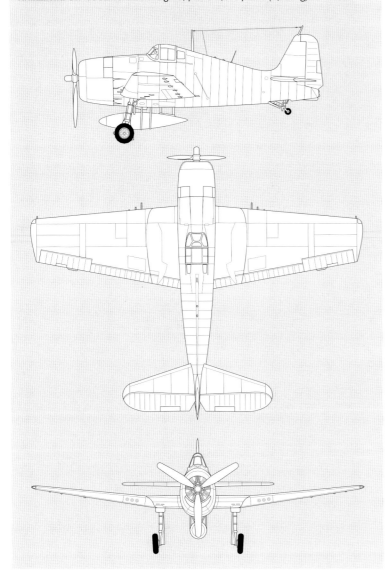

BELOW: Two Grumman F6F-3 Hellcats form up over Long Island Sound. The red outline around the national insignia dates this scene to sometime between June and August 1943.

OPPOSITE: An F6F skids into the crash barrier after blowing a tire on landing aboard the escort carrier USS *Nassau* (CVE-16).

hydraulically charged and electrically fired, not manually operated as in older fighters. The F6F-5 could also carry 2,000 pounds (908kg) of external ordnance.

To accommodate the huge power plant, the Hellcat's cockpit was raised. As a result, it afforded good pilot visibility, despite the large R-2800. This was an incredibly important asset for a fighter plane: in combat, the pilot who sees an enemy fighter first usually prevails. Pilots did complain, however, about the Hellcat's noisy cockpit, especially on long missions. The noise was due, in part, to the large engine.

Many aces are associated with the Hellcat. The air battles over the islands of Saipan, Guam, and Tinian—known collectively as the "Great Marianas Turkey Shoot"—demonstrated how effective the Hellcat really was in the Pacific theater. The Japanese air fleet never recovered from its devastating defeat during this American assault on the Marianas.

F6Fs saw action in the European theater. The British operated the Hellcat, designated Hellcat I and Hellcat II, against the German Luftwaffe. After the war, the Blue Angels, the Navy flight demonstration team, chose the Hellcat as its first aircraft in 1946. Some Hellcats saw action with the French during a conflict in Indochina, while a few others were used as radio-controlled drones in the Korean War.

North American P-51 Mustang

For many, the North American P-51 Mustang is the most beloved fighter aircraft of World War II. Yet, had its airframe not been paired with the Rolls Royce Merlin engine, the Mustang would not have become such an enduring classic.

When James H. "Dutch" Kindelberger and John Leland "Lee" Atwood left Douglas to join North American Aviation in 1934, the company had not yet sold an airplane. The company was started in 1928 as an investment holding company for various aviation interests, and both Kindelberger and Atwood brought their experience from working at the Douglas DC transport program to the small Maryland company. Newly appointed North American President and General Manager Kindelberger promptly moved the company to California and refocused its energy on the production of small, single-engine, military trainers for the Army Air Corps. This decision led to many lucrative government contracts. When the onset of World War II increased the need for airplanes, North American, the little company that once had no sales, came to supply more military aircraft than any other American manufacturer, a record that stood until 1967.

In 1940, the British Purchasing Commission approached North American about producing the Curtiss P-40 under license. Instead, Kindelberger presented a North American proposal based on contemporary European designs that he claimed would outperform the P-40. Kindelberger and a team consisting of Atwood, Edgar Schmued (a recent émigré from Germany with experience at Messerschmitt), Raymond H. Rice, and others designed an all-metal aircraft with a low-drag airframe, a retractable undercarriage with a steerable tailwheel, and a semimonocoque fuselage. The wings had a NACA-inspired sectional laminar flow airfoil with trailing edge flaps and ailerons. It was North American Aviation's first fighter.

After approving the concept, in May 1940 the British Purchasing Commission placed an order for 320 planes, designated NA-73. The first prototype was finished in 117 days. The entire aircraft was built in five sections, a novel approach that saved time and money. It was designed to use the same power plant as the P-40—the V-1710 liquid-cooled Allison engine. With aerodynamics in mind, the engine was housed in a cowl molded to fit like a glove. The radiator was placed underneath the aircraft, slightly aft of the cockpit, an ideal aerodynamic solution to the longstanding liquid-cooled radiator placement dilemma. Not only did this arrangement minimize drag, but hot air

RIGHT: The North American P-51 fuselage was manufactured in three sections: engine, main, and tail. Here, engine sections with their Packard Merlin engines already installed are moved along a specially built conveyor system.

OPPOSITE: The P-51 Mustang is considered America's best all-around propeller-driven fighter. The Mustang had it all: speed, maneuverability, high-altitude performance, reliability, range, and firepower. The bubble-canopied P-51D was the most produced variant. Here it is depicted in the markings of 363rd Fighter Squadron, 357th Fighter Group stationed at Leiston, England.

leaving the radiator's exhaust gate actually created enough thrust to increase the aircraft's speed.

The first realization of Dutch Kindelberger's vision, named the "Mustang" by the British, was delivered to England in November 1941. The British were impressed by the Mustang's overall ability, but it performed poorly at high altitudes. Without a supercharger, the Mustang was deemed most suitable for low-altitude photoreconnaissance and close ground support below 15,000 feet (4,572m). Still considering the aircraft a solid design, the RAF followed through with a sizable purchase.

While successfully engaging in its low-altitude duties for the RAF, the P-51 Mustang finally received attention from the United States. With the events at Pearl Harbor and the United States' escalating involvement in the war, the Army looked to North American. In 1942 the Army ordered 310 P-51As, retaining the name Mustang, and 500 A-36s (these were called Apaches), with dive brakes incorporated into the wings for dive-bomber and ground attack missions. The A-36 saw extensive action in the Italian campaign (1943 to 1945).

In October 1942, British engineers refitted five Mustangs with Rolls Royce Merlin engines—the same engine that powered the Supermarine Spitfire. With its new Merlin 65 two-stage supercharger, fuel injection, and a constant-speed, four-bladed propeller, the Mustang came into its own. The high-altitude Merlin, paired with the Mustang's superior airframe, improved the aircraft's rate of climb and maximum speed dramatically. Best of all, accommodating the Merlin in the Mustang was a fairly simple operation. Only minor adjustments—such as relocating the carburetor to a spot underneath the nose, which was shared by the supercharger's intake scoop—were required.

Finally, the Merlin-powered Mustang, starting with the P-51B variant, had the power to demonstrate the extraordinary range, speed, and maneuverability its designers had anticipated.

The new engine/airframe combination was such a success that North American had to develop another source for Merlin engines. In a reverse lend-lease move, the American Packard Motor Car Corporation was chosen to build the Rolls Royce Merlin 65 under license. Now Mustang production really got moving, and many variants were produced for the Allies. Modifications throughout the program included improvements for a 360-degree visibility bubble canopy, which necessitated the addition of an extended dorsal fin that improved directional stability. The D was also updated with rearward radar that alerted pilots to approaching enemy aircraft. More than 15,000 Mustangs were built for the war effort, at one point to the tune of twenty-two Mustangs per day. In the end, nearly 2,000 P-51Bs and 8,000 P-51Ds were built.

Earlier Mustangs had been armed with four wing-mounted .50-inch (1.3cm) machine guns; later variants could carry up to six guns, three in each

ABOVE: A P-51 fuselage is lowered onto its wing assembly. North American was one of the first companies to use modern manufacturing methods, such as movable assembly lines, to make aircraft assembly more efficient. The aircraft's sections were manufactured sequentially; sections were transported throughout the facility by a series of floor and ceiling conveyors.

LEFT: Nearly complete P-51 Mustangs are positioned along the final assembly line. By streamlining production, North American Aviation was able to turn out nearly one finished Mustang an hour at its peak.

North American P-51D Mustang Specifications

Type: Single-seat interceptor, long-range escort fighter
Power plant: One 1,695-horsepower Packard V-1650-7 Merlin liquid-cooled engine (P-51D)
Performance: Maximum speed, 438 miles per hour (705kph) at 25,000 feet (7,620m); service ceiling, 41,900 feet (12,771m); maximum range, 2,080 miles (3,347km)
Weight: Empty, 7,125 pounds (3,235kg); maximum takeoff weight, 12,100 pounds (5,493kg)
Dimensions: Span, 37 feet (11.3m); length, 32 feet 3 inches (9.8m); height, 13 feet 8 inches (4.2m); wing area, 233 square feet (21.4m^2)
Armament: Six .50-caliber MG-35-2 machine guns, plus up to a 1,000-pound (454kg) bomb load or six 5-inch (12.7) rockets

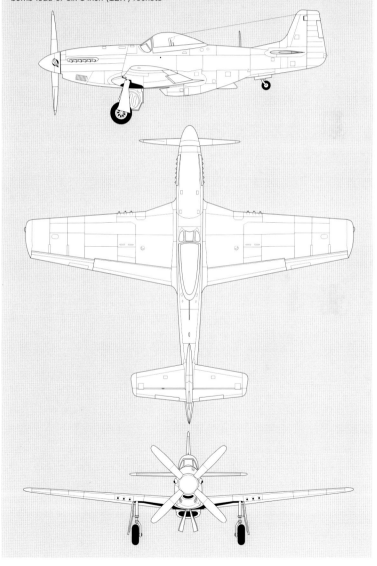

wing. Depending on the variant, 1,000 to 2,000 pounds (454–908kg) of external stores could be carried on exterior pylons.

Active in the European theater, the Mustang had the longest range of all the American fighters. Mustangs could escort American bombers from bases in Britain all the way into the heart of Germany and back, and their deployment was a significant turning point in the war, at least from Reichsmarschall Hermann Göring's perspective. In interviews after the war, Göring said that he knew Germany had lost the war when he saw Mustangs over Berlin. Mustangs also saw action in the Pacific theater. After the war, several nations purchased Mustangs for their air forces, and many of the planes returned to duty for the Korean War.

In 1944, the famed design evolved into a twin-engine, long-range fighter. Two Mustang fuselages were mounted on a lengthened laminar flow wing. This F-82 Twin Mustang was designed for trans-Pacific escort duties and was quite successful; it was used in combat during the Korean War. The Mustang also earned historical significance: it was the last propeller-driven fighter aircraft used by the Army Air Force.

ABOVE: As testament to the Mustang's success as a fighter plane, it enjoyed a long service career, with some serving in Air National Guard units well into the 1950s.

Northrop P-61 Black Widow

As early as 1940, the Luftwaffe was conducting crippling nighttime bombing operations over France and England. The Allies desperately needed to produce an aircraft with the capabilities to deter these attacks. To this end, the Northrop P-61 Black Widow was designed with emerging radar technology and an electronic weapons-firing system; and it was the only World War II fighter designed and built specifically for all-weather night operations. With two Pratt & Whitney R-2800 radial engines, the P-61 was also the largest fighter aircraft to serve the Army Air Force in World War II.

The P-61's revolutionary design was the creation of John "Jack" Northrop and Walter J. Cerny. A seminal figure in American fighter aircraft evolution, as a young man Northrop began his career with the Loughead Aircraft Manufacturing Company. ("Loughead" was later changed to the phonetic "Lockheed" by the founding brothers.)

After serving in the Army during World War I, Northrop returned to aviation design: at first again with Lockheed then, in 1923, with Douglas. In 1928, Northrop founded Avion Corporation with partner W.K. Jay. Despite the company's success with an all-metal, seven-passenger monoplane, the Depression doomed Avion. The company was sold to United Aircraft and Transport Corporation, leaving Northrop free to establish the Northrop Company in 1932, with funding from Donald Douglas. In 1939, Northrop left the first company to bear his name to start a self-funded enterprise, Northrop Aircraft Inc.

Northrop's forte was research. He was intent on designing an aircraft that was essentially a giant wing, thereby reducing drag for maximum aerodynamics and performance, an airframe ideal that was not fully realized by the military until many years later. He also furthered the study of monocoque, multicellular wing construction.

The P-61 Black Widow exemplified Northrop's attention to research and construction principles. It was a revolutionary design based on requirements officially released by the military in October 1940. The Army wanted a high-altitude night fighter that demonstrated high- and low-speed capability, could take off and land on a short runway, used radar, and carried extensive armament.

On May 26, 1942, the first of two XP-61 prototypes made its first flight. This led to the procurement of thirteen YP-61s for further testing. The first production version, the P-61A, was a cantilevered mid-wing monoplane with two booms. It was originally designed for three crew members: a pilot, a radar

RIGHT: The four electrically operated .50-caliber machine guns in the turret of a P-61 Black Widow receive the once over from a Northrop armorer. These machine guns, along with its 20mm cannons, helped make the P-61 one of the most heavily armed fighter planes of the period.

OPPOSITE: Despite its size—nearly that of a medium bomber—the Northrop P-61 was a remarkably agile aircraft. It was the United States' first all-weather night fighter and incorporated a surprisingly high-tech weapons system for the time. By utilizing radar to guide itself to the target, the Black Widow could effectively bring its awesome firepower to the task.

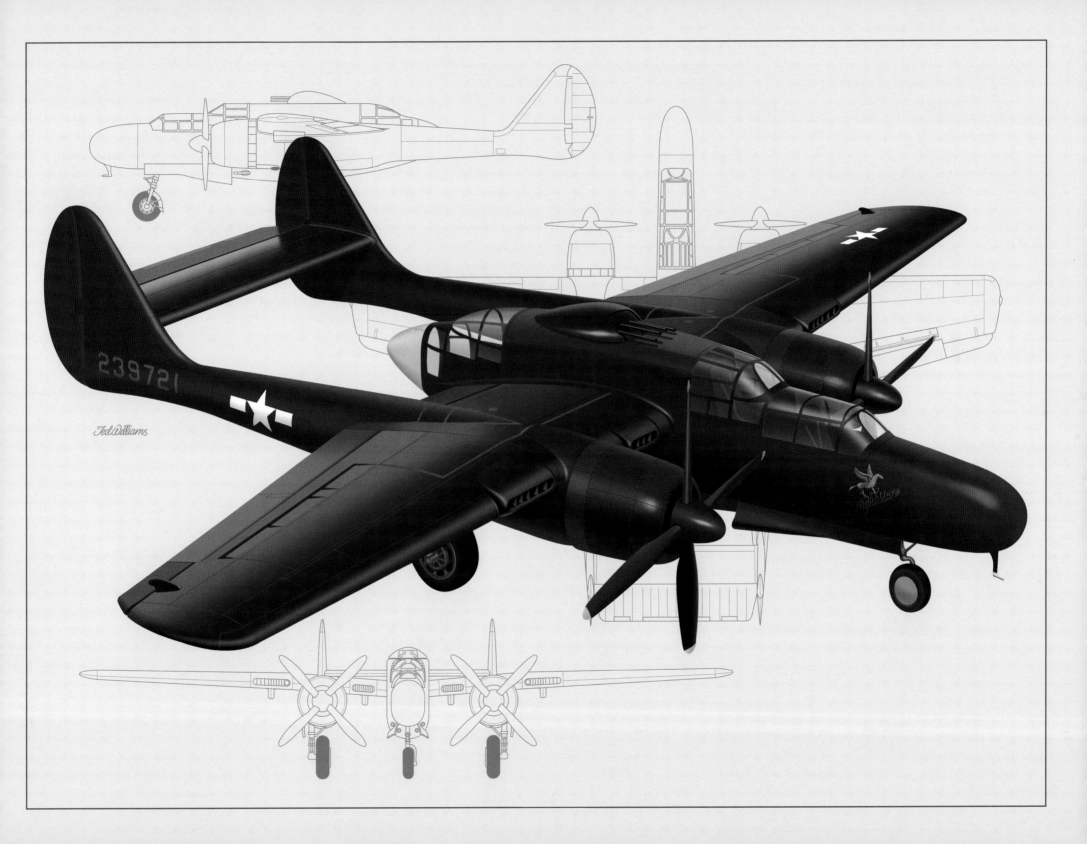

operator, and a rear gunner, all of whom wore goggles with red lenses before each flight to enhance their night vision. At first, a redesign of the P-61's airframe eliminated the rear gunner's position. The dorsal turret that housed the rear gunner had caused intolerable buffeting, an intense airframe vibration brought on by an inability to smoothly penetrate the airstream at high speeds. After a design alteration to fix the buffeting problem, the turret and rear gunner reappeared in later models.

The P-61's distinctive elongated nose housed a radar system that allowed the P-61 to operate in all weather conditions and at night. Radar surpassed the limitations of human eyesight. Now a pursuit aircraft could track, attack, and destroy a target even when the pilot and gunners could not see it with their own eyes. If a fighter pilot's greatest asset is his eyesight, the P-61 was certainly a revolutionary design that augmented its pilot's advantage with radar. The enemy, who could no longer depend on the cover of night or inclement weather to shield his presence from the far-seeing radar, was at a distinct disadvantage. Yet the complexity of the radar's operation necessitated that the Black Widow have a crew. The pilot could not fly the plane and monitor the radar at the same time. It would require too many simultaneous, high-stress tasks for one individual. This consideration would become even more crucial in the jet age.

Two hundred P-61As were delivered to squadrons in late 1943. By 1944, 450 P-61Bs had gone into production. The B variant, with a longer nose, was only a slight improvement over the A. The P-61B introduced four 310-gallon (1,173L) external fuel tanks that increased fuel capacity and extended the aircraft's range.

The final variant produced in quantity was the P-61C. All P-61s were powered by twin Pratt & Whitney R-2800 Double Wasp 18-cylinder, two-row, radial air-cooled engines. The C was upgraded to a more powerful R-2800-73, with a General Electric CH-5 turbo-supercharger and a Curtiss electric propeller. The P-61C also employed air brakes on the top and bottom of the wing. Operated by a foot pedal, these brakes helped the pilot steady the fast-moving aircraft while diving on a target. Of the 517 P-61Cs ordered, only forty-one were completed before the war ended.

A P-61E was designed as a day fighter to no consequence, and thirty-six P-61s, redesignated F-15As, were developed for unarmed photoreconnaissance. The P-61 saw action throughout Europe and the Pacific. The Navy operated P-61s in the Pacific theater.

The aptly named Black Widow carried devastating firepower. The ideal armament configuration for the P-61 included four electrically fired 20mm cannons and four .50-caliber machine guns with interrupter switches to protect the aircraft's twin tail and propellers. The guns were located underneath the

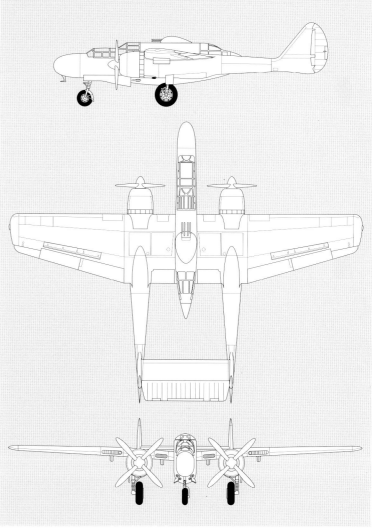

aircraft and in a top turret so as not to disrupt the crew's night vision during firing; however, many P-61s were produced without the turret and its machine guns. Additionally, the B and C variants, for instance, could carry a 6,400-pound (2,906kg) payload.

For its size, the P-61 was a surprisingly maneuverable aircraft. Either painted Army olive drab or black, the P-61 was as large as a medium bomber. The night-fighting behemoth boasted a turning radius equal to that of the Supermarine Spitfire; it was even able to best a Grumman F6F Hellcat in a tight turn. Its combat effectiveness can also be traced to the specialized night-fighting training provided to the three-member crew.

The war's end also brought an end to the P-61's career, but its accurate weapons system, its use of radar, and its proficiency at performing in adverse conditions was a harbinger of things to come. In the jet age, the fighter pilot's role rapidly changed from basic gun fighting to the operation of an aircraft capable of deploying an array of sophisticated tactical weapons systems.

ABOVE: Painted gloss black for nighttime operations, a Black Widow taxis to the ramp. The P-61 Black Widow's Pratt & Whitney R-2800 engines required large, four-bladed propellers to distribute engine torque.

OPPOSITE: Northrop engineers add final touches to the assembly of a Pratt & Whitney R-2800 in the left nacelle of a P-61 Black Widow. A placard, at left, reminds the worker of the P-61's production priority.

Grumman F8F Bearcat

With its reputation as the "Ironworks," especially in the production of the F4F Wildcat and F6F Hellcat, Grumman introduced the next in its family of fighting felines in 1945. The F8F was Grumman's last piston-engine, propeller-driven fighter developed for the Navy, as well as the Navy's first aircraft to utilize the bubble canopy for improved pilot visibility. Thirteen hundred F8Fs were completed before war production ceased: in all, several prototype models, 873 F8F-1s, and 365 F8F-2s were built.

Late in the war, Japan responded to the American air threat over the Pacific with new aircraft. Late arrivals from the Japanese, including the Mitsubishi J2M and the Kawanishi N1K, were faster and better protected than earlier-generation Zeros. The United States needed to update its aircraft to keep pace with these Japanese developments.

William Schwendler, chief engineer at Grumman, put a team together to develop a pursuit aircraft that would be powerful like the Hellcat, but small like the Wildcat, while maintaining maximum pilot defenses (armor, self-sealing fuel tanks) and standard required naval equipment and armament. To counter the evolving Japanese aircraft, priority was placed on low-altitude performance, handling capabilities, and rate of climb; the military's specifications even de-emphasized range in favor of speed and handling. The Navy wanted a "hot" airplane that could operate from smaller carriers.

The resulting F8F single-seat, cantilevered, low-wing monoplane was actually smaller than the Wildcat. Its pressurized cockpit felt cramped compared with the ample space provided for a Hellcat pilot, but this inconvenience was quickly forgiven once the Bearcat demonstrated its overall performance gain. The first XF8F-1 prototype flew in August 1944 and performed well. With rapid climb and acceleration, it was faster than its predecessors, and had the ability to make tight turns that would have been impossible in an F6F Hellcat.

Already successfully paired with many military airframes at the time, a Pratt & Whitney R-2800 Double Wasp 18-cylinder radial air-cooled engine delivered awesome power and turned the Bearcat's four-bladed, twelve-foot-seven-inch (3.8m) constant-speed Aeroproducts propeller. Grumman choose to construct the F8F with a heartier aluminum skin than was typically used in aircraft production. This offered added strength and airframe longevity—not a surprising design decision from the Ironworks. As an additional performance measure, the aircraft was flush-riveted and spot-welded to reduce surface drag.

OPPOSITE: The Grumman F8F Bearcat was a very fast fighter plane designed to counter the increasing threat from Japanese kamikaze attacks. It was also the Navy's last prop fighter. Created with the smallest possible military airframe that could mount a Pratt & Whitney R-2800, the Bearcat could climb from a standing start to 10,000 feet (3,048m) in about ninety seconds, and it delivered a devastating punch from its four 20mm cannons.

Ever concerned with pilot protection, Grumman introduced safety wingtips on the Bearcat. These innovative wingtips would come off if the aircraft approached nine Gs. The theory was that the wingtips would detach at a predetermined location should extreme G forces threaten the structural integrity of the aircraft. Jettisoning the wingtips would prevent the wings from breaking at a random location when subjected to intolerable forces, an eventuality that would render the aircraft uncontrollable. These near-hollow tips also reduced weight, further improving the Bearcat's performance. After a tragic in-flight incident involving the innovative safety feature, the wingtips were rigged with a trigger to ensure that both wingtips would detach simultaneously. Although well intentioned, the safety wingtips were never really put to use. At the time, Navy pilots seldom put themselves, or their aircraft, in situations approaching nine Gs.

Although the war was near its end, frontline squadrons began to receive F8F-1s in May 1945. General Motors' Eastern Aircraft Division had also been contracted to build 1,876 Bearcats, these models designated F3M-1, but the order was canceled. Additional F8F-1s followed in 1946 and 1947, but the F8F-2 was the only other variant produced in quantity. A larger tail added stability to the -2 models. Several F8F-1s and F8F-2s were equipped as night fighters, and many F8F-2s were used for photoreconnaissance.

Only four machine guns carrying 300 rounds per gun were mounted in the F8F's folding wings. When it was discovered that Japanese aircraft in the Pacific were being downed with less ammunition than the Hellcat's six guns were dispensing, it was wisely decided to reduce the Bearcat's armament. The loss of the guns offered considerable weight savings and ammunition efficiency. In later models, the Bearcat was equipped with four 20mm cannons in lieu of machine guns. In addition, all Bearcats were able to carry a 2,000-pound (908kg) payload.

The F8Fs never saw combat in War World II, but they were supplied to France during a conflict in Indochina. From 1951 to 1954, the Bearcat was deployed effectively as land-based ground support, despite its limited range. The F8F did not see action in the Korean War, and by July 1955 it was removed from the U.S. Navy. Some models in the Thai Air Force, however, saw service as late as 1960.

Once removed from active service, demilitarized Bearcats were used in air racing. In 1969, Darryl Greenmayer and his F8F-2 broke the world speed

record for propeller-driven aircraft that had been set in 1939 by Fritz Wendel, a Messerschmitt representative. Greenmayer flew his Bearcat at 480 miles per hour (772kph).

Designed for combat in the Pacific theater, and, in particular, to meet the threat posed by Japanese kamikaze attacks, the Bearcat was never able to demonstrate its true capabilities before the war ended. No matter its place in history and war, the Bearcat remains the quintessential radial-engine, propeller-driven fighter plane. Frequently compared to the Mustang, which is often named as the best propeller-driven aircraft with a liquid-cooled engine, it is not a true one-to-one comparison, since each aircraft was designed for a different mission.

Perhaps the Bearcat's most important contribution was its late availability. Its superior characteristics allowed the Navy to use it as a solid interim aircraft during a transitional period in military aviation. The Bearcat kept the Navy supplied with a reliable fighter design while it began to accept the jet into its naval air fleet.

OPPOSITE: This Grumman F8F Bearcat is fitted with gun pods under the wings. These pods were an attempt to establish the Bearcat as a ground attack aircraft; however, in the Korean conflict it quickly became evident that the Bearcat's lack of range, even with an auxiliary centerline fuel tank, hampered its effectiveness in the ground attack role.

ABOVE: Of all the Grumman designs from World War II, the Bearcat's cockpit offered the pilot the best view. Shown here is number 337, an F8F-2 with a shorter vertical stabilizer. It is also fitted with underwing hardpoints for mounting 5-inch rockets.

Grumman F8F-2 Bearcat Specifications

Type: Single-seat naval fighter
Power plant: One 2,100-horsepower Pratt & Whitney R-2800-34W 18-cylinder air-cooled radial engine
Performance: Maximum speed, 421 mph (677kph) at 19,700 feet (6,005m); service ceiling, 38,700 feet (11,796m); maximum range, 1,105 miles (1,778km)
Weight: Empty, 7,070 pounds (3,210kg); maximum takeoff weight, 12,947 pounds (5,878kg)
Dimensions: Span, 35 feet 10 inches (10.9m); length, 28 feet 3 inches (8.6m); height, 13 feet 10 inches (4.2m); wing area, 244 square feet (22.4m^2)
Armament: Four .50-caliber machine guns or four 20mm cannons

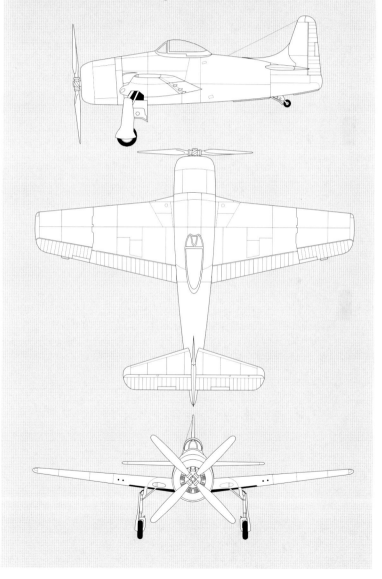

Bell P-59 Airacomet

The Bell P-59 Airacomet made history as the first American jet-propelled aircraft. Although not a successful fighter, the P-59 was a vital link to the first jet fighter produced for operational service, the Lockheed P-80 Shooting Star. Designed for use in World War II, the P-59 never saw combat. Its performance could not match propeller-driven aircraft such as the Lockheed P-38 Lightning or the North American P-51 Mustang, each an excellent example of a reliable, mass-produced aircraft with a winning victory ratio. Yet the benefits of jet propulsion, once perfected, were irrefutable. The piston engine's heyday was coming to an end.

Because the United States joined World War II later than its Allies, American jet development lagged behind the efforts of the British. Frank Whittle designed a jet engine for the RAF in 1930. His findings published, Germany and Italy rapidly began developing their own jet technology. The German Messerschmitt Me 262, the first jet to participate in combat during World War II, took flight in 1939.

In April 1941, General Henry H. "Hap" Arnold, commander of the United States Army Air Force, was the first American to witness the Whittle jet engine when it was put to use in the Gloster E.28/39 prototype. Impressed, Arnold arranged to have design examples of the engine provided to the United States in reciprocity for the lend-lease program.

The United States was eager to explore the jet engine's potential. It was understood that a piston-engine aircraft could not exceed speeds much higher than 500 miles per hour (805kph). At 500 miles per hour and higher, the tips of the spinning propeller blades approach the speed of sound. At such high speeds, the propeller loses its ability to produce thrust. Additionally, the nature of the internal combustion reciprocating engine held speeds down to around 500 miles per hour. Higher air speeds could be attained only if a new propulsion system were to be developed.

In September 1941, the U.S. Army Air Force asked the Bell Aircraft Corporation to design an aircraft around the RAF jet engine now being built under license by General Electric, an industrial turbine expert. To date, there is still speculation about why Bell was chosen for this important project. Among the possible explanations: an appreciation of Bell's innovative designs, Bell's proximity to the General Electric facility that was already producing the engine, and Bell's relative inactivity in comparison to other World War II aircraft suppliers.

RIGHT: The Bell P-59 Airacomet was designed to carry three .50-caliber machine guns and one 37mm cannon in its forward fuselage gun bay. Note the large size of the cannon's magazine as compared with the magazines for the machine guns.

OPPOSITE: The Bell P-59 Airacomet was America's first jet-propelled fighter. Although it didn't perform much better than contemporary propeller-driven fighters, the Airacomet marked an important first in the development of jet aircraft.

The project was veiled in secrecy from the start. To ensure that other countries did not receive intelligence that the United States was developing a jet, the project was classified as top secret. Even the American public was unaware of the Airacomet's existence until 1944.

Three prototypes and thirteen pre-series aircraft were developed covertly at a secret location across town from Bell's Buffalo, New York, facility. The aircraft was designated P-59 after a program already in place to build a coaxial, two-seat fighter with a pusher propeller. Surreptitiously, development of the P-59 pusher design was discontinued in favor of the more significant jet fighter with the same designation.

In October 1942, the first P-59 was evaluated at Muroc Dry Lake, California, now Edwards Air Force Base. As a precaution, whenever a P-59 was on display, a fake propeller was attached to the nose to disguise it as a propeller-driven aircraft, thereby discouraging the curiosity of unauthorized onlookers. A twin-engine, cantilevered mid-wing monoplane with tricycle landing gear and a pressurized cockpit, the Airacomet featured two General Electric type I-A turbojet engines, each delivering 1,250 pounds (933kg) of static thrust, which were placed near the center of gravity at the wing roots. This location facilitated engine repair and replacement. To keep the tail clear of the jet exhaust, the empennage was high, a characteristic of the P-59 and other jets to come. The wing was engineered with a laminar flow airfoil.

Test pilots reported several positive characteristics of the new plane. The P-59 did not vibrate, as was common with piston-engine aircraft, and the turbulence produced by a spinning propeller was no longer a concern. Overall, the Airacomet could reach high speeds at high altitudes and it was not difficult to fly. However, the P-59 was never able to attain the speed anticipated.

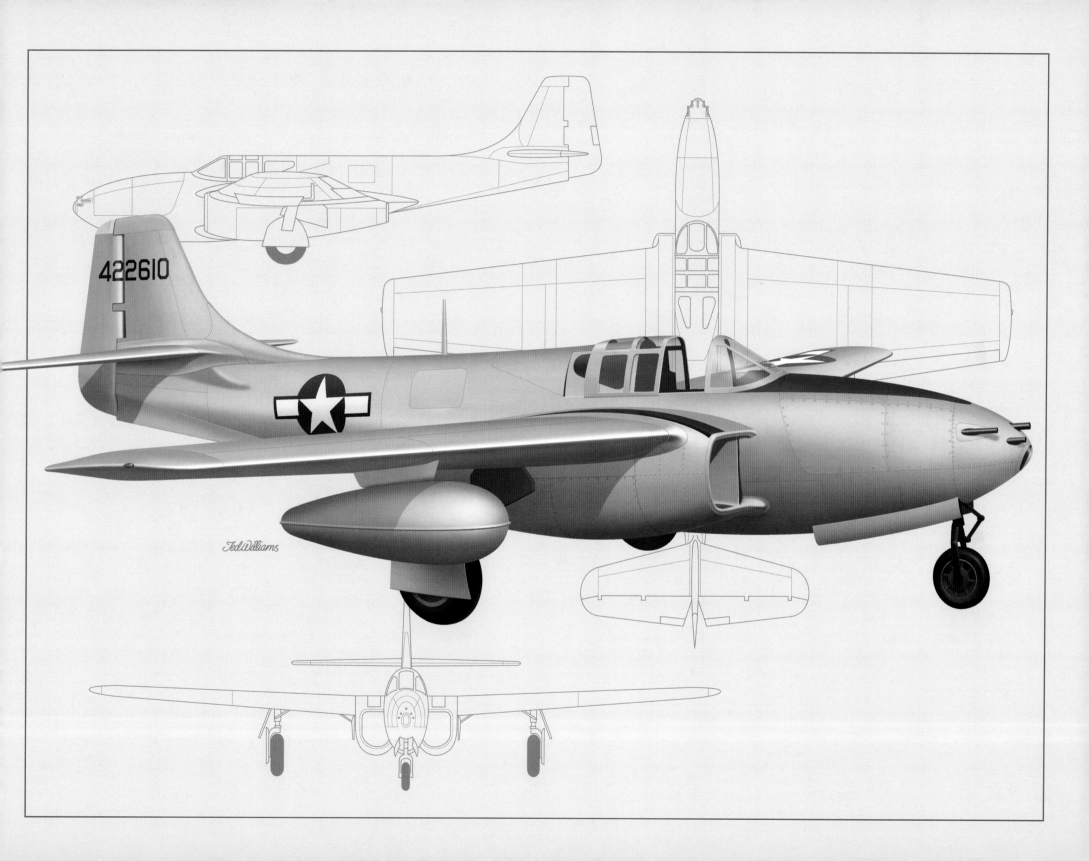

Testing revealed that the engine needed improvement; in particular, the hot exhaust stressed the turbine blades to ruin.

Over the course of the program, sixty-six Airacomets were built, many fewer than originally anticipated. The majority were P-59As, but thirty models with minor modifications, were classified as P-59Bs.

The P-59 was designed to have one 37mm cannon and three .50-caliber machine guns fitted in the nose, but the armament was typically not included because most P-59s were used for evaluation or as trainers to prepare pilots for the next military jet, the P-80. Overall, the Airacomet was primarily used for training and to study the advancement of jet propulsion.

The P-59 was tested and evaluated by both the Army and the Navy. The Navy determined that the P-59 was not suitable for carrier operations. The engines needed refinement if they were to provide the acceleration required to take off from a carrier. And visibility was poor.

Despite the P-59 Airacomet's failings, the jet engine proved to be the power plant of the future. Developed in one year, the P-59 program was indicative of how the jet age would develop: quickly. Indeed, the jet age would soon eclipse the era of propeller-driven aircraft. New engineering solutions and imaginative ideas would be responsible for the next chapter of aviation history.

OPPOSITE: This three-quarter rear view clearly shows the placement of the engine nacelles that house the Bell P-59's General Electric jet engines. A strake has been added to the underside of the fuselage to provide increased lateral stability.

BELOW: A close-up look at the business end of the P-59's twin turbojets. Early jet engines were maintenance intensive.

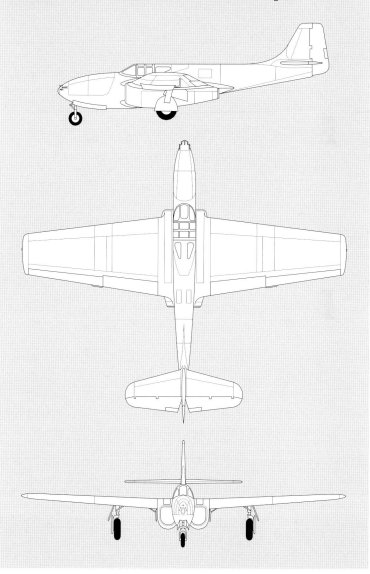

Bell P-59A Airacomet Specifications

Type: Single-seat jet fighter
Power plant: Two General Electric J31-GE-5 turbojet engines producing 2,000 pounds (908kg) of static thrust
Performance: Maximum speed, 409 mph (658kph) at 35,000 feet (10,668m); service ceiling, 46,200 feet (14,082m); maximum range, 240 miles (386km)
Weight: Empty, 7,950 pounds (3,609kg); maximum takeoff weight, 10,882 pounds (4940kg)
Dimensions: Span, 45 feet 6 inches (13.9m); length, 38 feet 1 inch (11.6m); height, 12 feet (3.7m); wing area, 358.8 square feet (33m^2)
Armament: One 37mm M4 cannon and three .50-caliber machine guns

Lockheed P-80 Shooting Star

Nine months after the first flight of the Bell P-59, Lockheed was approached by the U.S. Army Air Force to develop a jet design around the successful British de Havilland H-1B Goblin turbojet. Amazingly, Lockheed delivered a prototype just 143 days after project acceptance.

This quick turnaround was due to the efforts of Clarence L. "Kelly" Johnson and Hall L. Hibbard. These men had been fostering jet development long before the American military recognized the jet engine's potential.

Like the P-59 Airacomet, the XP-80 had a conventional aircraft design. It was a single-engine, single-seat, low-wing, cantilevered monoplane. The fuselage was a semimonocoque duralumin assembly built in two sections, similar to the P-59's construction. The XP-80's leading edge on the laminar flow wing slimmed to a knifelike profile, featuring hydraulic flaps and ailerons on the trailing edge. The wings were situated just slightly aft of the bubble canopy, with the air intakes for the engine at the wing roots. The XP-80 incorporated a retractable tricycle landing gear, a necessary configuration in the jet age.

The P-80 prototype had been designed to use the British de Havilland H-1B Goblin turbojet, but it proved not to be a good match for the airframe. Maximum speed at 20,000 feet (6,096m) for the XP-80 was clocked at 502 miles per hour (808kph). Although faster than any other USAAF aircraft available, the de Havilland engine, rated at 2,460 pounds (1,117kg) of static thrust, never produced the power promised. A second prototype, the XP-80A, was modified to accomodate the heavier General Electric J-33 prototype engine, which produced 3,850 pounds (1,748kg) of static thrust. The A variant was bigger overall. It was also heavier and longer, with a new wing fillet to correct undesirable roll characteristics discovered during XP-80 flight testing. The A model also featured a pressurized cockpit and additional fuel storage in wingtip tanks; the resulting silhouette became synonymous with the early jet age. Provisions for night flying and a heartier landing gear were also developed on the XP-80A.

The first XP-80A flew in June 1944. It was quickly followed by thirteen evaluation models, YP-80As, but World War II ended before any significant production was possible. Thus, only 676 P-80As were actually completed out of the original Lockheed contract to build 4,000. North American's contract to build P-80As for the war effort was canceled.

The P-80As saw several power plants. First production models were shipped with the J33-GE-9. This was replaced in later P-80As by the GE-11,

96th Pursuit Squadron

RIGHT: A Lockheed employee walks under the tailpipe section of a P-80 Shooting Star that is under construction. The fixture supporting the aircraft provides easy access to all parts of the airframe, and the aircraft's landing gear can be retracted or extended as needed.

OPPOSITE: The P-80 Shooting Star was the USAAF's first operational jet fighter and, in the Korean War, was the first USAF jet fighter to see combat. This example carries the markings of the 96th Pursuit Squadron, the famous "Hat in the Ring" squadron that traces its beginnings back to World War I.

capable of 4,000 pounds (1,816kg) of static thrust. A few final P-80As received the J33-A-17, built by the Allison division of General Motors. In 1947, a P-80B was developed to use the most powerful jet engine yet—an alcohol-and-water injected Allison J33-A-21 delivering 5,200 pounds (2,361kg) of static thrust. A Shooting Star flew to fame in June 1947 when Colonel Albert Boyd broke the world speed record. This specially modified XP-80R Shooting Star reached the then unbelievable speed of 623 miles per hour (1,002kph).

Many changes occurred during the P-80's lifetime. Not only was the swift emergence of the jet age a predominate concern, but a transformation in the military's command structure altered the P-80's lineage. In 1947, the U.S. Air Force was created as a standalone branch of the military, no longer affiliated with the Army. At this time the "P" designation for pursuit aircraft was changed to "F" for fighter. Hence, the P-80B became the F-80B.

The final Shooting Star variant to be produced in large numbers was the F-80C. The first lot of 238 F-80Cs was powered by the J33-A-23, which produced 4,600 pounds (2,088kg) of static thrust. The second lot, 561 aircraft, received the J33-A-35, rated at 5,400 pounds (2,452kg) of static thrust.

Armament was placed in the nose, alongside the radio equipment. Throughout the Shooting Star's career, it was outfitted with six .50-caliber

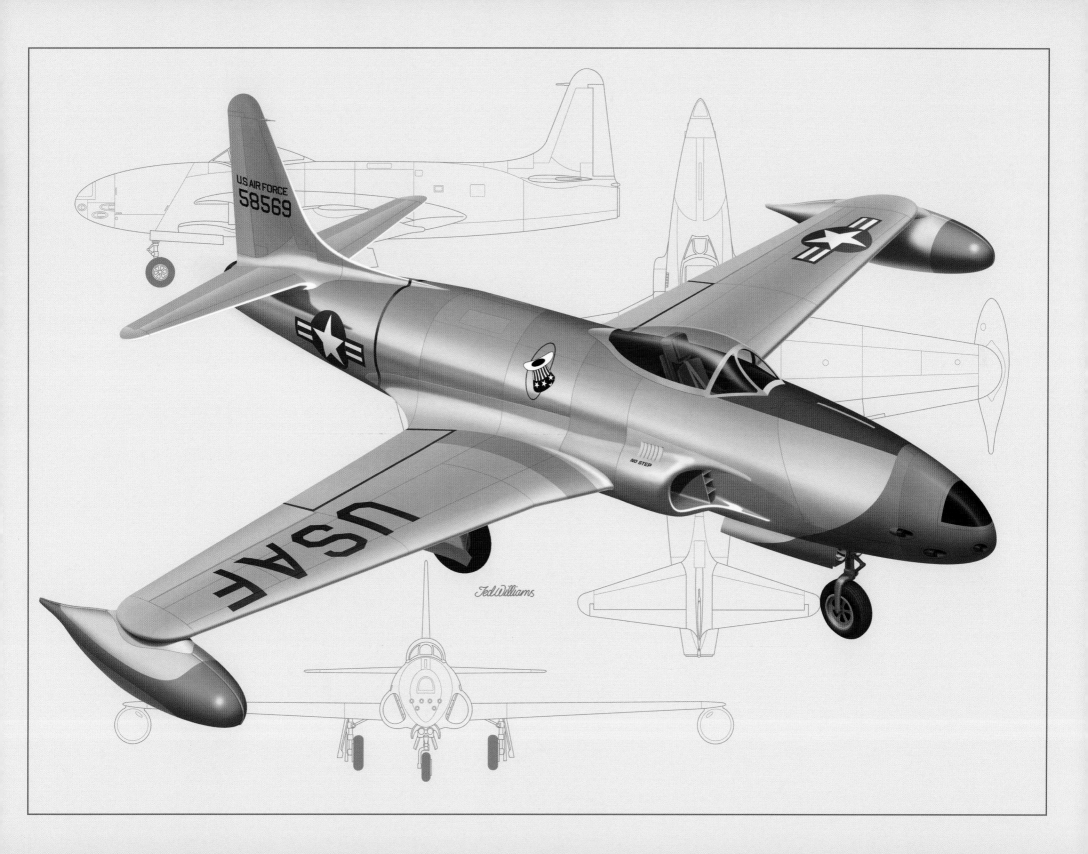

Lockheed P-80A Shooting Star Specifications

Type: Single-seat fighter and fighter-bomber
Power plant: One General Electric J33-GE-9 turbojet engine producing 3,850 pounds (1,748kg) of static thrust
Performance: Maximum speed, 558 mph (898kph) at 6,000 feet (1,829m); service ceiling, 45,000 feet (13,716m); maximum range, 540 miles (869km)
Weight: Empty, 7,920 pounds (3,596kg); maximum takeoff weight, 14,500 pounds (6,583kg)
Dimensions: Span, 38 feet 10 inches (11.8m); length, 34 feet 6 inches (10.5m); height, 11 feet 4 inches (3.5m); wing area, 237 square feet (21.8m²)
Armament: Six .50-caliber machine guns

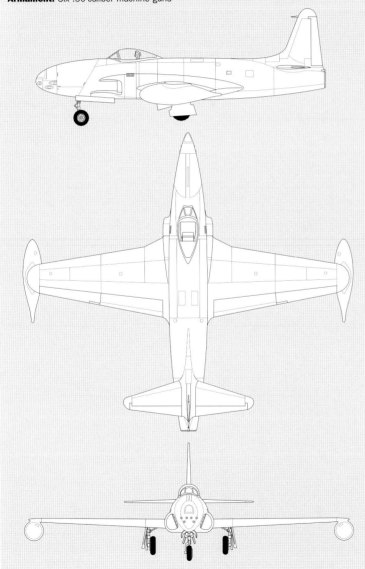

machine guns. Later variants could haul bombs and other weaponry on under-wing mounts.

Although the Shooting Star did not perform in World War II, it did answer the call to duty. At the start of the Korean War, the F-80 was the United States' primary frontline fighter aircraft. North American P-51 Mustangs and Vought FU4 Corsairs were also briefly used early in the Korean conflict, but it soon became apparent that piston-driven aircraft could no longer perform fighter duties alongside jet-propelled aircraft. A mere five years after World War II, the greatest fighter aircraft of that conflict were no longer contenders, especially once the Russian-designed Mikoyan and Gurevich MiG-15 jets joined the fray.

The Russian MiG, flown by the People's Republic of China Air Force, was an amazingly effective aircraft, made more so because U.S. intelligence did not know that the Soviet Union had developed such superior technology. Based on the aerodynamic studies performed by German engineers during World War II, the MiG's performance surpassed that of the Shooting Star. Yet on November 8, 1950, in the first air conflict between a Russian and American jet, the F-80C took the victory, thanks to its well-trained and cunning American pilot, Lt. Russell J. Brown.

Despite early victories, the Shooting Star was clearly outclassed. It spent the remainder of the Korean War supporting ground troops with rocket, bomb, and napalm attacks. It was removed from service after the Korean conflict.

The F-80's list of contributions is lengthy. It was the first operational jet aircraft produced in quantity for the U.S. Air Force and the first American aircraft to exceed 600 miles per hour (965kph) in level flight. It was also the first American jet-powered aircraft to score a victory in jet-to-jet combat.

BELOW: This Lockheed F-80C was forced down in the arctic. A ground crew was dispatched to recover the plane and it was decided to attach skis and fly it to the nearest base. Bright red tail and wing markings were applied to all aircraft operating in arctic regions for easy spotting in the event that a plane went down.

LEFT: F-80Cs in service with the National Guard receive routine maintenance. The Shooting Star's entire aft fuselage could be removed for easy access by ground crews.

McDonnell F2H Banshee

Developed from the Navy's first jet, the McDonnell FH-1 Phantom, the F2H Banshee served as a fighter, bomber, and photoreconnaissance platform in the Korean conflict. Not to be discounted, the Phantom prepared the Navy for carrier-based jet operations, and it was faster than the Navy's propeller-driven aircraft in service at the time. But the Phantom did have its drawbacks. Overall, it lagged behind the jets already in operation with the U.S. Air Force, such as the F-80 Shooting Star, which in turn also had severe performance deficiencies when toe-to-toe with the Russian MiG-15s.

Typically slower to implement new aviation technologies, the Navy turned its attention to the jet engine in 1943. Toward the end of World War II, the Navy possessed an impressive air arm. The Grumman cats—the Wildcat, Hellcat, and Bearcat—and the Vought F4U Corsair were some of the best fighter aircraft in service. Along with the valiant Navy pilots who flew them, all of these fighters quickly became legends as they swept the skies of enemy aircraft. Entrenched in wartime production, the predominant Navy suppliers of these legendary aircraft were not available to develop the Navy's first jet. As a consequence, McDonnell Aircraft Company, still a startup, earned the prized contract.

James McDonnell received his degree in aeronautical engineering from M.I.T. in 1925. After his formal schooling, he gained practical design experience at several aviation companies, including the Consolidated Aircraft Company. Like many other entrepreneurs, he was thwarted by the Depression. After an unsuccessful attempt at launching a business in the unstable economy of the late 1920s, McDonnell went back to work for other industry leaders, working his way to the Glenn Martin Company. After a time, his own McDonnell Aircraft Company was off to a meager, but solid, start in 1939.

In 1943, the Navy was looking for an aircraft powered by a jet engine that had a long range, but could operate at a manageable speed for carrier landings. The Navy Bureau of Aeronautics was so concerned about restraining the jet's top-end speed for naval operations that it approached McDonnell with this requirement. When McDonnell produced a proposal for a jet with unswept wings, the Navy pounced on it. This proposal led to the FH-1 Phantom.

Although the Phantom was miles ahead of its propellered fleetmates, it couldn't keep up with its Air Force contemporaries, much less the Soviet Union's aircraft. Now that the Navy was warming to jets and their unique characteristics, it commissioned a fighter to succeed the Phantom. Herman D.

RIGHT: A McDonnell F2H Banshee is catapulted from a carrier. As a safety precaution, the canopy was often kept open during takeoff to facilitate an emergency bailout.

OPPOSITE: The F2H Banshee presents its very distinctive silhouette. Despite mounting two early jet engines side-by-side, the McDonnell design team was able to create a graceful and visually appealing aircraft. It seems to follow the old adage, "if it looks good, it'll fly good."

Barkey and Al Utsch, led by McDonnell Vice President G.C. Covington, designed the next McDonnell on top of what was the Phantom. The new design was to be an all-around bigger aircraft with more powerful engines, greater lifting capacity, and increased armament.

Named the Banshee, the new design—a single-seat, twin-engine, fighter aircraft—had a laminar flow wing. Like the Phantom, the new plane incorporated the Westinghouse turbojet that was then in development for the Navy. As a safety and efficiency feature, the Banshee could fly on one engine if necessary. Pilots routinely powered down one engine on long flights to maximize fuel economy. As expected, the Banshee came standard with the Navy equipment required for carrier operations: folding wings, a reinforced undercarriage, and an arresting hook.

Not without justification, the U.S. Navy was reticent to switch to an all-jet air fleet. Early jet engines frequently could not produce enough power to take off from a short carrier runway. Unable to spool up quickly, the jets couldn't lift off the deck in time, resulting in many accidents. The Banshee demonstrated to the Navy that it urgently needed to modernize its aircraft carriers to safely handle the new higher-performance jets.

During this critical transition period, the British Navy solved many of the problems experienced by jet operations aboard traditional aircraft carriers. The British innovations led the way for a modernization of the carrier deck: modern aircraft, they reasoned, required modern carriers. These improvements consisted of fitting two steam catapults on the forward flight deck and adding

an angled deck to allow the carrier to retrieve aircraft while using the forward deck for storing and launching aircraft. The U.S. Navy quickly adopted these solutions and a systematic refitting program was initiated. The USS *Hancock* was the first U.S. carrier with these innovations.

Over the course of the Banshee program, 892 of the jets were built. The prototype flew on January 1947, garnering an initial production order for fifty-six F2H-1s. The F2H-1 was similar to the prototype, except for its redesigned tail. A total of 364 F2H-2s, all with a longer fuselage, increased fuel capacity (in auxiliary wingtip tanks), and larger engines, were ordered in May 1949. An F2H-3 was modified as a result of combat seen by F2H-2s in Korea. The F2H-4, of which 150 were built, was the final variant in the program. Night fighting and photoreconnaissance versions were also produced.

The Banshee carried four 20mm M-2 cannons, upgraded from the machine guns carried by the Phantom. All Banshees could carry an ordnance payload, which was put to use during the Korean conflict. In Korea, the Banshee served as a primary offensive aircraft and escort fighter. Later, the C and D variants could carry four Sidewinder missiles.

The success of any fighter design can by gauged by its ability to evolve to meet future mission requirements. The Banshee was able to do just that, staying in fleet service until 1959 and reserve service until 1965. Some photoreconnaissance variants even continued to perform into the early 1970s.

OPPOSITE: McDonnell Banshees, with their wings neatly folded, sparkle after a trip to the paint shop. Glossy paint creates less drag than a flat finish and it was easier to maintain aboard carriers at sea.

BELOW: For a brief period during the 1950s, naval aircraft like this Banshee were left with their natural aluminum finish. The Navy felt it needed a more appropriate paint scheme than the glossy dark blue it had used in the past. This unpainted Banshee houses an up-to-date radar system within its large radome.

McDonnell F2H-1 Banshee Specifications

Type: Single-seat naval fighter
Power plant: Two Westinghouse J34-WE-34 turbojet engines producing 3,250 pounds (1,476kg) of static thrust
Performance: Maximum speed, 587 mph (944kph) at sea level; service ceiling, 48,500 feet (14,783m); maximum range, 1,475 miles (2,373km)
Weight: Empty, 9,794 pounds (4,446kg); maximum takeoff weight, 22,312 pounds (10,130kg)
Dimensions: Span, 44 feet 10 inches (13.7m); length, 40 feet 2 inches (12.2m); height, 14 feet 5 inches (4.4m); wing area, 294 square feet (27m²)
Armament: Four 20mm cannons

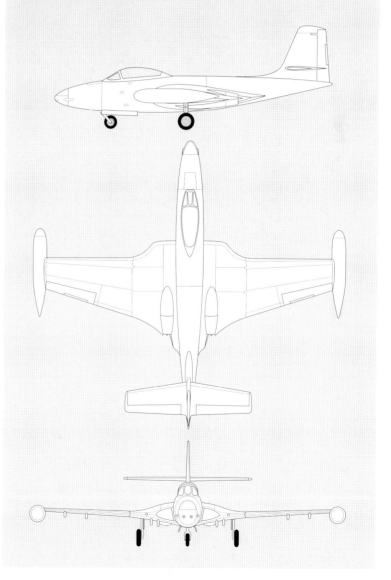

Republic F-84 Thunderjet

The F-84 Thunderjet was Republic's first entry into the jet age. With Alexander Kartveli at the helm, Republic's design was initiated in 1944, near the end of World War II. The design originally entailed rebuilding the P-47 airframe to incorporate a jet engine, but this plan was quickly discarded. In its wake, an entirely new airframe took shape.

The Thunderjet's gestation period coincided with the development of other early jet programs. In the years closely following World War II, there was plenty of competition among aircraft manufacturers, as each vied to develop the next jet design.

The Republic XF-84 Thunderjet made its first flight on February 28, 1946. It was the first new military pursuit aircraft to be evaluated after World War II. Only months later, the prototype broke a speed record, flying at 611 miles per hour (983kph), making it the fastest military aircraft in the United States. Kartveli's design decisions were true to the guiding principles that had led him to success with the P-47. The aircraft made efficient use of ducting and air intakes, a Kartveli specialty. To this end, it was the first jet to utilize a nose intake. As a consequence, the Thunderjet was a big airplane with thick wings (in contrast to the slim, knife-edge wings used on other early military jets): the majority of the aircraft's fuel had to be stored in the wings, since the center air intake took most of the fuselage space normally reserved for fuel storage.

The Thunderjet was certainly a modern aircraft. In addition to their thickness, the straight low-wings made use of a laminar flow airfoil. The horizontal tailplanes were mounted high on the empennage and the entire aircraft was covered in a duralumin skin. The cockpit was pressurized, assuring the pilot's comfort at high altitudes, and an ejection seat was provided for emergency bailout at high speeds. It would take a while for aircraft engineers and pilots to become familiar with the high-speed, high-altitude environment of the jet age.

The Air Force placed its first order for fifteen evaluation models and eighty-five P-84B production models in January 1946. These first Thunderjets came standard with wingtip tanks for auxiliary fuel storage, modern tricycle landing gear, and an Allison J35 jet engine with 4,000 pounds (1,816kg) of static thrust. By 1948, 226 F-84Bs were produced for the Air Force. An F-84C followed. It was nearly indistinguishable from the B, except for its more powerful Allison engine and slight modifications throughout. Ultimately, 191 F-84C were built before additional modifications led to D and E variants. Both

RIGHT: A Republic F-84 Thunderjet undergoes midair refueling, as seen from the fuel boom operator's position in the rear fuselage of the airborne tanker. The Thunderjet was the first USAF jet fighter equipped for midair refueling. In 1953, seventeen Thunderjets flew what was then a record-breaking continuous flight—4,485 miles (7,216km)—made possible by midair refueling. Midair refueling significantly increases a jet fighter's mission envelope by extending its range and loiter time.

OPPOSITE: The checkerboard design and red accents indicate that this F-84C served with the 308th Fighter/Bomber Squadron, 31st Fighter Group. Because the Thunderjet's engine intake and duct system occupied so much fuselage space, thicker wings with internal tanks were designed to carry the aircraft's fuel.

the D and the E variants were way ahead of their Thunderjet prototypes, benefiting from more powerful engines and better weaponry. An update to the E variant included an onboard radar system. Almost 1,000 of the D and E versions were produced: 154 Ds and more than 800 Es. The G was the variant produced in the greatest quantity, with more than 3,000 completed for use in the United States and NATO countries. The G featured autopilot, in-flight refueling, and advanced weapon capabilities.

Typical Thunderjet armament included four machine guns, but later variants were upgraded to six .50-caliber machine guns with a higher rate of fire: four mounted in the nose and two located in the wings. The Thunderjet proved to be a suitable rocket-launching platform as well. Several variants were outfitted with underwing retractable rocket launchers, and some were even fashioned to carry external bomb stores on ordnance racks that could be jettisoned. The F-84G was also able to carry tactical nuclear weapons.

Variants E through G saw action in the Korean War. Used as fighters, bombers, and on escort missions, they were put to daily combat use by USAF and UN forces throughout the conflict.

The F variant represented a major evolutionary development for the jet. The Air Force's experience with the swept-wing Soviet MiGs led to a design improvement to the Thunderjet. The F-84F was introduced in 1951. It featured a 40-degree swept wing and tail for increased performance, a longer fuselage, redesigned perforated airbrakes, and hydraulically powered controls. Renamed the Thunderstreak, the first production models were powered by a J65-W-3, with 7,220 pounds (3,278kg) of static thrust that was built under license by Wright. In total, Republic produced 2,711 F-84F Thunderstreaks before the end of 1958.

Republic F-84C Thunderjet Specifications

Type: Single-seat fighter

Power plant: One Allison J35-A-13 turbojet engine producing 4,000 pounds (1,816kg) of static thrust

Performance: Maximum speed, 620 mph (998kph) at sea level; service ceiling, 43,240 feet (13,180m); maximum range, 1,485 miles (2,389km)

Weight: Empty, 9,538 pounds (4,330kg); maximum takeoff weight, 19,689 pounds (8,939kg)

Dimensions: Span, 36 feet 6 inches (11.1m); length, 38 feet 1 inch (11.6m); height, 12 feet 7 inches (3.8m); wing area, 260 square feet (23.9m^2)

Armament: Six .50-caliber machine guns

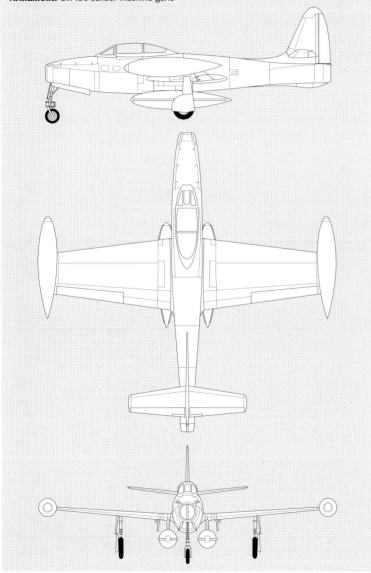

ABOVE: These swept-wing F-84Fs are connected to a giant muffler system. The system allowed Republic engineers to safely run up several engines at once without creating an environment that would surely deafen anyone within yards of the facility.

An RF-84F that was modified for reconnaissance followed. Named Thunderflash, it was refitted to carry up to four cameras in the nose. The central nose air intake was repositioned to the wing roots to provide space for the camera equipment. While designed for photoreconnaissance, the Thunderflash retained its armament, allowing it to be both offensive and defensive. In all, 718 were produced in this configuration.

Over the course of the entire program, approximately 7,886 F-84s were built, both for use by the United States and internationally. Several European nations purchased F-84s for military use. Domestically, all variants were taken from active service in the mid-1950s. The remaining Thunderjets, Thunderstreaks, and Thunderflashes were operated by the National Guard through the latter half of the 1950s.

In its Thunderjet incarnation, it was the last straight-wing subsonic fighter produced for use by the U.S. Air Force. Obviously a successful design, the F-84 was in use by some NATO countries through the 1970s. The F-84 platform's ability to evolve was demonstrated by its longevity; with three generations developed from a single concept, Kartveli created a benchmark for early jet aircraft.

RIGHT: Unmistakably an Alexander Kartveli design, the F-84 Thunderjet was the first early jet to utilize the extremely efficient nose air intake. The Thunderjet was also the first USAF fighter to carry a nuclear weapon.

Grumman F9F

Grumman had been a favored aircraft supplier to the Navy since the start of World War II, so it was no surprise that the Navy looked to Grumman for a jet design. The Panther program, culminating in the F9F-8 Cougar, produced planes with qualities typical of Ironworks offerings: they were sturdy, reliable, and easy to maintain.

Originally designed to utilize four Westinghouse 24C turbojet engines, the XF9F-1 looked nothing like the Panther. The XF9F-1 was an extremely big aircraft: 46 feet (14m) long, with room enough for the pilot and a radio operator to sit alongside each other in the cockpit. That original design was scrapped once it was determined that the aircraft would be unable to store enough fuel for a useful operating radius. An XF9F-2 came next. Called the Panther, this design incorporated a single Rolls Royce Nene J42-P-6 engine with 5,000 pounds (2,270kg) of static thrust. Another prototype was developed with an Allison J33-A-23 engine, already in use in operational Air Force jets, that produced 4,600 pounds (2,088kg) of static thrust.

The first production order included forty-seven F9F-2s with the Rolls Royce engine built under license by Pratt & Whitney and fifty-four F9F-3s with the Allison engine. However, nearly all the F9F-3s originally ordered and all subsequent orders for Panthers were built with the Pratt & Whitney engine. With an Allison engine, the F9F-3 never performed as well as the Pratt & Whitney–powered variant.

In total, 621 F9F-2s were produced. The next variant to be produced in quantity was the F9F-5. It featured a more powerful J48-P-6 water-injected Pratt & Whitney engine, again based on a Rolls Royce design, rated at 6,500 pounds (2,951kg) of static thrust. The fuselage was elongated and the vertical tail was raised for increased stability at high speeds. Though 109 F9F-4s were developed, unsuitable engine operation led them all to be converted to F9F-5s. Overall, by 1952 1,382 Panthers were accepted into service with the Navy.

Like any Grumman product, the Panther design was well thought out. The Panther was a straight-wing, single-seat aircraft with a strong structure. As with all its warbirds, Grumman was concerned with the maintainability of its aircraft. The Panther introduced the "sliding nose" concept, whereby the entire nose of the aircraft could be slid ahead three and a half feet (1m) along a track to expose the armament enclosed in the forward fuselage. Likewise, the aft section could disconnect from the fuselage for easy maintenance, an indispensable feature given the restricted space on a hangar deck.

RIGHT: The last production model of the Panther/Cougar series was the highly developed F9F-8. This variant had a slightly enlarged wing and cambered leading edge for improved cruise speed and slow speed handling, in-flight refueling capability, and advanced avionics. Here, an -8 is being towed to the ramp.

OPPOSITE: Grumman's first jet fighter—albeit with straight wings—presents a remarkably streamlined shape. The permanently mounted wingtips were a practical concession to the early fuel-guzzling jet engines. This F9F-2 Panther flew with VF-721 in Korea.

F9F-2
123645

NAVY

★ 106

Ted Williams

A

LEFT TOP: The straight-wing Panther planform was adapted with a swept wing and tail to become the F9F-6 Cougar; even the air intakes at the wing root were swept back slightly. The thin-walled structures on each wing are wing fences. Early swept-wing designs required these devices to channel the airflow directly across the chord of the wing.

LEFT BOTTOM: This F9F Panther has been modified for photoreconnaissance. It has a longer nose with camera windows to accommodate photography equipment. Because of the camera set-up and its reconnaissance function, the aircraft does not carry machine guns.

The Panther's pressurized cockpit included a novel air-conditioning unit and a single-piece bubble canopy with a quick-release mechanism. An ejection seat was to become standard equipment on all early jets. For space-efficient storage on the carrier and hangar deck, the Panther's wings folded. As powerful as it was, the Panther nevertheless had to be catapult-launched off the carrier, a practice still in use for modern Navy jets.

Panthers were used extensively throughout the Korean War. Introduced to the Korean conflict on July 3, 1950, the Panther provided close air support for the UN troops fighting in Korea. On November 9, 1950, a Panther would claim its first victory, shooting down a MiG-15. After April 1951, the jet took on a multimission role. The Marine Corps operated Panthers from bases scattered around the Korean peninsula. The Panther's 240-gallon (908L) wingtip fuel tanks, four nose-mounted 20mm M-3 cannons, and its ability to deliver rockets and bombs made it an ideal ground-support weapon.

An F9F-6 was developed with swept-back wings. Strikingly different from the Panther, it was renamed the Cougar, reflecting its feline heritage. The aircraft's silhouette and armament remained the same, but the 35-degree swept-back wings improved performance dramatically, raising the top speed to 654 miles per hour (1,052kph) in level flight. An F9F-8 Cougar followed. It had an even more powerful engine and a larger wing area, with a longer fuselage that allowed for increased fuel capacity. Like the Panther and Cougar models before it, several F9F-8s were modified for photoreconnaissance. In total, 1,985 Cougars were built.

The Panther was out of service by 1957. Cougars modified into trainers stayed in service as late as 1974. This design was the first jet used by the Blue Angels. The Navy's demonstration team flew the Panther from 1952 to 1955, and the Cougar from 1955 to 1958.

The jet age brought a new reality to aircraft development. Above all, to ensure maximum performance, jets needed to be kept lightweight without compromising the strength of the airframe's construction. Meanwhile, it was a constant design challenge to generate enough power and to carry sufficient fuel onboard to meet speed and range requirements. With these needs in mind, Grumman and the Navy continued to search out new fighter design solutions for many years come.

Grumman F9F-2 Panther Specifications

Type: Single-seat fighter

Power plant: One Pratt & Whitney J42-P-6/8 turbojet engine producing 5,000 pounds (2,270kg) of static thrust

Performance: Maximum speed, 526 mph (846kph) at 22,000 feet (6,706m); service ceiling, 44,600 feet (13,594m); maximum range, 1,353 miles (2,177km)

Weight: Empty, 9,303 pounds (4,224kg); maximum takeoff weight, 19,494 pounds (8,850kg)

Dimensions: Span, 38 feet (11.6m); length, 37 feet 3 inches (11.4m); height, 11 feet 4 inches (3.5m); wing area, 250 square feet ($23m^2$)

Armament: Four 20mm cannons and a 2,000-pound (908kg) bomb load

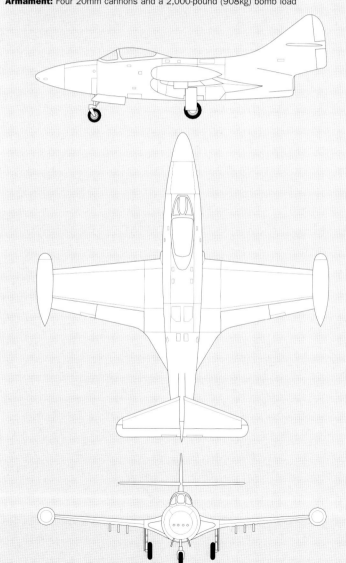

RIGHT: Bomb carts rest in the foreground after being used to load 250-pound (114kg) bombs onto a squadron of Marine Corps Panther jets in preparation for a ground attack mission in Korea.

BELOW: Four of the first six Panthers assigned for duty with the Blue Angels fly in formation.

North American F-86 Sabre

Considered one of the most successful early jet fighter aircraft, the North American F-86 Sabre developed out of the Fury program. The Fury was a straight-wing jet designed by North American for Navy carrier use. While the Fury was a lackluster performer, the Sabre came to exemplify an era. This was hardly surprising, considering that North American Aviation was the company that gave flight to the P-51 Mustang.

Not only was the Sabre an outgrowth of the Fury program, but NACA research and recently disclosed aerodynamic studies performed by World War II German Messerschmitt 262 engineers also contributed to the Sabre's design. This research helped the Sabre's design team—John Leland "Lee" Atwood, Edgar Schmued, Raymond Rice, and L. P. Green—create a fast, easy-handling machine suitable for operation in the UN's police action in Korea. As the Sabre design clearly illustrated, in the late 1940s engineers placed an emphasis on attaining the fastest speed at level flight. In pursuit of this goal, the Sabre's designers also used test data from the Bell X-1 program, which contributed to later Sabre variants.

The first XP-86 flew on October 1, 1947; by May 1948, the P-86 was operational. During an April 26, 1948, test flight, a Sabre made history as the first American jet to break the sound barrier while in a dive. The jet age was advancing in leaps and bounds. Notable were the Sabre's swept-back wings. The P-86 was the first American military aircraft to employ the 35-degree sweep. In conjunction with the developing jet engine, swept-back wings allowed for greater speeds—approaching the speed of sound, or Mach 1, in level flight. The swept-back wings eliminated buffeting, a dangerous high-speed flight characteristic that could cause catastrophic failure of the airframe's integrity.

Over the course of the Sabre development program, multiple variants were tested. From first version to final production model, five different engines were used: a Curtiss-Wright, an Avro, a Rolls Royce model, and two different General Electric engines. Initially, a General Electric Allison J35-C-3 turbojet rated at 3,750 pounds (1,703kg) of static thrust was chosen to power the first prototype.

The Sabre, so named in March 1949, was a bigger airplane than its brother, the Fury, but it was still a single-seat aircraft with a cantilevered low-wing. Features of the Sabre, redesignated F-86, included airbrakes, hydraulically operated trailing-edge ailerons, and automatic leading-edge slats. The tricycle

OPPOSITE: The USAF was looking for a design to counter the MiG threat; it found it in North American Aviation's swept-wing Sabre. The "MiG Killer" shown here is an F-86E with the Korean War markings of the 25th Fighter Interceptor Squadron, 51st Fighter Interceptor Wing, operating out of Suwan, Korea.

landing gear was retractable and the two rear wheels fit snugly up into the wings. An ejection seat and pressurized cockpit provided pilot safety and comfort. An F-86A achieved a new world speed record in September 1948, when Major Richard L. Johnson flew his F-86A Sabre at 670 miles per hour (1,078kph).

The Sabre went into production as the F-86A. In all, 554 F-86As, were built and classified as fighter-bombers. This variant housed six .50-caliber machine guns in the nose, and featured an underwing apparatus that was capable of carrying a 2,000-pound (908kg) bomb load or six rockets. The A underwent many upgrades for power and speed, eventually giving way to the F-86D, the next variant produced in quantity, with 2,504 leaving the factory. This model was modified for an all-weather mission envelope. Its features included improved radar with autopilot, larger tail surfaces, and a General Electric J47-GE-17 delivering 5,425 pounds (2,463kg) of static thrust. The D also eliminated the machine guns in favor of twenty-four 2.75-inch (7cm) rockets for use in interception missions. Two all-weather variants, the 341 K and the 981 L, followed the D variant. NATO participants in the Korean War flew the F-86K, while the L was an improved D produced for American use. E, F, and H variants incorporated evolutionary improvements to the fighter-bomber version.

The Sabre maneuvered well and handled with ease and grace. Its powered controls were a delight to pilots; there was no need to manhandle a roll. And, appearing on the F-86F, a flying tail further prevented compressibility. The all-flying tail incorporated the horizontal stabilizer and the elevators into a single unit to assure better pitch control at supersonic speeds. The Sabre was also appreciated by fighter pilots because of its good visibility.

Sabres saw extensive action in the Korean War. Although its performance was inferior to that of the MiG-15, with a better-trained pilot, the Sabre could hold its own. It ended the conflict with a respectable ten-to-one victory ratio.

Over its design cycle, 8,681 Sabre models were manufactured in facilities around the world—a record quantity for an American jet fighter. Only the Phantom II has come close to this production figure. Although all U.S. production ceased in December 1956, some NATO nations were still flying Sabres as late as 1970—not surprising, considering the quantity produced and put into use by twenty-six nations worldwide.

RIGHT: The sight of F-86 Sabre jets flying in the classic "finger four" formation is nothing less than spectacular.

OPPOSITE TOP: This view of the USAF North American F-86 Sabre in a steep, banking turn clearly shows the 35-degree swept wing and tail configuration that helped the F-86 acquire the nickname "MiG Killer."

OPPOSITE BOTTOM: Maintenance personnel from the 335th Fighter Interceptor Squadron serving in Korea work on a Sabre's General Electric J-47 at a maintenance depot in Korea. The engine is easily exposed by removing the aft fuselage.

Type: Single-seat fighter

Power plant: One General Electric J47-GE-13 turbojet engine producing 5,200 pounds (2,361kg) of static thrust

Performance: Maximum speed, 675 mph (1,086kph) at 25,000 feet (7,620m); service ceiling, 48,300 feet (14,722m); maximum range, 765 miles (1,231km)

Weight: Empty, 10,950 pounds (4,971kg); maximum takeoff weight, 16,357 pounds (7426kg)

Dimensions: Span, 37 feet 1 inch (11.3m); length, 37 feet 6 inches (11.4m); height, 14 feet 8 inches (4.5m); wing area, 288 square feet (26.5m²)

Armament: Six .50-caliber machine guns, plus a 2,000-pound (908kg) bomb load

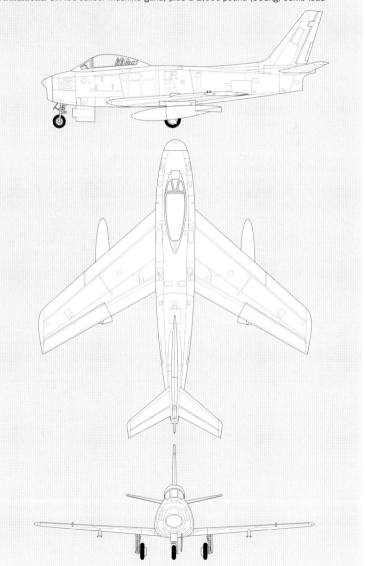

Vought F7U Cutlass

Of all the aircraft covered in this book, the Vought F7U holds a dubious place in the history of the American fighter plane. Possibly one of the most dangerous fighter aircraft accepted into service, the Vought F7U Cutlass claimed the lives of many pilots over the short span of its evaluation period and while performing standard frontline duties. The Cutlass' design was years ahead of its time, putting into practice features that were unimaginable by many, no other fighter aircraft in service with the Navy could compare with the Cutlass' innovation. But out on the leading edge of technology, the consequences of the Cutlass' teething problems were also unlike anything previously experienced by the Navy; yet, to its credit, the Navy had the tenacity to address these problems and to come up with solutions that went against conventional wisdom.

Innocuously enough, the U.S. Navy opened a competition for a new fighter aircraft in 1945. The specification was for an aircraft capable of a speed of 600 miles per hour (965kph) and with an operational ceiling of 40,000 feet (12,192m). From designs submitted by firms such as Curtiss, Douglas, Martin, McDonnell, and North American, the revolutionary Vought Cutlass was selected; it was an unusually bold choice for the U.S. Navy.

The first flight of the XF7U-1, one of three XF7U prototypes, took place on September 29, 1948, at the Naval Air Test Center (NATC) at Patuxent River, Maryland. The prototype showed potential, but its evaluation period was cut short when, just a few days later, the plane crashed, killing the test pilot. Still, Vought won an order for fourteen F7U-1 production models based on the Navy's initial impressions of the design's merit.

Like the prototype, the production model was designed around several naval aviation firsts. Among its noteworthy accomplishments: it was the U.S. Navy's first swept-wing jet; it was the first jet designed from its inception to utilize afterburners; and it was the first truly tailless aircraft to go into production in the United States.

Why tailless? The Vought design team was betting that removing any vestiges of a traditional empennage would allow the Cutlass to climb and fly faster. Also, in 1945 compressibility was becoming a real problem for pilots traveling at the faster jet speeds. Pilots had been experiencing this notorious condition as early as World War II in propeller aircraft like the P-38, but the jet engine only amplified the need for a solution. So far, strategically placed drag inducers and powered controls had been attempted as possible ways to break

OPPOSITE: This tailless design from Vought created quite a sensation in the press. Although not the most successful of the early Navy fighters, the F7U Cutlass introduced many firsts to qualify it as an important link in the evolution of the American fighter plane. This F7U is depicted in the orange and blue of VF-83.

the grip of compressibility. Vought, however, approached the problem with a most drastic solution. Since compressibility affected the horizontal control surfaces of the tail plane, eliminating the tail altogether should eliminate compressibility. But with the tail missing, the Cutlass designers also discovered that a long nose was needed to balance the center of gravity.

As for swept wings, the Navy had been reticent to adopt them, believing that the increased performance would be impossible to tame for carrier operations. At a 38-degree sweep, the Cutlass' wing was fashioned into a low aspect ratio trapezoidal configuration. Leading edge slats, incorporated in the full length of the wing, provided additional lift at lower speeds. Since the horizontal tailplanes were eliminated, a set of ailerons and elevators, called "ailevators," were added along the trailing edge to provide pitch-and-roll control. All slats were hydraulically operated by the first 3,000-psi, high-pressure hydraulic system utilized by the Navy. Another naval innovation included the steerable nosewheel of the tricycle landing gear.

Powering the F7U-1A was pair of J34 Westinghouse turbojets, with each engine and its afterburner providing 4,250 pounds (1,930kg) of static thrust. An afterburner adds fuel to the engine's exhaust; this mixture is then burned along with the extra oxygen produced by the jet engine, nearly doubling the engine's thrust. They cannot be used continuously, however, as they require massive quantities of fuel.

Soon after, an F7U-2 was commissioned. The F7U-2 was to be propelled by more powerful Westinghouse engines, but this order was canceled in favor of the F7U-3, which was substantially larger than the original design. It featured more powerful J46 Westinghouse engines and afterburners that produced 6,100 pounds (2,769kg) of static thrust. It also incorporated structural considerations for carrier landings, including a redesigned cockpit for better visibility, a stronger foundation, and a redesigned nose gear.

While the F7U-3 was armed with four 20mm cannons, a F7U-3M version was modified to carry an additional four Sparrow missiles. This variant was the first fighter aircraft outfitted with air-to-air, radar-guided missiles. A photoreconnaissance variant, the F7U-3P, was also developed, with one remaining in service until 1959.

Safety problems weren't the only issues that disrupted the Cutlass program. The engines would flame out when the cannons, mounted above the air intakes, were fired. This problem was solved by not allowing the right and left

RIGHT TOP: The clean lines of an early in-flight Vought F7U Cutlass prototype are strikingly modern. The aircraft has a long test probe affixed to its nose for gathering flight data for evaluation. The Cutlass was the first swept-wing jet accepted into service with the U.S. Navy for carrier operations.

RIGHT BOTTOM: The tailless Vought Cutlass had a long, but sturdy, steerable nose gear strut, and its two wheels made taxiing easier. In this view, it is easy to see the removable rocket pod mounted to the fuselage.

guns to fire at the same time, thus preventing a gun-blast pressure wave from building up and stalling the engine. Many aircraft were lost as a result of this odd occurrence before it was corrected. Moreover, the Cutlass' extremely high nosewheel was the source of many disastrous landings, and the aircraft was woefully underpowered.

Cutlass production ceased in 1955 and the aircraft began to be phased out as early as 1956. It was replaced by another revolutionary Vought design, the Crusader. Yet, despite all its problems, the Cutlass was popular with naval aviators. Safety horror stories and maintenance debacles aside, the Cutlass was highly adept at aerobatics and high G-force maneuvers.

Although the Cutlass never developed into an ideal aircraft, many of the technologies and ideas it put into practice were successfully realized in later aircraft, some becoming standard on today's modern air fleet.

BELOW: Crewmembers bring a Cutlass to the flight deck on the forward elevator. Coming from storage aboard the hangar deck, the aircraft's large, 38-degree swept-wing panels are still in the folded position.

Vought F7U-3 Cutlass Specifications

Type: Single-seat, carrier-based fighter
Power plant: Two Westinghouse J46-WE-8A afterburning turbojet engines producing 4,600 pounds (2,088kg) of static thrust
Performance: Maximum speed, 680 mph (1,094kph) at 10,000 feet (3,048m); service ceiling, 40,000 feet (12,192m); maximum range, 660 miles (1,062km)
Weight: Empty, 18,210 pounds (8,267kg); maximum takeoff weight, 31,642 pounds (14,36kg)
Dimensions: Span, 38 feet 8 inches (11.8m); length, 44 feet 3 inches (13.5m); height, 14 feet 7 inches (4.5m); wing area, 496 square feet (45.6m^2)
Armament: Four 20mm cannon and four air-to-air missiles

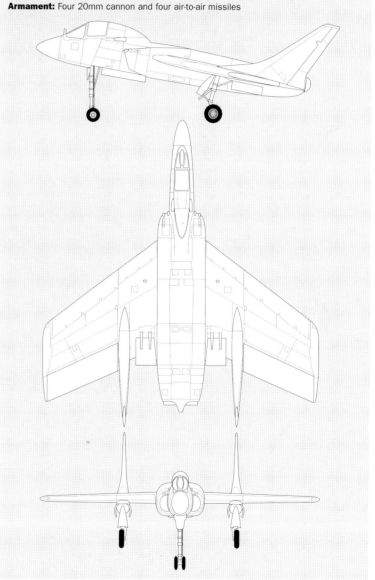

Northrop F-89 Scorpion

In March 1945, the U.S. Army Air Force put out a specification for a long-range, all-weather fighter with bombing capabilities. The Army Air Force was looking for a jet-powered aircraft with the night-fighting capabilities of the Northrop P-61 Black Widow. Several manufacturers responded with designs, including Curtiss, Northrop, Goodyear, Douglas, Consolidated, and Bell. Curtiss-Wright's design for a mid-wing model with Westinghouse engines was finally chosen. Still, the Army was intrigued by Northrop's design.

Fortunately for Northrop, the Curtiss XP-87 program was discontinued: the design had simply been too ambitious. It was the heaviest aircraft developed by Curtiss and, overburdened as it was, could not reach the speeds required. Most troubling, the XP-87 had experienced extreme buffeting. Sadly, mired in corporate problems, the Curtiss Aeroplane Division was bought by North American after failing to sell its all-weather fighter/bomber to the military. The Curtiss XP-87 Blackhawk was the last design from one of the oldest names in aviation—one of the few remaining manufacturers with ties to the Wright Brothers.

With the Curtiss program coming to an end, Northrop provided two prototypes of its long-range all-weather fighter, the XP-89 Scorpion. With the Black Widow to its credit, Northrop already understood a night-fighter interceptor's special needs; however, Northrop's success with its Scorpion design was bittersweet. The XP-89 was the last Northrop design before the retirement of Jack Northrop as head of the company he had founded in 1939.

The Northrop XP-89 made its first flight in August 1946. It was a cantilevered, mid-wing monoplane with a traditional laminar-flow wing to enable steady low-speed maneuverability and landing in varied conditions. The high tail and long nose of its sleek fuselage was its most visually striking element. Inside the aircraft's long nose was housed both the sensitive radar equipment and either four or six 20mm cannons. At the time, the A-1 radar was a sizable unit made up of vacuum tubes, necessitating the prominent proboscis. The tail was raised high on the horizontal tailplane to prevent the afterburners' destructively hot exhaust from harming the aircraft; hence, the "Scorpion" moniker.

The Scorpion was a twin-engine aircraft; each Allison J35-A-9 was capable of producing 4,000 pounds (1,816kg) of static thrust and was paired with an afterburner mounted under the wing in its own nacelle, attached to the

RIGHT: An F-89C has just been moved off the outdoor assembly line at the Northrop facility in Ontario, California. Northrop took advantage of the mild California weather and moved the output end of its final assembly line outdoors to free up indoor factory space for sub assemblies.

OPPOSITE: The F-89 Scorpion was the first jet-propelled, all-weather interceptor. Built in large numbers, the Scorpion was specifically designed to counter the threat of a Russian bomber attack on the U.S. mainland. This F-89D has combination missile launcher/fuel tank wing pods.

XF-89's fuselage. (Note the military redesignation from Pursuit to Fighter.) The air intakes were located directly in front of each nacelle.

The entire structure was covered in an aluminum alloy, and the aircraft featured retractable tricycle landing gear, a pressurized cockpit, and ejection seats. Manned by a pilot and a radar operator, the XF-89's bubble canopy provided good visibility for the pilot. The aircraft also included "decelerons," a Northrop exclusive, which performed a dual function. Attached to the trailing edge of the wing, decelerons were ailerons that opened as if on a hinge and could act as either normal ailerons to control the roll access or as airbrakes.

A YF-89A version followed the first prototype, with improved radar and more powerful Allison J35-A-21A engines rated at 6,800 pounds (3,087kg) of static thrust. A limited order of F-89As went into production, and delivery took place in late 1950. The first eight were F-89As, but the bulk of the order—forty models—was converted to F-89Bs, with a redesigned tail. In September 1951, 164 F-89Cs followed with even larger Allison engines, and an onboard fire-control system developed by Hughes. Its permanently attached wingtip tank superstructure was later divided into two sections. The forward section

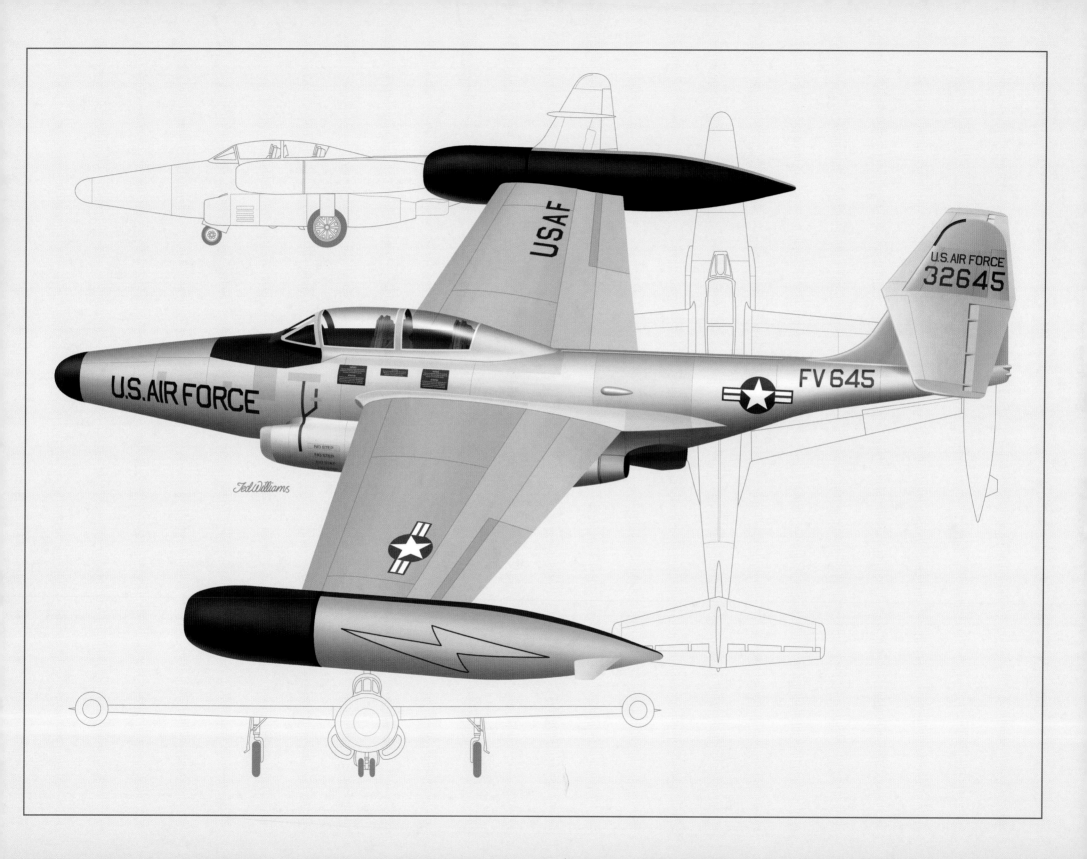

contained air-to-air missiles in a rocket pod and the rear section held a 300-gallon (1,136L) fuel tank. An F-89D was created to correct an airframe weakness. The D variant was duplicated in the greatest quantity. A total of 682 saw service. The D eliminated the canons in favor of an increased rocket load; it could carry up to 104 rockets, making it one of the most heavily armed planes in the Air Force.

An F-89H and J closed out the series. The 156 H series aircraft were equipped to carry Falcon air-to-air guided missiles, another Hughes innovation. Some 350 F-89Js were modified to carry Genie MB-1 nuclear missiles. On July 19, 1957, the U.S. Air Force entered the nuclear age. On a historic test flight, an F-89J fired the first nuclear warhead from an aircraft.

ABOVE: A U.S. Air Force Northrop F-89C is being prepared for a gunnery mission over the southern California desert. Armorers remove belts of 20mm cannon cartridges from ammunition boxes prior to loading this Scorpion's six cannons.

OPPOSITE: A ground crewman stands by with a fire extinguisher while a test pilot starts up an XF-89 prototype. Experimental aircraft were highly unpredictable. It was not unusual for a prototype to malfunction, catch on fire, or even explode.

Known for its excellent range and immense fuel storage capacity, the Scorpion program initially struggled with design flaws and accidents; however, each variant corrected these flaws and improved the aircraft so it was able to serve as a valuable weapon until it was relieved from frontline duty in 1961. Some Scorpions remained in service with the Air National Guard until 1969.

With revolutionary improvements to the radar, autopilot mechanism, and, of course, the introduction of jet propulsion, the Scorpion could track, attack, and destroy its target without needing to see it, now even more effectively than the famous Northrop arachnid, the Black Widow. The F-89 Scorpion was a deadly interceptor in all weather conditions, day or night, at a time when the United States was first beginning to feel the threat of the Cold War.

Northrop F-89D Scorpion Specifications

Type: Two-seat, all-weather fighter

Power plant: Pair of Allison J35-A-35 turbojet engines producing 7,210 pounds (3,273kg) of static thrust

Performance: Maximum speed, 600 mph (965kph) at 10,600 feet (3,231m); service ceiling, 49,200 feet (14,996m); maximum range, 1,370 miles (2,204km)

Weight: Empty, 25,194 pounds (11,438kg); maximum takeoff weight, 42,240 pounds (19,177kg)

Dimensions: Span, 59 feet 8 inches (18.2m); length, 53 feet 10 inches (16.4m); height, 17 feet 7 inches (5.4m); wing area, 562 square feet (51.7m^2)

Armament: 104 2.75-inch (70mm) folding-fin rockets

North American F-100 Super Sabre

With the North American F-100 Super Sabre, the U.S. Air Force went supersonic. The F-100 heralded the supersonic age and the next wave of jet aircraft. Gone were the days of one man, one gun. Military aircraft were no longer simply gunships. Designed as a sophisticated weapons platform with an electronic system controlling functions that were once manual, the F-100 was the first of the "Century Fighters," a series of American fighters that were all designated with numbers in the one-hundreds.

Named Sabre 45 by the factory because of the 45-degree sweep to the wing and tailplane, the design was proposed to the military as an all-weather fighter/bomber. With its origins in the F-86 Sabre, an aircraft beloved by the Air Force, the Super Sabre was accepted with one caveat: the XF-100, as it was designated, was to be developed as a daylight interceptor that could reach supersonic speeds in level flight.

The prototype, a single-seat, single-engine cantilevered low-wing monoplane, quickly earned the updated designation of YF-100A as design improvements and evaluation ensued. It was powered by a Pratt & Whitney two-stage J57-P-7 that produced 9,700 pounds (4,404kg) of static thrust, easily amplified to 14,800 pounds (6,719kg) of static thrust by its afterburner. The jet engine was finally delivering the kind of power the early engineers had anticipated. On the YP-100A's first test flight, its pilot, George Welch, accomplished supersonic flight, adding the sobriquet "Super" to the Sabre line.

The Super Sabre was an engineer's airplane, exhibiting advancements throughout. The cockpit was pressurized and air-conditioned with a hinged canopy that pivoted from its base at the rear, opening upward. The cockpit featured a standard-issue ejection seat. Inside, the instrument panel was ergonomically designed, with all controls easily within reach; outside, the engine's egg-shaped air intake was placed horizontally to streamline the aircraft's nose.

Mounted low, the swept-back wings and tail had inboard ailerons on the trailing edges. The slats on the leading edge were automatically activated; later variants were modified to include hydraulic slats on the trailing edge, and the horizontal swept tailplanes constituted an all-flying tail. An airbrake was located underneath the fuselage, and the nosewheel had two tires to improve its taxiing ability and ground maneuverability.

The F-100 was the first production aircraft to use titanium extensively throughout its construction. Preferred because of its lightness and durability, titanium was nonetheless expensive. But the North American design team,

**405th Tactical Fighter Wing
(while deployed in Thailand)**

OPPOSITE: The Super Sabre was the USAF's first supersonic fighter. Known as the "Hun" by its pilots, the first of the "Century Fighters" could sustain Mach 1 in level flight. This second-generation fighter was a handful and demanded great skill on the pilot's part. Its power to weight ratio was awesome for its time. The F-100D is shown here with the markings of the 510th Tactical Fighter Squadron, 405th Fighter Wing, based in Thailand.

headed by Dutch Kindelberger, spared no expense in creating its supersonic marvel.

The first production F-100A flew on October 29, 1953, and a total of 203 of these day fighter models were manufactured. An F-100C, D, and F followed, culminating in 2,089 aircraft. Armament consisted of four 20mm M-39 cannons with 200 rounds each. The forward-firing guns were mounted below the air intake. All variants could carry ordnance under the wings.

The F-100C fighter/bomber had what were known as "wet wings." The fuel in the wings was stored without rubber fuel cells, greatly increasing fuel capacity. Later, the F-100C was given the ability to carry tactical nuclear weapons, which were delivered by a Low Altitude Bombing System (LABS). In 1956, the USAF Thunderbirds were issued F-100Cs. It was the first supersonic aircraft used by a military demonstration team.

The D variant was equipped with the first autopilot system designed for use in supersonic flight. The D also featured a larger vertical tail and inboard flaps to help tame landing speeds. Focusing on its dual capacity as a fighter and a bomber, the F-100D's capabilities exceeded the requirements of the day fighter role for which it had been originally designed. The D variant employed LABS, as well as the newer M-1 bombing system, and it could carry a camera pod mounted on a centerline connection, for information-gathering missions. The F-100D was the most-produced variant of the Super Sabre series.

A two-seat version, the F-100F, holds the record as the first jet fighter aircraft to fly over the North Pole. France, Denmark, and Turkey are among the countries that operated the F-100 Super Sabre.

The first jet fighter dispatched to Vietnam, the F-100 was the Air Force's primary air supremacy fighter. The F-100 provided close air support until newer jets, such as the F-4 Phantom II, took over the Wild Weasel operations (a dangerous mission pioneered by the Super Sabre pilots that was designed to suppress enemy surface-to-air missile threats). Wild Weasel–modified aircraft were equipped with an exclusive radar-detecting device that launched strike missiles at targets identified by their radar emissions.

The Super Sabre program initially experienced accidents that stalled production and caused poor first impressions. However, any flaws that may have developed as a result of its rush into production were quickly corrected and the F-100 developed into an aircraft affectionately called the "Hun" (short for its "one-hundred" designation) by the men who flew it.

"QUALITY MUST BE BUILT INTO A PRODUCT
IT CANNOT BE INSPECTED INTO IT"

OPPOSITE: F-100 Super Sabres, the first of the "Century Fighters," on a final assembly line at North American Aviation's Los Angeles plant. The novel, horizontal, egg-shaped air intake is visible on the aircraft's nose.

LEFT TOP: F-100s were used to test early heat-seeking Sidewinder missiles. The Super Sabre was fitted with special rails for high speed missile launch testing. Later, Super Sabre variants would be equipped for Wild Weasel operations.

LEFT BOTTOM: Painted in the Southeast Asia camouflage scheme, this F-100 from the 612th Tactical Fighter Squadron, 35th Tactical Fighter Wing, is parked in a revetment on March 7, 1971, at Phu Cat Air Base in Vietnam, prior to a ground support napalm mission.

North American F-100D Super Sabre Specifications

Type: Single-seat fighter/bomber
Power plant: One Pratt & Whitney J57-P-21A afterburning turbojet engine producing 16,500 pounds (7,491kg) of static thrust
Performance: Maximum speed, 864 mph (1,390kph) at 35,000 feet (10,668m); service ceiling, 45,015 feet (13,721m); maximum range, 1,500 miles (2,414km)
Weight: Empty, 20,638 pounds (9,367kg); maximum takeoff weight, 34,832 pounds (15,814kg)
Dimensions: Span, 38 feet 9 inches (11.8m); length, 47 feet (14.3m); height, 15 feet (4.6m); wing area, 385 square feet (35.4m^2)
Armament: Four 20mm cannon and up to 7,040 pounds (3,196kg) of tactical air/ground ordnance carried on six hardpoints

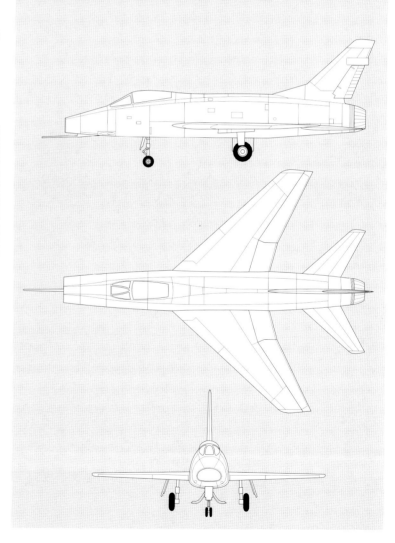

Douglas F4D Skyray

In 1947, the Navy's Bureau of Aeronautics, known as BuAer, released a specification for a delta-wing aircraft based on German aeronautical research surrendered after World War II. German engineers, in particular Dr. Alexander Lippisch, had determined that a delta wing increased the speed and climb of a jet aircraft. Specifically, the Navy was looking for a delta wing interceptor/fighter with short range and high performance for carrier deployment. While several manufacturers competed for the bid, Douglas received the contract. The Douglas design for the F4D Skyray would become the Navy's first aircraft capable of reaching 700 miles per hour (1,126kph).

Donald Wills Douglas was one of the pioneers who caught the aviation bug when the flying machine was still in its infancy. Douglas's early credits included studying and teaching aeronautics at M.I.T., working on the Connecticut Aircraft Company team that designed the Navy's first dirigible, and performing the duties of chief engineer for the Glenn L. Martin Company. Douglas' first company was a partnership with the wealthy sportsman David R. Davis. Their enterprise, the Davis-Douglas Company, quickly reorganized into the Douglas Company in July 1921 after Davis, who lost interest in the aviation venture, sold his shares to Douglas. Today, the Douglas Company is best known for its successful DC series of transport aircraft.

Ed Heinemann and C.S. Kennedy led the Douglas design team responsible for the Skyray. The Skyray was designed as a quick aircraft with a rapid rate of climb for intercepting enemy aircraft and protecting the fleet. The team chose to implement a swept-back, low-aspect ratio mid-wing with round wingtips—not a true delta wing, yet able to achieve supersonic performance. This distinctive wing shape resembled a manta ray, earning the Skyray its name. As with all Navy aircraft, the wings folded for carrier storage. The horizontal tail was eliminated entirely—the aircraft was tailless, with a wing large enough to have all the elevators and ailerons on its trailing edge.

From the start, engine selection and development troubled the Skyray program. The original plan called for a Westinghouse J40 axial-flow, afterburning turbojet with air intakes in the wing roots, but this engine proved problematic. The first XF4D-1 prototype made its maiden flight from Edwards Air Force Base on January 23, 1951. Instead of the J40, however, it was powered by an Allison J35-A-17 with 5,000 pounds (2,270kg) of static thrust.

A second prototype was also flight-tested with the Allison engine. Although the prototypes handled well, they were underpowered. In 1953, the

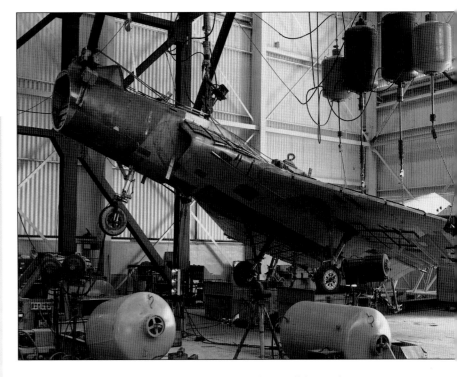

aircraft finally received the Westinghouse J40, rated at 11,600 pounds (5,266kg) of static thrust with afterburners. On October 3, 1953, the J40 propelled the Skyray to 753 miles per hour (1,212kph), a new world record. But despite this achievement, the engine was still unstable and was replaced by the Pratt & Whitney J57 turbojet with 9,700 pounds (4,404kg) of static thrust (14,870 pounds [6,751kg] of static thrust with afterburner).

The basic Skyray had a standard retractable tricycle landing gear, but it also included a tailwheel to protect the rear structure of the fuselage during its high-nose landings and takeoffs. The cockpit was located far forward and featured a clamshell-like canopy and ejection seat. Radar and a weapons-firing system were also located in the nose.

The first production F4D-1 flew in June 1954 and the bulk of the order was delivered for service in 1956. By 1958, Douglas had produced 420 F4D-1s for the Navy and the Marine Corps. In 1956, at the height of production, the Douglas facility could complete two Skyrays a week; in 1957, the number increased to three per week. Engine enhancements continued throughout the program. Final production models left the factory with a more powerful J57-P-8 turbojet, also known as P-8B. This engine produced 10,200 pounds (4,631kg) of static thrust and 16,000 pounds (7,264kg) with afterburners.

The Skyray possessed remarkable climbing ability. It could reach 49,000 feet (14,935m) in two minutes and thirty-six seconds, a feat demonstrated by

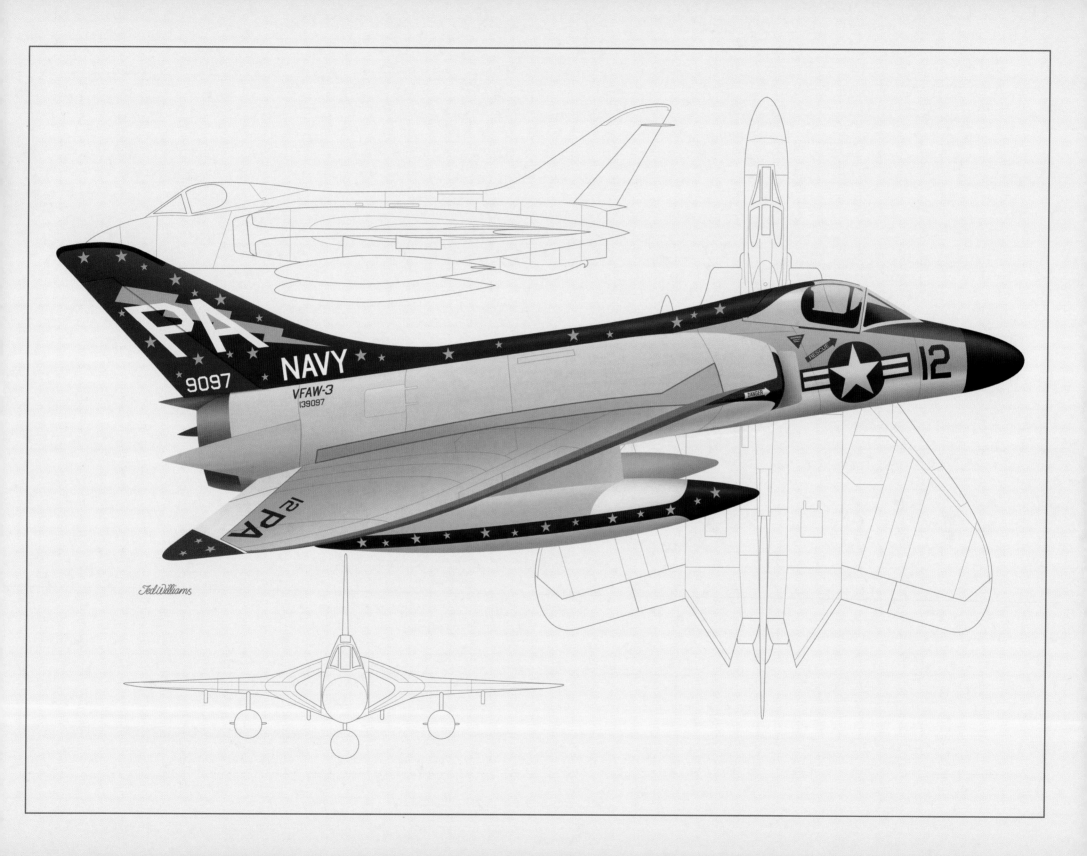

Douglas F4D Skyray Specifications

Type: Single-seat fighter-bomber

Power plant: One Pratt & Whitney J57-P-8 turbojet engine producing 15,000 pounds (6,810kg) of static thrust

Performance: Maximum speed, 695 mph (1,162kph) at 36,000 feet (10,973m); service ceiling, 55,000 feet (16,764m); maximum range, 1,200 miles (1,931km)

Weight: Empty, 10,024 pounds (7,268kg); maximum takeoff weight, 25,000 pounds (11,340kg)

Dimensions: Span, 33 feet 6 inches (10.2m); length, 45 feet 3 inches (13.8m); height, 13 feet (4m); wing area, 557 square feet (51.2m^2)

Armament: Four 20mm cannons plus a 4,000-pound (1,816kg) bomb load

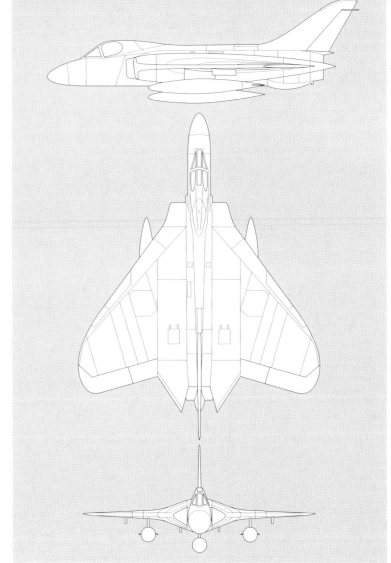

Marine Corps Major Edward N. LeFaivre in May 1958. Standard armament included four wing-mounted 20mm cannons. The wings were equipped with underwing connections that could carry a 4,000-pound (1,816kg) load of bombs, rockets, or drop tanks.

In 1956, Douglas manufactured a redesigned F5D-1. Called the Skylancer, it had a bigger J57 jet engine and longer range. The Skylancer's top speed was 953 miles per hour (1,534kph), nearly 300 miles per hour (483kph) faster than the Skyray. Only four models were produced before the program was canceled in favor of a supersonic aircraft already in production by Vought. All four were used for evaluation and testing; two models were claimed by NASA for space program research.

During its service life, the F4D Skyray never entered combat and was taken out of service in 1962, stepping aside for jets designed with multimission capabilities.

In its day, the Skyray was a successful example of a second-generation jet. Its sophisticated systems, supersonic speed, and interception capabilities were assets to the Navy's carrier air fleet. In the early 1950s, no other Navy fighter aircraft could fly as fast or as high, or could get higher faster. It's well known that the Skyray programs endured numerous maintenance challenges, particularly with the engine and the skin. Its double-layer skin, although light, was fragile, and was often damaged in flight. In addition, many pilots contended that it was a demanding aircraft to fly. But in a time of rapid advancements in aviation engineering, the Skyray was the first Navy airplane to really push the envelope.

ABOVE: A Skyray flies over the California coastline, displaying its delta-wing configuration.

OPPOSITE: Douglas employees at work in the pickup position and mating area at Douglas' El Segundo plant in California. The Skyray had an abundance of access panels to facilitate both assembly and maintenance.

Lockheed F-104 Starfighter

The U.S. military was finally getting comfortable traveling at the speed of sound. Both the Air Force and the Navy had aircraft that could handle Mach 1, but the United States needed an aircraft that could best the Russian designs. Experience in Korea proved that America needed a faster fighter plane, and designer Kelly Johnson heard the call. Lockheed's F-104 Starfighter was the first American jet capable of sustained flight at twice the speed of sound.

Developed in 1952 in the famous Lockheed design facility known as the Skunk Works, the Starfighter was built for speed. Johnson's team was looking for inventive ways to get the most speed possible out of a streamlined airframe. The XP-104 was a small aircraft compared to most early 1950s jets. Design practices of the day called for big aircraft with large delta wings, but the Starfighter had a surprisingly short wingspan—only 21 feet (6.4m), with negative dihedral. The small, low-aspect ratio, mid-mounted wings appeared incapable of lift, which was, in fact, a legitimate concern. To lower the aircraft's stall speed from 198 miles per hour (319kph), the leading edges would tilt forward to provide more lift at takeoff and landing. Notches in the trailing edge flaps (in production models only) forced a portion of the engine's high-pressure air over the top of the wing, augmenting lift.

Not only were the wings short, they were also unusually thin. With only a maximum thickness of 4.2 inches (10.7cm), the ailerons and hydraulic flap actuators were designed to fit into the small wing cavity. Yet, while miniaturized, each mechanism was powerful enough to withstand the extreme forces experienced at high speeds. Another salient wing feature, especially noticeable to the ground crew, were the sharp leading edges. While parked on the ground, a protective covering was required to prevent ground personnel from getting cut by the knifelike edge, should someone accidentally bump into the wing.

The wings were attached to the aircraft unconventionally as well. Instead of the typical spar construction, the wings were attached to sleevelike members that fitted around the fuselage frame.

Every detail on the Starfighter was scrutinized for ways to gain speed. The tail was designed in a new "T" shape. This arrangement was determined to be the best match with the airframe for travel at higher speeds. Because the ejection seat could not clear the high T-shaped tailplane, the engineers at the Skunk Works came up with an ejection seat that expelled the pilot underneath the aircraft. This was an acceptable solution at the high altitudes where the

479th Tactical Fighter Wing

RIGHT: This publicity shot from Lockheed features test pilot Herman "Fish" Salmon next to an evaluation Starfighter. In early promotional photos, the F-104 Starfighter's engine inlets, with their specially designed shock cones, were covered for secrecy.

OPPOSITE: The Lockheed Starfighter presents the classic silhouette of the 1950s jet age. The F-104's streamlined profile and its Mach 2 performance earned it the nickname "the missile with the man in it." Pictured here is an F-104C from the 479th Tactical Fighter Wing.

Starfighter was designed to operate, but in low-altitude crisis situations, such as during takeoff or landing, downward ejection could be deadly.

The needle-nosed XF-104 made its initial flight in 1954. Its fuselage was slim, with only enough space for the pilot, the fuel, and the engine and its afterburning unit combo, which took up half the space inside the main body of the aircraft. Although designed to use the new General Electric J79 turbojet, with 14,800 pounds (6,719kg) of static thrust with afterburning, delays forced the prototype to fly with the less powerful Wright XJ65-W-6. Once the J79 became available, seventeen evaluation models with the proper engine, a longer fuselage, and sturdier landing gear, designated YF-104, followed. A device called a shock cone was located in each air intake. This cone would shift to regulate the airflow for maximum efficiency at varying speeds.

Called the "missile with a man in it," the Starfighter was the first aircraft to break the sound barrier in a climb. On May 7, 1958, a YF-104 with the J79 climbed to more than 91,000 feet (27,737m); and on May 11, another test pilot took a YF-104 to 1,404 miles per hour (2,259kph). But this speed and climb came at a price. The Starfighter had a very short range. Without auxiliary fuel tanks or refueling, the Starfighter's basic range was only 300 miles (483km).

The F-104A entered service in 1958 and an F-104B was developed as a two-seat model for training, but the Air Force was concerned that the Starfighter was too fast. Of that first batch of Starfighters produced for the USAF, forty-nine crashed. These accidents, with the resulting fatalities and

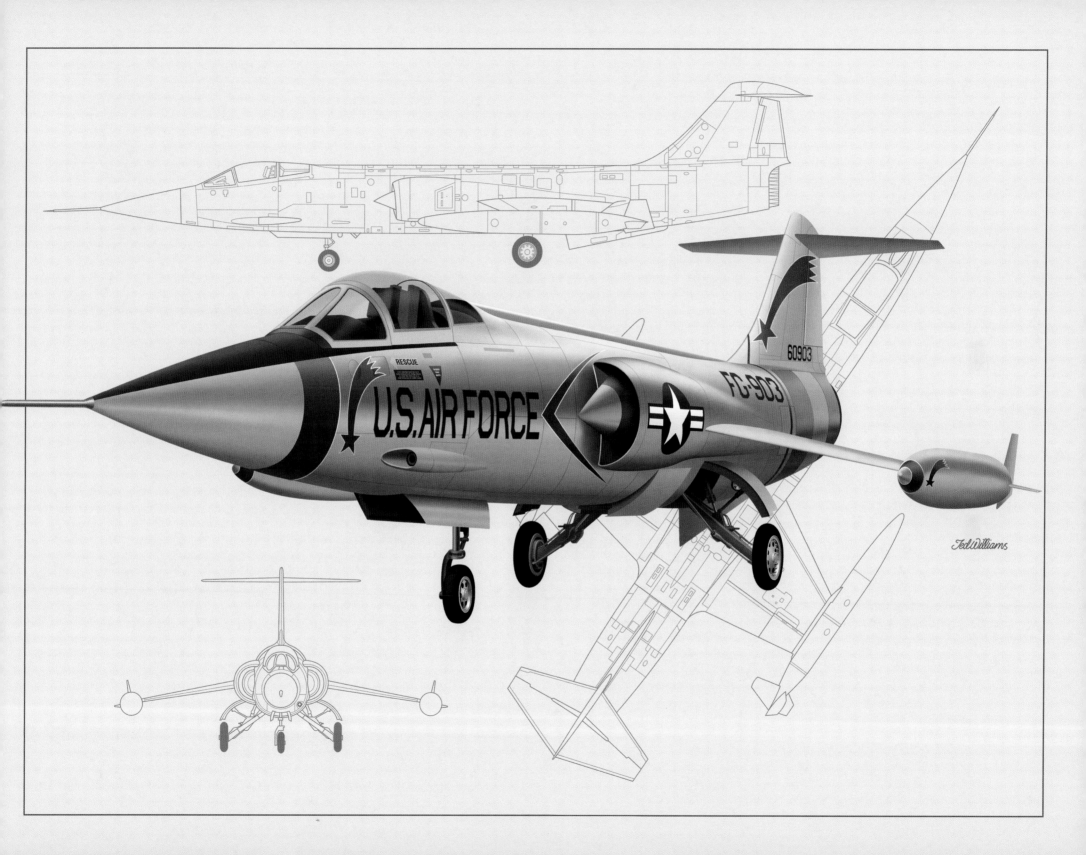

injuries, were attributed to the temperamental nature of the short wings at low speeds and low altitudes, the downward ejection seat, and the Starfighter's extreme climb and blink-of-an-eye acceleration. Fifty-six F-104Cs were developed to be tactical bombing versions capable of inflight refueling. The F104Cs could carry a 4,000-pound (1,816kg) payload or drop tanks. The F-104D was the F-104C's companion two-seat trainer. Twenty-one F-104Ds were produced. A QF-104A was developed in limited quantities: these were designed to serve as target drones.

In 1959, the Navy received and tested three Starfighters for evaluation, but did not pursue the program. Another three Starfighters were developed for testing by NASA. Designated NF-104A, they were modified with tail-mounted rockets that delivered 6,000 pounds (2,724kg) of static thrust. In 1963, one of these NASA-modified models set a world altitude record of 119,000 feet (36,271m). Yet, while flying one of the NF-104As on December 10, 1963, test pilot Charles "Chuck" Yeager was involved in a near-fatal accident.

Another noteworthy accomplishment in a Starfighter is credited to a female pilot. In November 1963, Jacqueline Cochran, an aviation legend, flew a Starfighter to Mach 1.8, a women's world speed record. Earlier, during World War II, Cochran was instrumental in forming the Women's Airforce Service Pilots (WASPs).

The Starfighter was armed with the General Electric M61 Vulcan 20mm cannon. With the invention of an electrically operated rotating barrel, the

ABOVE: A pair of F-104As bank left over the Oakland Bay Bridge in California. The wingtip tanks have been replaced with rails to fire Sidewinder air-to-air missiles.

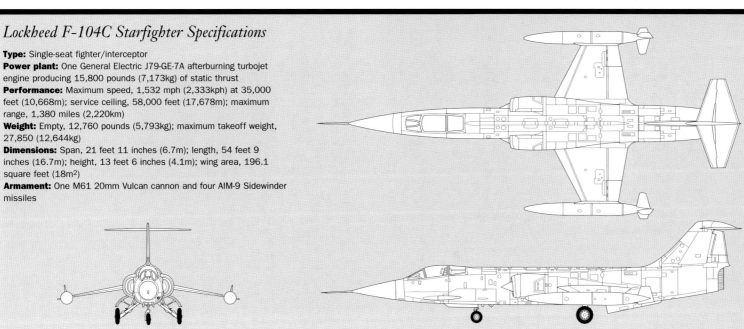

Lockheed F-104C Starfighter Specifications

Type: Single-seat fighter/interceptor

Power plant: One General Electric J79-GE-7A afterburning turbojet engine producing 15,800 pounds (7,173kg) of static thrust

Performance: Maximum speed, 1,532 mph (2,333kph) at 35,000 feet (10,668m); service ceiling, 58,000 feet (17,678m); maximum range, 1,380 miles (2,220km)

Weight: Empty, 12,760 pounds (5,793kg); maximum takeoff weight, 27,850 (12,644kg)

Dimensions: Span, 21 feet 11 inches (6.7m); length, 54 feet 9 inches (16.7m); height, 13 feet 6 inches (4.1m); wing area, 196.1 square feet (18m²)

Armament: One M61 20mm Vulcan cannon and four AIM-9 Sidewinder missiles

General Electric Company created a weapon of awesome firepower, dispensing 4,000 rounds per minute. At this rate of fire, a pilot needed to take special care not to use up the gun's supply of ammunition: the Vulcan could expend its entire store of 725 rounds in just seven seconds. After experiencing operating problems with the Vulcan, later variants flew without it. The Starfighter was also the first fighter aircraft to carry a heat-seeking AIM-7 Sidewinder air-to-air missile on each wingtip.

From 1965 to 1968, the F-104C saw action in Vietnam, but newer aircraft, with longer range and greater ordnance, quickly usurped the Starfighter's frontline status. A fleet of Starfighters had also been put on standby during the Cuban missile crisis in 1962 and remained in the Florida area to protect the United States' southeastern coastline until 1969.

The F-104G was modified for export and production under license to Germany and NATO nations. The G variant featured a more reliable J79 engine, a bulkier tail, connection points for additional armament, and a British-designed Martin-Baker ejection seat that could fire upward over the T-tail unit. Despite limited use in the United States, the Starfighter became one of the most prevalent fighter aircraft in use around the world throughout the 1960s.

The Starfighter was a modern marvel. Although deemed too "hot" by the U.S. Air Force, Kelly Johnson's Starfighter did what it was designed it to do: go fast—really fast. It even looked fast. The super-aerodynamic airframe was equipped with radar and modern gun-sight technology. The F-104 could climb 60,000 feet (18,288m) per minute and maintain a maximum speed of Mach 2.2. Although not a stellar performer in its role as interceptor, it paved the way for today's Air Force and Navy supersonic air fleets.

BELOW: The first XF-104 (FG-786), without inlet shock cones, flaunts its sleek design. The prominent probe attached to the nose gathers data during supersonic testing (removed operationally); an auxiliary generator powers the onboard systems while the aircraft is being refueled for a second test run.

RIGHT: This overhead view of an FG-786 calls attention to the very short, twenty-one-foot (6.4m) wingspan of the Starfighter. The T-tail was another remarkable innovation brought to this design by Lockheed's talented engineer Clarence "Kelly" Johnson.

Vought F8U Crusader

When Vought—once part of United Aircraft Corporation, then later the Vought Systems Division of LTV Aerospace Corporation—received the Navy's contract to build its next daylight fighter/bombing jet aircraft, the Navy needed a supersonic fighter that could land at a manageable 115 miles per hour (185kph), making it suitable for carrier operations. After the turbulent Cutlass program, the Vought F8U Crusader was a welcome success for the Navy. It spawned numerous variants, until it was superseded by the multimission McDonnell F-4 Phantom II.

Russ Clark led the design team that developed the F8U. The requirements for flight at Mach 2 were demanding enough without the added considerations for naval operations. Clark's team pursued several avionic technologies and construction innovations to create an exceptional aircraft that met Navy specifications. The team's brainchild would go on to win the Collier Trophy for its pioneering efforts in the advancement of aviation science.

The first XF8U-1 prototype was available for flight testing in 1955. It was powered by a Pratt & Whitney J57 turbojet with afterburner. Brought to Edwards Air Force Base, the XF8U-1 was the first prototype to slip into the speed of sound on its maiden test flight. After five years of testing, this benchmark aircraft was requested by the Smithsonian for display, a testament to its importance as a history-making plane.

The Crusader's most unusual feature was its swept-back, two-position, variable-incidence wing. This innovation provided the extra lift needed at slower speeds and regulated the angle of approach during landings, further eliminating the punishing impact a heavy aircraft places on its landing gear, without compromising visibility. The wing, which was attached to the rear spar by a hinge, was operated by hydraulic pistons that adjusted the incidence of the wing, thereby varying the angle of the wing up to 7 degrees. When raised, the wing essentially acted like an airbrake, keeping speeds manageable for carrier deck operation, and at takeoff a raised position helped produce extra lift. During flight at higher speeds, the changeable wing was positioned flush with the fuselage. To this day, the Crusader is the only military aircraft to employ this feature.

The wing was also reinforced to carry 1,348 gallons (5,102L) of fuel in an internal fuel compartment. This volume of fuel gave the Crusader an impressive range. And the Crusader was capable of inflight refueling. A refueling probe was inserted behind the cockpit to the pilot's left.

The airframe was constructed out of advanced, lighter alloys. The tail was built with titanium, an extremely strong, lightweight material able to endure high temperatures and resist oxidation, an added benefit for naval aircraft stationed near salt water. The alloy used to cover the fuselage included a high concentration of magnesium, another lightweight, heat-resistant material.

These exotic metal components were wrapped around a standard-shape fuselage, sculpted to take advantage of a boundary layer that was optimized for speed by the Area Rule, giving the fuselage a pinched, "wasp waist" look. First proposed by Richard T. Whitcomb, a researcher with NACA, the Area Rule states that reducing a jet fuselage's circumference at the spot where the wings attach minimizes the drag experienced at near-supersonic speeds. This drag had been preventing early jets from traveling at and past Mach 1.

In 1957, 318 F8U-1s were ordered, followed by a 1958 order for 187 F8U-2s with a more powerful J57. And 152 F8U-2N Crusaders were modified for specialized night operations. This included improved radar, infrared capabilities, and an autopiloting mechanism. Last in the program, 286 F8U-2NEs were produced to carry a greater payload of bombs, rockets, or missiles.

Additional models were built for export to France, and many early production models were refitted with newer technology.

In 1962, the Crusader's designation changed from F8U to F-8 to adhere to the standardization called for by the Department of Defense. The existing variants were redesignated with ascending letters of the alphabet: F-8A replacing F8U-1, F-8B instead of F8U-1E, F-8C for the F8U-2, and so on. All Air Force and Navy aircraft now use this naming convention.

The Crusader was typically armed with four 20mm cannons, and the capability to launch offensive air-to-air missiles was quickly adopted. All variants could carry a variety of weaponry under the wings.

During the Vietnam War, the F-8 Crusader became known as the "MiG master" after downing a confirmed eighteen MiGs.

BELOW: A squadron of Vought Crusaders prepares for a catapult launch in 1955. The Crusader in the foreground, with its outer-wing panels folded down and its wing in the fully lifted position, is ready for takeoff. The Crusader's wing was an efficient lifting body. There are eight recorded occurrences of pilots taking off with the outer-wing panels left in the folded position. Upon realizing this, the pilots simply unfolded the panels and continued their missions.

The Crusader set many noteworthy records during its tenure. Before becoming the first man to orbit the Earth, Marine Corps Major John H. Glenn set a transcontinental speed record when, in 1957, he flew a specialized RF-8A/F8U-1P Crusader from the East Coast to the West Coast in three hours and twenty-three minutes.

The F-8 Crusader was the last aircraft built as an offensive gun platform. This "last gunfighter" had a relatively short service life, eventually being overtaken by newer aircraft that were designed for all-weather offensive and defensive missions, close air support, bombing, and photoreconnaissance for a complete multirole envelope. These newer fighters would rely on a missile-based system, rather than on guns, reflecting the way the U.S. military believed the battle for air superiority would be waged in the future.

LEFT TOP: Vought developed this Crusader as a prototype for an improved missile-fighting variant in response to a military specification. Called the "Crusader III" or "Super Crusader," the aircraft was given a number of improvements, such as a redesigned air intake. The Super Crusader was never produced. Other newer designs from different manufacturers were chosen for production instead.

LEFT BOTTOM: An auxiliary power cable and fuel line ready an F-8 Crusader for flight. At the moment, its wing is down in the static/cruise position. An XC-142A—a turboprop tiltwing transport for vertical takeoff and landing (VTOL)—waits beside the Crusader. The XC-142A was a collaboration between LTV Aerospace Corporation, Ryan Aeronautical Company, and the Hiller Aircraft Company. Only five were ever built.

Vought F8U-1 Crusader Specifications

Type: Single-seat, carrier-based fighter

Power plant: One Pratt & Whitney J57-P-4A afterburning engine producing 10,000 pounds (4,540kg) of static thrust

Performance: Maximum speed, 1,155 mph (1,858kph) at 36,000 feet (10,973m); service ceiling, 52,350 feet (15,956m); maximum range, 1,425 miles (2,293km)

Weight: Empty, 17,836 pounds (8,098kg); maximum take-off weight, 34,000 pounds (15,436kg)

Dimensions: Span, 35 feet 8 inches (10.8m); length, 54 feet 3 inches (16.5m); height, 15 feet 9 inches (4.8m); wing area, 350 square feet (32.2m^2)

Armament: Four 20mm Colt Mk-12 cannons with 144 rounds per gun and a rocket pack for thirty-two 70mm HVAR rockets

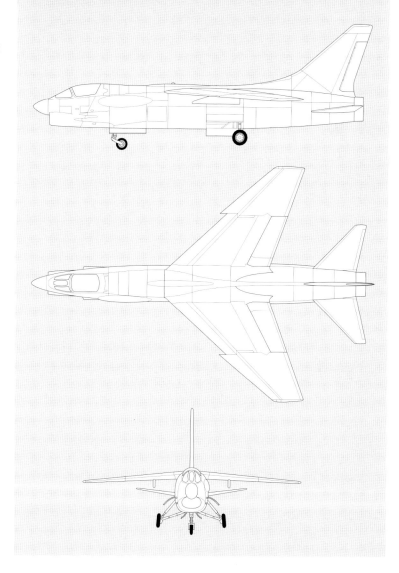

Republic F-105 Thunderchief

The Republic F-105 Thunderchief is the largest single-engine, single-seat fighter in the history of military fighter aviation—not a surprising distinction considering it was designed by Alexander Kartveli, whose big P-47 helped sweep the skies of enemy aircraft in World War II. At more than sixty-four feet (19.5m) long and nineteen feet (5.8m) tall, the Thud, as it became known, was a vital aircraft during U.S. operations in Vietnam.

The Thunderchief began its life as an advanced project to develop the next generation F-84F Thunderstreak. Under the supervision of Kartveli, it was designed as an all-weather, supersonic, long-range fighter/bomber with the ability to carry nuclear weapons in an internal bomb bay. However, because of its durability, the Thunderchief found itself performing some of the most dangerous air strikes in Vietnam.

Drafting began in 1952, and by 1954 Republic's contract to build fifteen evaluation models was finalized. On October 22, 1955, the first prototype, the YF-105A, took to the skies. The aircraft exceeded the speed of sound. On May 26, 1956, the next prototype, the YF-105B, flew even faster. With its more powerful Pratt & Whitney engine and NACA-inspired contoured fuselage, the YF-105B flew at twice the speed of sound, a feat that earned it the name Thunderchief.

In May 1958, the first shipment of seventy-one F-105B Thunderchiefs began to arrive at Air Force squadrons. The design of the airframe made use of the Area Rule. This wasp-waist shape mitigated the effects of supersonic drag, allowing the plane to perform at Mach 1 and beyond.

The mid-mounted wings—with high-speed spoilers on the top and full-span slotted flaps on the leading edge—and the low-mounted horizontal tailplanes were both swept back 45 degrees. The air intake at each wing root was swept forward in a new dramatic design. At the rear of the aircraft, underneath the fuselage, a ventral fin maintained lateral stability at higher speeds. Petal-type airbrakes surrounded the tailpipe, and operated in conjunction with airbrakes on each side of the cockpit.

Designed around a Pratt & Whitney turbojet, the first evaluation model, the YF-105A, received the Pratt & Whitney J57. The remainder of all preproduction and production F-105s received the J75. The J75 was a complex and powerful engine. Water injection and a sophisticated turbine system with afterburning could produce 23,500 pounds (10,669kg) of static thrust—burning 776 pounds (352kg) of fuel per minute.

The Thunderchief relied heavily on electronics. A sophisticated electronic control system, integrated throughout the aircraft, instantaneously provided updated information to the pilot. At the time, it was the most complex aircraft accepted into service, with vertical tape instruments for airspeed, vertical velocity, and altitude. Other indicators displayed roll, pitch, and yaw information. A forward-firing, 20mm Vulcan rapid-firing cannon was mounted on the left side of the aircraft's nose. The original internal bomb bay, although intended as a nuclear weapons store, was redesigned to hold a 390-gallon (1,476L) fuel tank or additional payload. In total, the Thunderchief could carry 4,000 pounds (1,816kg) of ordnance externally on four underwing connections and on the fuselage's centerline. Another 8,000 pounds (3,632kg) could be carried in its internal cavity. The load usually consisted of rockets, missiles, bombs, and napalm. The Thunderchief was the first American fighter that could drop its entire bomb load while flying at supersonic speeds.

Despite it size, the Thunderchief possessed good range. But the large Thunderchief required a long runway to achieve lift. Later, to expand its mission envelope, variants were modified to accept inflight refueling.

First available in 1959, 610 F-105D models were produced. They featured a more powerful J75 with 26,500 pounds (12,031kg) of static thrust, and more complicated, electronically controlled autopiloting functions and a weapons-

RIGHT: F-105Ds of the 4th Tactical Fighter Wing complete a midair refueling operation with a KC-135 jet tanker. Until the Vietnam War, all Thunderchiefs operated in their natural aluminum finish.

firing system. A longer nose housed a new radar system, the NASARR R-14A, which provided Doppler-assisted navigation. The final Thunderchief variant produced in quantity was the F-105F, a two-seat version intended for combat, with further modifications, such as a larger tail, for improved stability in flight. Overall, 833 Thunderchiefs, in the B, D, and F variants, were produced.

From 1965 to 1970, Thunderchiefs participated in daily operations over Vietnam in an air campaign called "Rolling Thunder," seeing action in more than 20,000 missions and bombing raids throughout North Vietnam. The Thunderchiefs encountered fierce anti-aircraft fire and surface-to-air missiles (SAMs), which claimed 350 Thunderchiefs and the lives of many of the American pilots who flew them. Better suited for bombing, the Thunderchief could nevertheless tangle with MiGs. Although the MiG was a better dogfighter, the Thunderchief, because of its rugged construction and the skill of its pilots, took twenty-seven combat victories against MiG-17s and MiG-21s.

A number of Thunderchiefs were modified for a program called Wild Weasel. Like the F-100 Super Sabre before it, some Thunderchiefs were equipped with an exclusive radar-detecting device that launched strike missiles at targets identified by their radar emissions. By 1971, F-105s were removed from the frontline and assigned to reserve units. The Thunderchief was never built for export. The F-105s Thunderchief was the last design by Alexander Kartveli before he retired in 1964. True to his legacy, it was a big, powerful aircraft that did its job well, while protecting the pilots who flew it.

ABOVE: Crewmembers use an MJ-1 bomb-loading vehicle to attach 750-pound (340kg) general-purpose bombs to the centerline pylon of a "Thud" from the 333rd Tactical Fighter Squadron, 355th Tactical Fighter Wing at Takhli Air Base in Thailand.

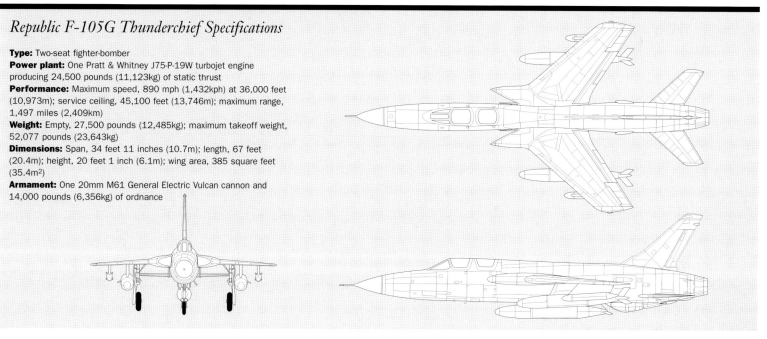

Republic F-105G Thunderchief Specifications

Type: Two-seat fighter-bomber
Power plant: One Pratt & Whitney J75-P-19W turbojet engine producing 24,500 pounds (11,123kg) of static thrust
Performance: Maximum speed, 890 mph (1,432kph) at 36,000 feet (10,973m); service ceiling, 45,100 feet (13,746m); maximum range, 1,497 miles (2,409km)
Weight: Empty, 27,500 pounds (12,485kg); maximum takeoff weight, 52,077 pounds (23,643kg)
Dimensions: Span, 34 feet 11 inches (10.7m); length, 67 feet (20.4m); height, 20 feet 1 inch (6.1m); wing area, 385 square feet (35.4m²)
Armament: One 20mm M61 General Electric Vulcan cannon and 14,000 pounds (6,356kg) of ordnance

McDonnell F-4 Phantom II

On the heels of Vought's "last gunfighter," McDonnell's F-4 Phantom II could be labeled the "first missile fighter." With no gun or cannon on board, the F-4, with its four Sparrow missiles, was designed to Navy specifications for carrier use, but it rapidly attracted the attention of the military's other flying organizations. Proficient at all tasks put to it, the two-seat, twin-engine, multimission aircraft saw service in the hands of Navy, Marine, and Air Force pilots—only one of a few successful crossover programs in the history of the armed services.

McDonnell's second design to carry the Phantom name is perhaps the most successful example of American fighter aircraft evolution. In service from 1958 until 1996, more than 5,000 Phantom IIs were built for active service worldwide. First presented to the Navy as an improved F3H Demon, the F-4 developed into the first true multirole aircraft in the military's inventory. Named after McDonnell's original Phantom program, which resulted in the first jet accepted into carrier service, the Phantom II was judged the victor in a fly-off against the Vought Crusader III.

At the Navy's request, the program first leaned toward attack characteristics; then, however, the McDonnell group, led by Herman D. Barkey, was asked by the Navy to return to the original all-weather fighter/bombing interceptor concept. On May 27, 1958, the first of two F4H-1 prototypes took flight. An order for twenty-one evaluation models followed. These models were used for carrier trials. During this testing period, these first Phantom IIs shattered many world records. A record-breaking two hour forty-seven minute, coast-to-coast flight, a climb to 98,556 feet (30,040m), and thirteen additional speed and climb milestones are credited to early Phantom IIs.

In 1962, the Phantom II was redesignated F-4 by the Department of Defense's standardization committee. The first production model was the F-4B. From June 1961 to March 1967, 649 of this variant were built, the first delivered to naval squadrons in October 1961. Two General Electric J79s, generating 15,900 pounds (7,219kg) of static thrust with afterburning, powered the F-4B past Mach 2. The J79 turbojet offered more power for its weight than any other engine available at the time. An elaborate intake ducting system was required to coax optimum performance from the two turbojets. A microprocessor-controlled system, the first of its kind, ensured proper airflow through the square air intakes on either side of the fuselage, just aft of the cockpit. As an added safety bonus, the Phantom II could fly on one engine.

VMFA-531 Grey Ghosts

RIGHT: Navy and Air Force F-4 Phantom IIs await final assembly. In the factory, dummy missiles were used for last minute mounting adjustments. In the foreground is a row of J79 turbojet engines. In full afterburners, these engines were capable of developing up to 17,000 pounds (7,718kg) of static thrust.

OPPOSITE: This overhead view of a McDonnell Phantom II showcases the striking lines of the big fighter. In its day, the F-4 was one of the most successful American fighter planes, credited with 70% of the aircraft downed in air combat during Vietnam. This one carries the markings of the "Grey Ghosts" of VMFA-531, a Marine Corps fighter/attack squadron.

This Mach 2 design had a low-mounted delta wing, swept back at a sharp 45-degree angle and tilted upward slightly toward the tips. The horizontal tailplanes, delta-shaped and swept back to match the wing, slanted downward and the entire empennage extended above the afterburner.

An aluminum alloy was used throughout the fuselage construction, while heat-resistant titanium was used to protect the aft areas from engine exhaust. A remarkable autonomous radar system allowed the Phantom II to search out its target and fire without any logistical assistance from the ground control.

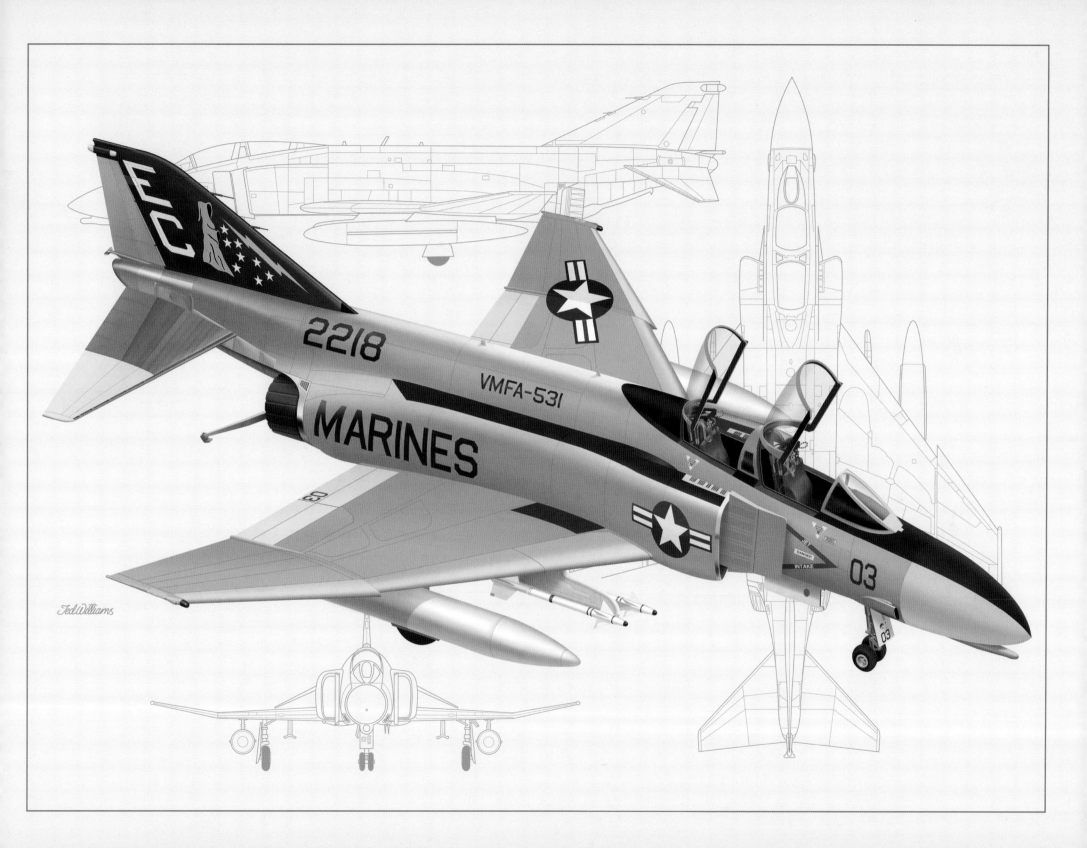

The Marine Corps operated an F-4B modified for photoreconnaissance. Large quantities of an F-4J variant, with structural enhancements and increased power plants, were produced for the Navy and the Marines. Additional navalized variants were introduced before the Phantom II was removed from frontline service in the mid-1990s.

The Air Force contracted for 583 F-4Cs as frontline tactical fighter/bomber/interceptors. Initially designated the F-110 Specter by the Air Force, the name was changed to the standardized F-4 Phantom II designation. Alterations were made to this model to accommodate land-based operations and Air Force preferences, including the addition of the more powerful J79-GE-15, which produced 17,000 pounds (7,718kg) of static thrust with afterburning. A total of 503 RF-4Cs, originally designed for the USAF, were modified for photoreconnaissance, and a production order of 825 improved F-4Ds quickly followed. Other variants followed with modifications for the needs of each branch of the American military and for export to other countries. Even though the Navy was at first the intended recipient, more Phantoms were actually built for the Air Force.

Both the Navy Blue Angels and the Air Force Thunderbird demonstration teams flew the F-4 from 1969 to 1973, capturing the public's imagination with stunning displays of the plane's performance capabilities and assuring the Phantom II's reputation as a premier fighter plane.

Phantom IIs began to be deployed to Vietnam in 1966. It did not take long for an operational flaw to surface. Contemporary thinking had concluded that offensive missile systems would eliminate the need for pilots to engage in dog-

ABOVE LEFT: A McDonnell RF-4C, a reconnaissance version of the Phantom II, carries a large nose boom for testing and evalution; it collects exact yaw, roll, and pitch data. The bulge underneath the nose accommodates camera equipment. The Phantom II's dihedral wingtip and anhedral horizontal stabilizer are clearly visible from this angle.

ABOVE RIGHT: Crewmembers stand aside as a F-4 Phantom II comes in on its final approach. The aircraft's tail hook is extended and it is ready to trap aboard the ship. The four arresting wires are clearly outlined on the carrier deck.

OPPOSITE: Air Force F-4 Phantom IIs in the main assembly area at the McDonnell factory during the height of the Vietnam conflict.

fighting tactics as practiced in World War II and Korea. Yet over the jungles in Vietnam, the North Vietnamese Air Force would often engage the American fighters. In such close quarters, the American pilot would either quickly run out of missiles or fail to get "lock-on"—either case rendering him defenseless. An early solution was to add underwing gun pods to augment the missile stores, but the gun pods did not have a stable mounting, impairing marksmanship. As a result, the F-4E variant was developed with a General Electric M61 20mm cannon mounted in the forward fuselage.

The F-4Gs took over the Wild Weasel program from the F-105 Thunderchief, becoming the premier destroyers of surface-to-air missile (SAM) sites. In 1991, Phantoms resumed Wild Weasel operations during Operation Desert Storm because they were still the most effective aircraft for the job of searching out and destroying SAM batteries.

The Phantom II was the most versatile weapons platform ever created by the aircraft industry. Attesting to this, more than 5,000 F-4s, in many variants, were produced in the United States. The last F-4 built was an F-4EJ assembled at a Mitsubishi plant in Japan in 1981. It was the 5,195th F-4 Phantom manufactured worldwide.

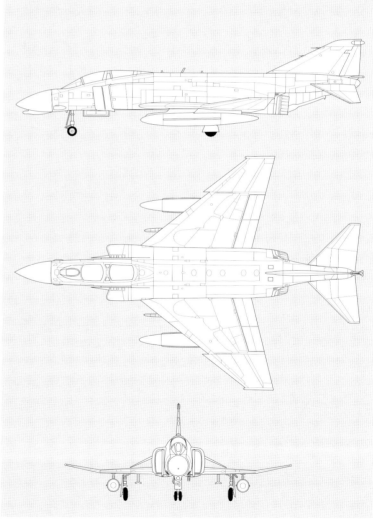

McDonnell F-4N Phantom II Specifications

Type: Two-seat, carrier- and land-based fighter

Power plant: Two General Electric J79-GE-8 afterburning turbojet engines producing 16,000 pounds (7,264kg) of static thrust

Performance: Maximum speed, 1,583 mph (2,547kph) at 48,000 feet (14,630m); service ceiling, 62,000 feet (18,898m); range 500 miles (805km)

Weight: Empty, 29,535 pounds (13,409kg); maximum takeoff weight, 61,795 pounds (28,055kg)

Dimensions: Span, 38 feet 5 inches (11.7m); length, 63 feet (19.2m); height, 16 feet 3 inches (5m); wing area, 530 square feet (49m^2)

Armament: Up to eight air-to-air missiles and a 16,000-pound (7,264kg) bomb load

Grumman F-14 Tomcat

As the 1950s drew to a close, the United States became aware that its Cold War foe, the Soviet Union, was developing deliverable, tactical, thermonuclear weapons. The U.S. Navy now needed an aircraft that could protect its task forces, one that could attack and destroy incoming enemy aircraft at a safe distance from the fleet's position. This need prompted the development of aircraft programs in the 1960s that emphasized speeds of Mach 2 and the creation of sophisticated weapons systems with the ability to counter the new, deliverable, tactical nuclear threat.

The F-14 Tomcat was developed once it was realized that the General Dynamics' F-111—Secretary of Defense Robert McNamara's favored design, chosen for its supposed suitability for both the Navy and Air Force—was not performing as anticipated. The F-111 was too heavy for carrier operations and it lacked the performance stats required from a fighter/interceptor. In misguidedly trying to develop a universal aircraft, General Dynamics fell short with the F-111 in many areas.

To remedy the situation, in 1967, Grumman designer Mike Pelehach came up with a design that incorporated the same power plant and missile system as the F-111, but in a new Grumman-designed airframe. Once it was clear that the Navy's F-111 program was doomed, Grumman presented its proposal to the Navy, eventually participating in the 1968 carrier-based Tactical Fighter Experimental (TFX) design competition to select the F-111's naval replacement.

Although other companies had submitted variable-geometry wing designs, Grumman was given the coveted contract to produce its Tomcat. A major supporter of the Grumman design was Vice Admiral Tom Connolly. While deputy chief of naval operations, Connolly had championed the Grumman design throughout the turbulent discussions and failed programs, such as the multiservice F-111 supported by McNamara, that had preceded the new Grumman "cat." His staunch support gave the aircraft the nickname "Tom's cat," hence Tomcat.

The successful Grumman concept was designed around a twin-engine, two-seat aircraft with variable-geometry wings. Grumman tested several possible configurations before it arrived at the Tomcat as it is recognized today. Designed to be a superior fleet defender, the Tomcat has developed into a multipurpose aircraft. Versatility is key for naval air operations, since each carrier can only operate and maintain a limited number of aircraft; a multirole aircraft

widens an aircraft carrier's mission envelope. To this end, the Tomcat spread its wings and took flight after being accepted into service in 1972.

The mechanism that pivots to change the geometry of the Tomcat's wing panels from a full forward position to a swept-back, delta configuration was constructed out of titanium. Grumman developed a new welding process to manufacture the specialized pivot. The titanium is actually welded together in a vacuum in order to bond it at the molecular level. This process ensures the long service life of the wing-joint assembly responsible for the variable geometry. And, unlike the F-111's manually operated system, a computer system on board the Tomcat continually monitors inflight parameters and automatically adjusts the wings to the appropriate position for optimal performance in varying conditions. The wing's flaps and control surfaces are also controlled by this system. The pilot can choose to disengage the automatic wing control, but the computer will not permit the pilot to position the wings in a way that could jeopardize the aircraft or endanger its occupants.

For carrier operations, the wings are moved forward for maximum lift during takeoff, landing, and low-speed flight. In flight, the wings can sweep from 20 to 68 degrees. It is in its full swept-back position, 68 degrees, that the potential of this twin-engine speed king is realized. The F-14 can fly at speeds well over Mach 2, thus fulfilling its original design concept. At supersonic speeds, the Tomcat's twin vertical tail fins provide directional stability, and help keep the aircraft longitudinally stable should one of the engines fail.

Though the Tomcat was designed to use the same Pratt & Whitney TF30 turbofan as the F-111, this engine was considered to be temporary. Under development by the Navy and Air Force, the Advanced Technology Engine (ATE) was scheduled to replace the Pratt & Whitney turbofan, but the ATE never materialized. So, in 1984, the GE F110 replaced the Pratt & Whitney engine.

An all-weather interceptor, the Tomcat can carry short-range, mid-range, and long-range Phoenix missiles, and it is equipped with a firing system that assures target acquisition at any speed. The Tomcat also has the phenomenal ability to simultaneously track up to twenty-four targets, while launching six missiles to attack six different targets.

Because of the complexity of the weapons it carries and its navigational system, the Tomcat requires a two-person crew: one person to fly the aircraft and the other to operate and monitor the many sophisticated avionics systems. The Naval Flight Officer (NFO) in the rear seat acts as a Radar Intercept

Grumman F-14A Tomcat Specifications

Type: Two-seat, carrier-based, multirole fighter

Power plant: Two Pratt & Whitney TF30-412A afterburning turbofan engines producing 20,900 pounds (9,489kg) of static thrust

Performance: Maximum speed, 1,584 mph (2,516kph) at 40,000 feet (12,192m); service ceiling, 56,000 feet (17,069m); maximum range, 2,000 miles (3,218km)

Weight: Empty, 39,310 pounds (17,847kg); maximum takeoff weight, 70,426 pounds (31,973kg)

Dimensions: Span, unswept, 64 feet 1 inch (19.5m), swept, 38 feet 2 inches (11.6m); height, 16 feet (4.9m); length, 62 feet 8 inches (19.1m), wing area, 565 square feet (52m^2)

Armament: One 20mm M61A-1 General Electric Vulcan cannon; fuselage pallets for four AIM-54 Phoenix air-to-air missiles or recesses for four AIM-7 Sparrow or AIM-120 advanced medium-range air-to-air missiles; two AIM-9 Sidewinder air-to-air missiles or one Sidewinder plus one Phoenix or Sparrow missile

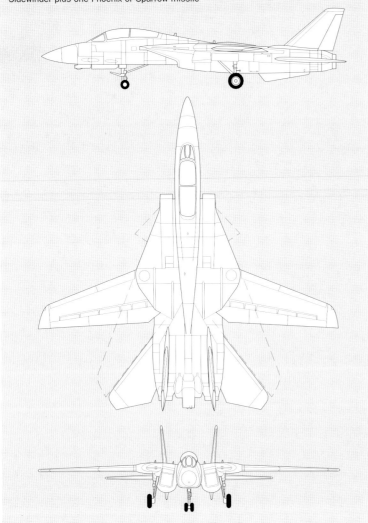

RIGHT TOP: Looking like a giant, skinned prehistoric bird, a Grumman F-14 Tomcat hangs in midair in the process of an airframe drop test. The most structurally demanding aspect of carrier operations for any naval fighter are the punishing landings it must withstand over the course of its service life. Grumman designed a series of special drop tests for the F-14. More than 500 drop tests were performed at a sink rate of 24.7 feet/second (7.53m/s).

RIGHT BOTTOM: A multitude of umbilical attachments provide the F-14 with internal power to test the avionics and weapons systems in a specially designed electronics testing facility.

Officer (RIO) and is responsible for operating the navigational, target-tracking, and weapons systems, while providing essential flight information to the aviator in the front seat.

For close encounters with enemy fighters, the Tomcat is armed with an M61 Vulcan cannon. The United States learned a valuable lesson during the Vietnam conflict, when it chose to eliminate the guns from its fighter planes. Today, all American fighter planes carry a gun for its own defense and to ensure that each aircraft is appropriately outfitted to perform its duties as an air superiority weapon in any situation.

ABOVE: F-14 Tomcats on the final assembly floor. Note the circular housing for the revolving radar antennae awaiting assembly to one of Grumman's E-2 Hawkeyes, the Navy's AWACS (Airborne Warning And Control System) aircraft.

The Tomcat boasts a long and distinguished service record. In 1981, Tomcats downed two Libyan Sukhoi SU-22s over the Gulf of Sidra, and in 1991, they were deployed as part of Operation Desert Storm. In 1995, Tomcats were used as bombers in Bosnia.

The F-14 Tomcat is an ideal carrier aircraft, and an ideal replacement for the Phantom II. Its variable-geometry wings give it the ability to meet the demands of carrier operations, while exceeding goals not usually achievable by a carrier-based fighter. Highly suitable for close support, ground attack, and fleet protection, the F-14 will endure well into the twenty-first century.

McDonnell Douglas F-15 Eagle

The F-15 Eagle has been the reigning American air superiority aircraft since the 1970s. Nearly a century's worth of trial and error with good and bad fighter designs led to the supremely successful McDonnell Douglas F-15 Eagle.

The MiG-25 prompted the Eagle's development. When the MiG-25, known to NATO intelligence as Foxbat, participated in an international air show in 1967, the American military did not have a comparable aircraft. To remain a contender, the Air Force issued a specification in 1967, which was actually an update to a program initiated in 1965. The specification outlined several guidelines, including good visibility, maximum weight of 40,000 pounds (18,160kg), speeds of Mach 2.5, a radar-assisted weapon system, and other specific flight characteristics and maintenance expectations.

In December 1969, the 37,500-page McDonnell Douglas proposal (the McDonnell and Douglas companies had merged in 1967) was chosen over designs from Republic Fairchild and North American Aviation. Among the pages of the massive document was the extensive computer analysis used to determine the best structural and design options for operating within the Air Force's parameters and budget.

The first F-15A flew on July 27, 1972. The Air Force chose not to produce any Eagles with an XF designation. All flight testing occurred on the first production models developed for evaluation purposes. On the whole, flight testing went well; however, as with any new design, some bugs surfaced. Although these were nowhere near disastrous, slight alterations to the wing, the horizontal stabilizer, and the airbrake were initiated to correct minor instabilities discovered during testing. These modifications included the distinctive raked wingtips and dogtooth stabilizers now seen on all Eagles. Some early evaluation Eagles were painted with patches of fluorescent orange to make it easier to spot them in the sky.

The Eagle was designed around a surprisingly simple airframe. Titanium and aluminum alloys were used extensively throughout, as were newer materials like boron epoxy and graphite. These lightweight materials allow the Eagle to be as big as it is and still be highly maneuverable. The 45-degree swept wing is a fixed-shoulder wing. Leading edge flaps were eliminated; all ailerons and flaps are located on the trailing edges only.

Many allowances for maintenance were designed into the aircraft. The wings and tail are easily interchangeable, and it is possible to replace an

RIGHT: An overhead view of the two-place cockpit of the Strike Eagle, the latest ground attack version of the F-15. The complexity of flying the airplane and operating the electronics weapons systems necessitated the addition of a second seat for the Electronics Weapons Officer (EWO).

OPPOSITE: The aerodynamically efficient airframe of the F-15 is evident in this view. Its amazing speed, climb rate, and maneuverability, augmented by its sophisticated avionics and weapons system, make the Eagle the best all-around fighter built to date. Shown in the two-tone non-specular gray camouflage scheme, this aircraft is from the Air Defense Tactical Air Command (ADTAC) 48th Fighter Interceptor Squadron stationed at Langley Air Force Base, Virginia, in 1982.

engine in less than thirty minutes. Major components are accessible without removing adjoining components, and ground crew personnel can get to all integral systems via numerous access panels.

The brand new Pratt & Whitney turbofan jet engine was chosen to power the Eagle. Although production was delayed while the TF-100 was finalized, it was worth the inconvenience. The Eagle was the first fighter aircraft with a favorable power-to-weight ratio. This equation is the secret behind the Eagle's unsurpassed acceleration and rapid rate of climb, both of which can be attributed to the turbofan's innovative construction. The engine components were made out of a powdered metal that was molded by heat and high pressure. The end result is an engine that can withstand much higher temperatures while offering awesome thrust. Air is supplied to the twin engines through air intakes with automated variable inlet control.

Yet it is the Eagle's advanced weapons systems, avionics, and navigation system that make the aircraft excel. Once the technology was developed to

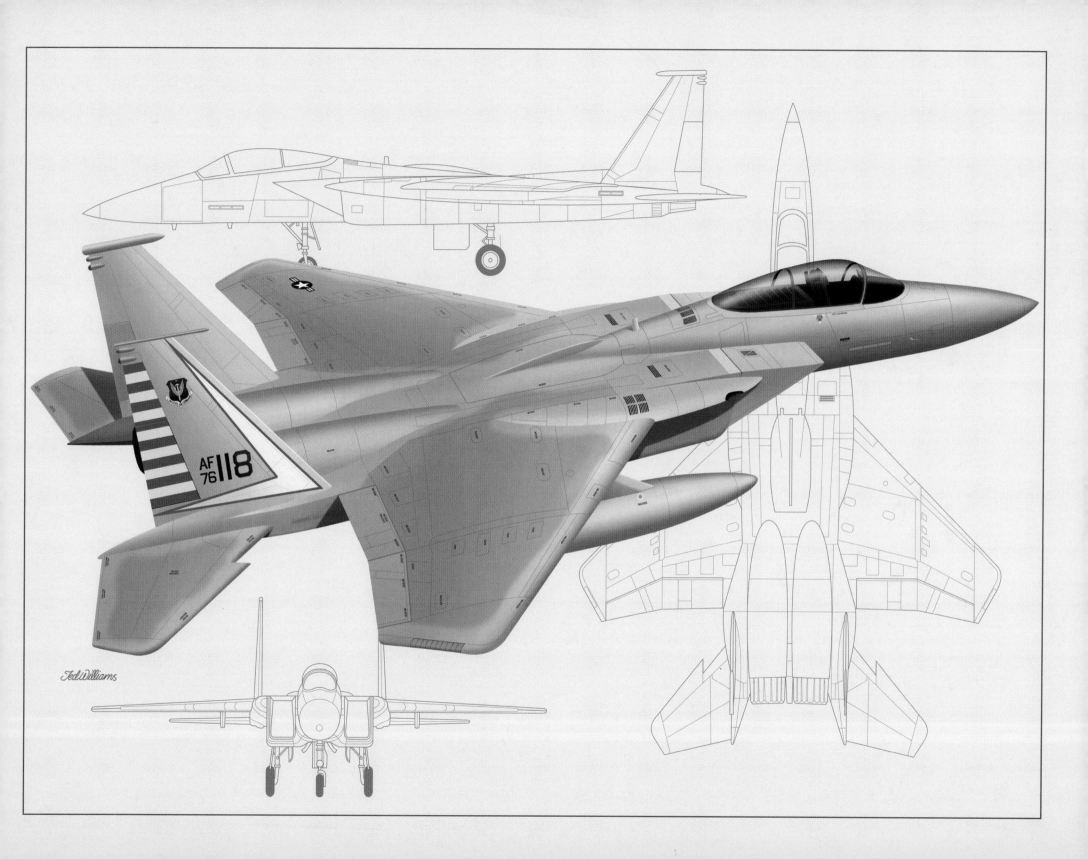

reduce the size and power draw of electronic components, aviation engineers embraced the electronic age. Now, fully computerized, the Eagle can provide the pilot with instantaneous information and real-time response.

Nearly all the aircraft's processes are controlled by its avionics. A Heads-up Display (HUD) and Visual Situation Display (VSD) help the pilot track enemy aircraft and monitor the aircraft's in-flight condition without the distraction of taking his eyes off the scene in front of him by looking down into the cockpit. All vital information is illuminated on the windshield. Pulse-Doppler Radar enables a single pilot to fly the aircraft and operate the complex inertial navigation and weapons system simultaneously, while another radar system alerts the pilot if enemy aircraft is approaching from his "six."

The Eagle has excellent target management: it can single out a specific target from a group or lock on to a target while continuing to search for more. All weapons are fired or launched from the stick. Action buttons line the throttle for a highly effective point-and-shoot method known as "hands on throttle and stick" (HOTAS).

From its inception, the Eagle was designed to be an all-weather, multimission air superiority aircraft. Part dogfighter, part missile platform, part ground support, the F-15 is armed with a 20mm Vulcan cannon, and is equipped to carry radar-guided and heat-seeking air-to-air missiles or drop tanks under the wings and on the centerline. FAST (Fuel and Sensor Tactical) packs allow ground crews to mount additional ordnance and external fuel tanks in fifteen minutes.

Over the course of the program, several variations have come to fruition. The F-15A was developed for the Israeli Air Force; the F-15B is a two-seat companion to the A; the F-15C accounts for the bulk of the single-seat models in service; and the F-15D is a two-seat version of the C. The F-15E Strike Eagle is a two-seat model optimized for ground attack operations. The Strike Eagle performed well in Desert Storm, ending the conflict with a zero-combat-loss record. An F-15J variant was developed for Japan.

The Eagle is a remarkable fighter aircraft. It can accelerate to supersonic speeds while in a straight climb; it can sustain a high-G turn at twice the speed of sound; it can fly from the United States to Europe solely on the fuel it carries; and it can perform as a tactical interceptor, dogfighter, and bomber. But all of this functionality comes at a price. At more than $30 million apiece, you get what you pay for.

The F-15 Eagle was built to replace the F-4 Phantom II, and in time it too will be replaced by the F-22 Raptor, the newest aircraft in a distinguished line of internationally acclaimed air superiority fighters.

OPPOSITE TOP: A pair of F-15 Eagles patrol the "No Fly Zone" over the Iraqi desert. The fighters are fully armed with missiles and carry three auxiliary fuel tanks to lengthen their loiter time while on patrol.

OPPOSITE BOTTOM: An F-15 Eagle touches down with its speed brake deployed. This brake is designed to slow the aircraft on landing by creating extra drag.

LEFT: The vertical performance of the McDonnell Douglas F-15 Eagle is awesome. It can attain Mach 1 in a vertical climb.

McDonnell Douglas F-15A Eagle Specifications

Type: Single-seat air superiority fighter

Power plant: Two Pratt & Whitney F100-PW-100 afterburning turbofan engines producing 23,810 pounds (10,810kg) of static thrust

Performance: Maximum speed, 1,678 mph (2,574kph) at 47,000 feet; service ceiling, 60,000 feet (18,288m); maximum range, 3,570 miles (5,744km)

Weight: Empty, 28,000 pounds (12,712kg); maximum takeoff weight, 56,000 pounds (25,424kg)

Dimensions: Span, 42 feet 9 inches (13m); length, 63 feet 9 inches (19.4m); height, 18 feet 5 inches (5.6m); wing area, 608 square feet (56m^2)

Armament: One 20mm M61A-1 General Electric Vulcan cannon (940 rounds), four AIM-7 Sparrow missiles or eight AIM-120A plus four AIM-9 Sidewinder missiles

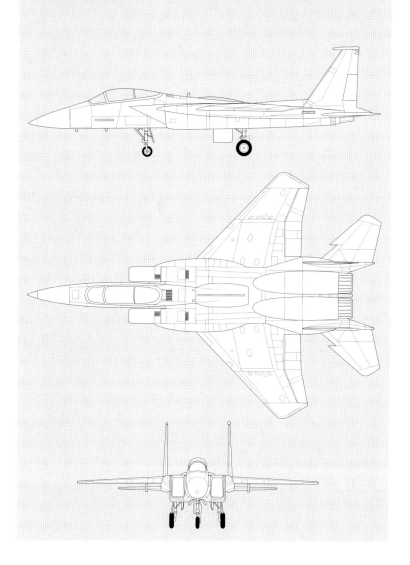

General Dynamics F-16 Fighting Falcon

The General Dynamics F-16 Fighting Falcon was designed to fill the U.S. Air Force's need for a small, lightweight aircraft that was optimized for aerial combat. It was to have one other important characteristic: affordability. Although the Air Force was already moving forward with the formidable F-15 Eagle program, that aircraft's $30 million-per-unit price tag was straining military budgets.

In January 1972, the Air Force commenced with the Lightweight Fighter (LWF) program. It was looking for the perfect lightweight fighter: a small, agile aircraft that utilized new technologies for maximum performance, while keeping an eye on maintenance and costs. In response to the LWF documentation, the Air Force received five proposals. A General Dynamics and a Northrop submission were tied for the win, until General Dynamics finally received the nod for the design that would go on to become the F-16 Fighting Falcon. Northrop's proposal was not dropped; it was picked up by the Navy and developed as the F-18 Hornet.

General Dynamics was not a new name to the military, having been a valued supplier of submarines and missiles since World War II. The company got into the airplane business when it merged with Convair, the Consolidated Vultee Aircraft Corporation, in 1954.

The Air Force favored the Fighting Falcon for several reasons. In particular, it used the same Pratt & Whitney F100 turbofan already in use in the Eagle. This repurposing was a moneysaver since the F100 had already undergone testing and tweaking during the Eagle program, and its use in the Fighting Falcon would unify engine maintenance.

Weighing in at only 13,600 pounds (61,744kg) empty, the first evaluation YF-16 flew on February 8, 1974. Striking features included a blended-wing body that allowed for better aerodynamics and more internal space for fuel; strakes to maintain flight stability by preventing stall conditions at the wing root during a high angle of attack; a cockpit designed for supreme visibility and featuring a reclined seat proven to reduce the effects of extreme G-forces on the human body; and the fly-by-wire (FBW) system.

The Fighting Falcon demonstrated astounding agility due, in part, to its aft center of gravity, which is offset by the FBW. With FBW, to change flight attitude, the pilot uses the aircraft's controls in the normal fashion; however, instead of the usual mechanical translation of the stick movement, this input is sent to a computer, which in turn moves the control surfaces of the aircraft.

With today's basically unstable designs, the computer makes infinitely faster decisions than the pilot is capable of making for optimum control of the aircraft. To ensure the stability of the system, FBW employs three redundant systems. Without computer intervention, today's high-technology fighters simply could not fly.

The Fighting Falcon is a single-engine, 40-degree swept fixed-wing aircraft with an all-moving tailplane. The leading and trailing edge flaps are regulated by the FBW. Again, the FBW's onboard processing unit has the ability to determine the best flap configuration for every flying condition—the FBW, not the pilot, triggers the flaps while in flight.

The first run of production Fighting Falcons, the F-16A, was available by December 8, 1976. The A variant received the next generation Pratt & Whitney turbofan, the F100-PW-200, radar, and armament that increased its weight and size. By 2000, nearly 4,000 F-16s, and its multiple variants, had been produced for many nations around the world. The Fighting Falcon has been purchased by the following countries: Belgium, Denmark, Egypt, the Netherlands, Norway, Pakistan, Venezuela, South Korea, and Israel. In 1981, the Israeli Air Force was the first to put F-16s into combat. Production sites in the Netherlands and Belgium helped General Dynamics' Fort Worth, Texas, facility fulfill international orders for F-16s. The F-16B was developed as a two-seat version of the A with a necessary fuel-capacity reduction to make space for the longer, tandem cockpit.

In 1981, the Multi-stage Improvement Program (MSIP) was initiated. This program entailed the standardization of all existing and future F-16s with newer technologies such as Low Altitude Navigation Targeting Infrared for Night (LANTIRN) system, and improved radar able to detect multiple targets among obstacles in all weather conditions. Global positioning technology and a Precision Location Strike System (PLSS) also exponentially increased the Fighting Falcon's combat effectiveness.

After 1983, the Fighting Falcon variants C and D replaced the A and B. The C benefited from the MSIP modifications and evolutionary improvements to the turbofan engine. The F-16D is a two-seat version of the C variant. The F-16E was introduced in 1982. Classified as a Dual Role Fighter (DRF), the F-16E was developed to have a longer range and to carry more ordnance. With its longer fuselage and double-delta wings, the E's silhouette differs from the other Fighting Falcon variants.

HR

AF
80 542

RESCUE

Jed Williams

General Dynamics F-16A Fighting Falcon Specifications

Type: Single-seat, multirole fighter

Power plant: One Pratt & Whitney F100-PW-200 afterburning turbofan engine producing 23,800 pounds (10,805kg) of static thrust

Performance: Maximum speed, 1,320 mph (2,124kph) at 40,000 feet (12,192m); service ceiling, 50,000 feet (15,240m); range, 575 miles (925km)

Weight: Empty, 14,567 pounds (6,613kg); maximum takeoff weight, 35,400 pounds (16,072kg)

Dimensions: Span, 31 feet (9.4m); length, 47 feet 7 inches (14.5m); height, 16 feet 5 inches (5.m); wing area, 300 square feet (27.6m^2)

Armament: One 20mm cannon plus a 10,500-pound (4,767kg) bomb load

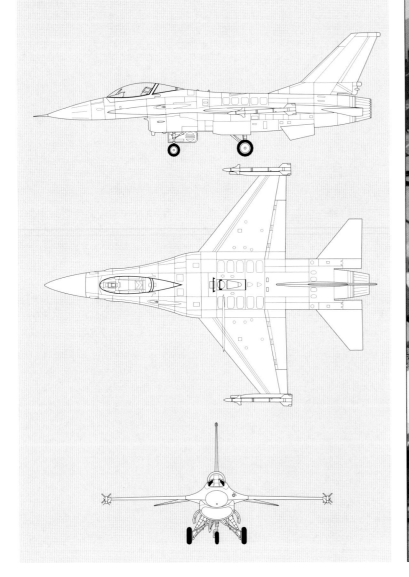

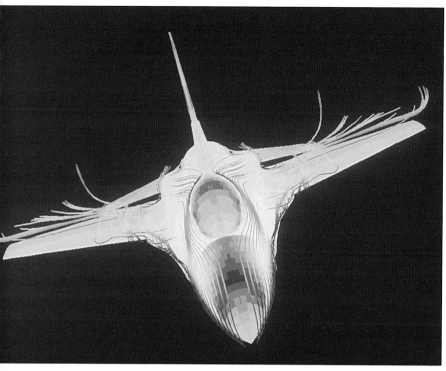

OPPOSITE: An overhead view of the General Dynamics F-16 Fighting Falcons production facility at Fort Worth, Texas.

LEFT TOP: Computer simulation is used to augment expensive wind tunnel testing. Today, aircraft designers rely heavily on digital simulation and computer models.

LEFT BOTTOM: The Pratt & Whitney F-100 turbofan engine, used in the F-16, being tested in full afterburner at the 57th Component Repair Squadron's engine test facility at Nellis Air Force Base.

RIGHT: This view of an F-16 shows the aircraft's heads-up display (HUD). All flight data is displayed on a transparent screen, which does not obstruct the pilot's forward visibility. This feature also eliminates the need to constantly look down into the cockpit to monitor instruments. The muzzle of the 20mm Vulcan can be seen to the right.

The Fighting Falcon has many exceptional characteristics, including the ability to sustain several consecutive 9-G turns. In fact, the aircraft can withstand G-forces that would instantly kill the pilot, but the F-16's electronics system is regulated to ensure that the aircraft does not carry out a maneuver outside survivable human limitations.

All Fighting Falcons are equipped with detection systems that alert the pilot to possible hostile targets and allow him to select the most appropriate defensive actions. The Radar Warning Receiver (RWR) is one such system, and a typical action is "jamming," which obscures a radar signal detected by the F-16 by adding noise to the radar transmission or erroneous coordinates to confuse the enemy radar operator. The pilot controls the F-16 with an ergonomic, side-mounted stick. Positioned to keep the arms in a natural resting position, the side-mounted stick allows for maximum wrist and arm support during high-G maneuvers.

The Fighting Falcon participated in Operation Desert Storm. Armed with a 20mm cannon and an assortment of missiles, it was used more frequently than any other aircraft in the conflict.

Opposing the idea that only a big aircraft can perform well, the F-16 is a highly capable air superiority contender in a smaller form. In conjunction with the F-15 Eagle, the F-16 can deliver its air superiority capabilities swiftly, and with precision, at a moment's notice.

Lockheed Martin F-22 Raptor

The future of American air superiority is the Lockheed Martin F-22 Raptor. Possessing all the qualities of today's top American fighters, the Raptor is a stealth aircraft with advancements that will allow it to dominate the skies.

In 1981, the United States Air Force began its search for an Advanced Tactical Fighter (ATF). The ATF was to be a supremely maneuverable supercruiser (having the ability to fly thirty minutes of a sixty-minute mission at supersonic speeds without afterburning) that utilized low-observable stealth technology.

With the ATF program progressing, several aircraft manufacturers banded together into teams to pool their talents, thereby increasing their chances at solving the problems associated with developing a superfighter. After a series of elimination rounds, two teams were chosen to square off against each other. The McDonnell Douglas/Northrop alliance presented the more unconventional looking design, perhaps engineered to catch the eye of the future-focused committee, but it was the Lockheed Martin/Boeing/General Dynamics team that received the final contract in 1991. It was a grueling, ten-year competition waged in the face of budget cuts and a changing international landscape that threatened the program's funding.

During the competition, each of the final teams built two prototypes. One was powered by the General Electric YF120 variable-cycle turbofan while the other received the competing Pratt and Whitney YF119 turbofan. Perceived as being easier and more cost effective to produce (among other criteria), the YF119 was selected to be the superfighter's power plant.

The Lockheed Martin design, the F-22 Raptor, includes a mix of proven technologies and revolutionary developments. At first glance, it is not difficult to see the Raptor's resemblance to the F-15 Eagle, the aircraft it is expected to eventually replace. Borrowing the best qualities of today's air fleet, the Raptor utilizes an active flight control system similar to the type already employed by modern fighters; this includes the navigation, weapons, and Heads-up Display (HUD) systems already in use on the F-15 Eagle, F-16 Fighting Falcon, and F-18 Hornet. Moreover, the Raptor's updated avionics system, by analyzing thousands of parameters every second, is able to interpret the pilot's actions, allowing the aircraft to choose the best response to ensure an optimal outcome, while protecting the plane and its occupant.

The Raptor is the first fighter aircraft designed, not modified, to use vectoring thrust. Vectoring thrust enables a seamless transition between aerial

OPPOSITE: The unconventional lines of the Raptor belie its brute power. Its twin-engine planform is similar to the F-15, but introduces the latest stealth technology. The F-22 takes stealth fighter performance to the next level with sustained supersonic cruise and greater load carrying capabilities. The Raptor promises to become the best American fighter plane of the twenty-first century.

combat maneuvers. This precise control is achieved by allowing the exhaust nozzles to swivel, directing the thrust for better performance. Furthermore, the Raptor can exploit high angles of attack and post-stall maneuvers without loss of control; its twin-tail empennage helps maintain stability during these extreme, high-speed flight maneuvers.

The Raptor is also the first American fighter to utilize stealth technology. For an aircraft to be classified as stealth, it must have the following characteristics: it must have an extremely low radar cross-section, a low heat signature, and a trim physical profile; it cannot carry any external stores; and its engines must be quiet-running, with nominal emissions and no identifiable exhaust smoke, or contrail. A stealth aircraft is, for all intents and purposes, invisible. This quality allows an aircraft to complete a mission without giving the enemy the forewarning necessary to launch effective countermeasures.

Complying with the needs of stealth engineering, all exterior surfaces on the Raptor are sculpted to deflect radar, and a radar-absorbing material (RAM) covers such easily detectable airframe and wing surfaces as edges or recessed features. RAM converts radar energy into heat, thus reducing the capacity of the enemy's radar to effectively track the object. A new type of RAM was developed specifically for the F-22, since a new substance was needed that would not deteriorate at the extreme temperatures experienced at the boundary layer of the supersonic aircraft.

Other, newer lightweight materials and installation techniques are used throughout the F-22's construction as well. The Raptor's trapezoidal wings, in particular, are fashioned out of a composite resin.

The Raptor also features an improved human environment. A life-support and oxygen delivery system monitors and maintains the pilot's physical condition and protects against the life-threatening effects of high G-forces; the system includes an improved flight suit that responds to the pilot's physical reactions to the changing G-forces, while regulating the wearer's body temperature.

The Raptor is armed with a 20mm M61 Vulcan cannon, albeit a lighter version than the M61 used on earlier American fighters, with better aiming technologies. Despite its advancing age, the M61 Vulcan is still the best gun available for air combat. Conforming to stealth regulations, the Raptor's radar-assisted air-to-air and air-to-surface missiles and all-weather Joint Direct Attack Munition (JDAM) payload is stored in internal bays. If the operation is

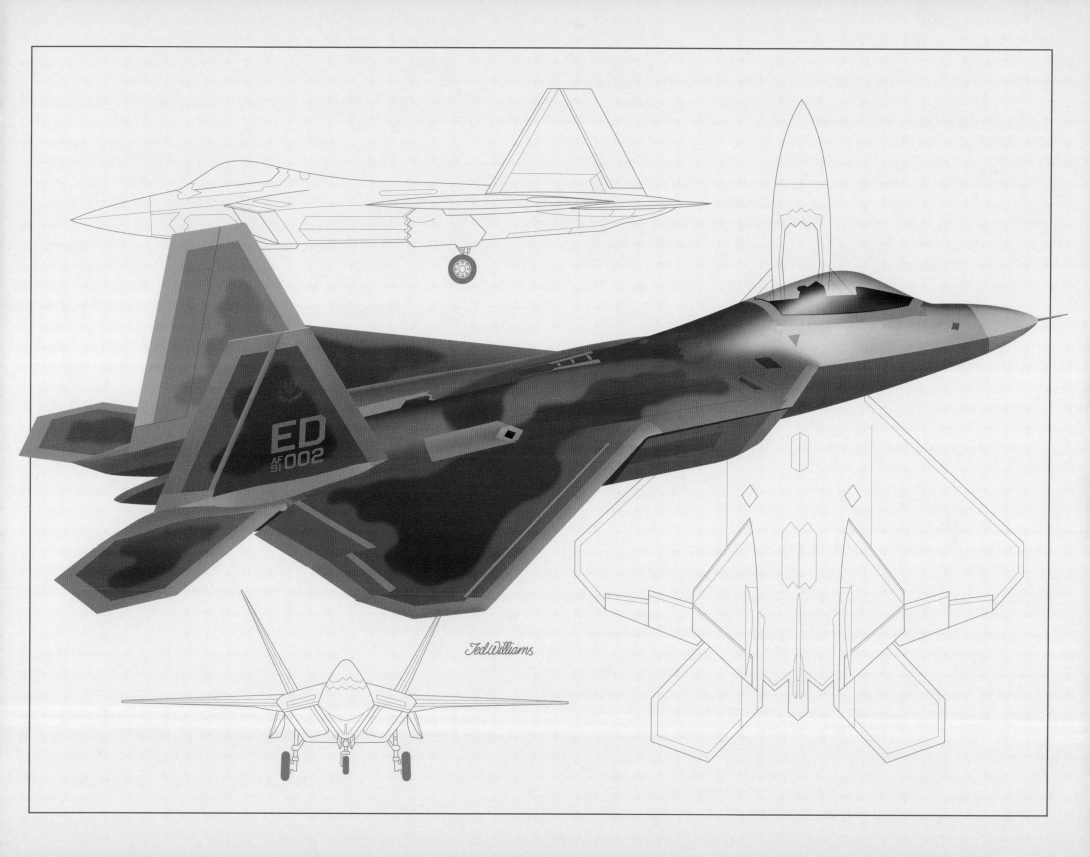

Ted Williams

Lockheed Martin F-22 Raptor Specifications

Type: Single-seat, advanced tactical fighter

Power plant: Two Pratt & Whitney F-119-100 afterburning turbofan engines producing 35,000 pounds (15,875kg) static thrust

Performance: Maximum speeds, 1,155 mph (1,858kph) at 30,000 feet (9,120m), Mach 1.7 with afterburner, Mach 1.58 supercruise; service ceiling, 50,000 feet (15,240m); range, 2,000 nautical miles (3,726km)

Weight: Empty, 30,000 pounds (13,608kg); maximum takeoff weight, 60,000 pounds (27,216kg)

Dimensions: Span, 44 feet 6 inches (13.5m); length, 62 feet 1 inch (18.9m); height, 16 feet 7 inches (5m); wing area, 838 square feet (77.9m^2)

Armament: One 20mm M61A2 General Electric Vulcan cannon (480 rounds); three internal bays for AIM-9 Sidewinders (one in each bay) and/or four AIM-120A or six AIM-120C AMRAAM AAMS and/or GBU-32 JDAM 1000 PGMs on hydraulic weapons racks in main weapons bay; four underwing stores stations at 125 inches (317mm) and 174 inches (442mm) from centerline of fuselage, capable of carrying 5,000 pounds (2,268kg) each.

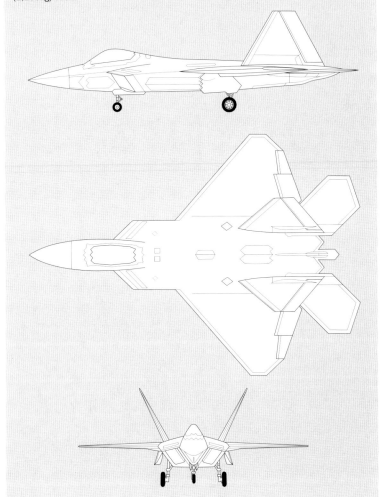

OPPOSITE TOP: A skin panel for the wing of the Lockheed/Boeing/General Dynamics team's YF-22 Advanced Tactical Fighter (ATF) prototype undergoes through-transmission ultrasonic (TTU) testing at the Boeing facility in Seattle, Washington. TTU is a non-destructive process that ensures the manufacturing quality of the skin, which is built from advanced composite materials.

OPPOSITE BOTTOM: Lockheed engineers visualize airflow patterns as they move over the model of an YF-22. Smoke is injected into a wind tunnel and illuminated by a laser to complete the test.

RIGHT: A Lockheed Martin YF-22 performs aerial refueling with a KC-135 as part of its intensive flight-testing program. This profile view of the Raptor shows the unique shape of the stealth airframe.

not stealth, 20,000 pounds (9,060kg) of external ordnance or 600-gallons (2,271L) of external fuel can be attached to the underside of the aircraft.

Projected to be operational in 2005, the twin-engine F-22 Raptor will be a superfighter unlike any other in the world. With a maximum speed of Mach 1.8, a supercruise speed of Mach 1.6, and a range of more than 750 miles (1,206.8km)—easily lengthened by in-flight refueling—the Raptor is an amazing evolutionary development from its pursuit biplane forefathers. In December 2001, five evaluation Raptors were in the process of flight-testing at the Air Force Flight Test Center, at Edwards Air Force Base.

Yet, like its Eagle predecessor, the Raptor is a costly venture. Much like the relationship between today's F-15 and F-16, the Lockheed Martin F-35 was chosen in October 2001 to supplement the future F-22 Raptor fleet. Developed for the Joint Strike Fighter (JSF) program (another government program initi-

ated to develop a modern fighter to a specific set of requirements), the F-35 will be a slightly lower-cost-per-unit multirole stealth fighter than the F-22. A specific variant was designed for the United States Air Force and a navalized version has been reinforced for carrier landings, while the Marine Corps will receive a STOVL (short takeoff vertical landing) variant of the F-35. Projected to be operational in 2008, the same family of Pratt & Whitney engine used by the Raptor will power all three F-35 variants. Together, by 2025, the F-22 Raptor and F-35 will provide the United States with an entirely all-stealth fighter fleet.

The ATF and JSF programs are not the end of fighter plane evolution. Other, newer aircraft designs are already challenging the idea of how an air-supremacy aircraft should look, perform, and, in the case of uninhabited combat air vehicles (UCAV), be flown.

Bibliography

Books

Angelucci, Enzo. *Airplanes from the Dawn of Flight to the Present Day*. New York: Greenwich House, 1982.

———. *Rand McNally Encyclopedia of Military Aircraft*. New York: Military Press, 1980.

Angelucci, Enzo, and Peter Bowers. *The American Fighter: The Definitive Guide to American Fighter Aircraft from 1917 to the Present*. New York: Orion Books, 1987.

Archer, Bob. *U.S. Air Force: The New Century*. Leicester: Midland Publishing, 2000.

Bilstein, Roger E. *Flight in America 1900–1983: From the Wrights to the Astronauts*. Baltimore, MD: Johns Hopkins University Press, 1984.

Bonds, Ray, Bernard Fitzsimons, Tony Hall, and Philip de Ste. Croix, eds. *The Great Book of Modern Warplanes*. New York: Portland House, 1987.

Bowers, Peter. *Curtiss Aircraft 1907–1947*. Annapolis, MD: Naval Institute Press, 1979.

Boyne, Walter J. *The Aircraft Treasures of Silver Hill*. New York: Rawson Associates, 1982.

Braybrook, Roy. *F-16 Fighting Falcon*. New York: Crescent Books, 1991.

Bugos, Glenn E. *Engineering the F-4 Phantom II: Parts into Systems*. Annapolis, MD: Naval Institute Press, 1996.

Davis, Larry. *P-12/F4B in Action*. Carrollton, TX: Squadron/Signal Publications, Inc., 1993.

———. *P-26 Mini in Action*. Carrollton, TX: Squadron/Signal Publications, Inc., 1994.

Dorr, Robert F. *Warbirds Illustrated No. 49: F-105 Thunderchief*. London: Arms & Armour Press, 1988.

Drendel, Lou. *Modern Military Aircraft: Thud*. Carrollton, TX: Squadron/Signal Publications, Inc., 1986.

Friddell, Phillip. *F-104 Starfighter in Action*. Carrollton, TX: Squadron/Signal Publications, Inc., 1993.

Ginter, Steve. *Naval Fighters Number Six: Chance Vought F7U Cutlass*. Simi Valley, CA: Naval Fighters, 1982.

Goodwin, Jacob. *Brotherhood of Arms: General Dynamics and the Business of Defending America*. New York: Times Books, 1985.

Grant, William Newby. *P-51 Mustang*. New York: Gallery Books, 1980.

Green, William, and Gordon Swanborough. *The Complete Book of Fighters: An Illustrated Encyclopedia of Every Fighter Aircraft Built and Flown*. New York: Smithmark Publishers Inc., 1994.

———. *US Army Air Force Fighters, Part 1*. London: MacDonald and Jane's Publishers, 1977.

Gunston, Bill. *American Warplanes*. New York: Crescent Books, 1986.

———. *History of Military Aviation*. London: Hamlyn, 2000.

———. *The Illustrated History of Fighters*. New York: Exeter Books, 1981.

Gurney, Gene. *The P-38 Lightning*. New York: Arco Publishing Company, Inc., 1969.

Jablonski, Edward. *Man with Wings: A Pictorial History of Aviation*. New York: Doubleday & Company, Inc., 1980.

Jenkins, Dennis R. *Grumman F-14 Tomcat: Leading US Navy Fleet Fighter*. Leicester: Midland Publishing, 1997.

———. *McDonnell Douglas F-15 Eagle: Supreme Heavy-Weight Fighter*. Leicester: Midland Publishing, 1998.

———. *WarbirdTech Series: McDonnell Douglas F-15 Eagle, Volume 9*. North Branch, MN: Specialty Press Publishers and Wholesalers, 1997.

Johnsen, Frederick A. *WarbirdTech Series: Republic P-47 Thunderbolt, Volume 23*. North Branch, MN: Specialty Press Publishers and Wholesalers, 1999.

Kinzey, Bert. *F-100 Super Sabre in Detail & Scale*. Blue Ridge Summit, PA: Tab Books, 1989

Knott, Richard C. *A Heritage of Wings: An Illustrated History of Navy Aviation*. Annapolis, MD: Naval Institute Press, 1997.

Larkins, William T. *U.S. Navy Aircraft 1921–1941/U.S. Marine Corps Aircraft 1914–1959: Two Classics in One Volume*. New York: Orion Books, 1988.

Lawson, Robert L., ed. *The History of US Naval Airpower*. New York: Military Press, 1985.

Mizrahi, J.V. *Carrier Fighters*. Northridge, CA: Sentry Books, 1969.

Mondey, David, ed. *The International Encyclopedia of Aviation*. New York: Crown Publishers, 1984.

Morris, James M. *History of the U.S. Navy*. Greenwich, CT: Exeter Books, 1984.

Robinson, Anthony, ed., updated by Michael J.H. Taylor. *In the Cockpit: Flying the World's Greatest Aircraft*. Secaucus, NJ: Chartwell Books, 1991.

Stafford, Gene B. *Thunderbolt in Action*. Warren, MI: Squadron/Signal Publications, 1975.

Sweetman, Bill. *Enthusiast Color Series: F-22 Raptor*. Osceola, WI: Motorbooks International, 1998.

Taylor, Michael J.H., ed. *Jane's Encyclopedia of Aviation*. New York: Portland House, 1989.

———. *Planemakers No.1: Boeing*. London: Jane's Publishing Company, 1982.

———. *The Chronology of Flight: 1940 to Present (The World's Greatest Aircraft)*. Philadelphia, PA: Chelsea House Publishers, 2000.

Taylor, Michael J.H., and David Mondey. *Milestones of Flight*. London: Jane's Publishing Company, 1983.

Thompson, Warren E. *WarbirdTech Series: Northrop P-61 Black Widow, Volume 15*. North Branch, MN: Specialty Press, 1997.

Tillman, Barrett. *MiG Master: The Story of the F-8 Crusader*. Annapolis, MN: The Nautical and Aviation Publishing Company of America, 1980.

Treadwell, Terry. *Ironworks: Grumman's Fighting Aeroplanes*. Osceola, WI: Motorbooks International, 1990.

Vought F4U "Corsair." Air Age Technical Library: Warplane Research. New York: Air Age, 1944.

Articles

Andrews, Hal. "The Navy's First Jet Fighter." *Air Classics*. Vol. 29, no. 1 (January 1993): 60–63.

Barrow, Jess C. "Teething Troubles with F4B-4." *Journal of American Aviation Historical Society*. Vol. 16, no. 2 (Summer 1971): 98–104.

Bauer, Daniel. "Marion Carl." *Air Classics*. Vol. 30, no. 5 (May 1994): 24–37, 60–65.

"The Beast from Burbank: P-38 Lightning." *Air Classics*. Vol. 3, no. 2 (1966 Annual): 34–41.

Beauchamp, Gerry. "Hawks for Hire." *Wings*. Vol. 8, no. 2 (April 1978): 24–38, 59–63.

Bledsoe, Larry W. "Symphony in Black: How and Why a Painting was Created to Honor America's Night Fighter Pilots of World War Two." *Air Classics*. Vol. 29, no. 7 (July 1993): 48–57.

"Boeing's Battling Biplanes." *Air Classics Quarterly Review*. Vol. 1, no. 2 (Fall 1974): 36.

Bowers, Peter M. "Airborne Cobra, Part II." *Airpower*. Vol. 9, no. 1 (January 1979): 10–31, 63.

———. "Airborne Cobra, Part III." *Wings*. Vol. 9, no.1 (February 1979): 26–37, 61.

———. "Boeing's First Fighters." *Wings*. Vol. 7, no. 4 (August 1977): 42-55.

———. "The First Pursuit." *Wings*. Vol. 6, no. 6 (December 1976): 8–23, 66–67.

Bowman, Martin W. "Korea's Jet Warriors." *Air Classics*. Vol. 31, no. 12 (December 1995): 12–33, 68–69.

Boyne, Walt. "Hawks for Hire." *Air Classics*. Vol. 6, no. 6 (August 1970): 6–18, 51, 59.

———. "Sever the Sky." *Air Classics*. Vol. 4, no. 3 (February 1968): 26–36.

Daniels, C.M. "Thunder-Maker." *Air Classics*. Vol. 7, no. 5 (July 1971): 18–36, 50–61.

Eberspacher, Warren, CCS. "Consolidated PB-2A, A Modern Solution for an Outdated Concept." *Skyways: The Journal of the Airplane 1920–1940* (January 2001): 2–11.

"The Elegant Curtiss Hawks." *Air Classics Quarterly Review*. Vol. 1, no. 2 (Fall 1974): 26.

Ethell, Jeff. "Magnificent Eagle." *Air Progress Pilot Reports*. Vol. 2, no. 1 (Spring 1981): 70–77.

"The Fledglings: Boeing's Early Navy Fighters." *Air Classics Quarterly Review*. Vol. 1, no. 2 (Fall 1974): 19.

Furler, E.F., Jr. "Bell's War Years." *Air Classics*. Vol. 21, no. 1 (January 1985): 58–69.

Gatlin, Wayne. "Flying the F-89." *Air Classics*. Vol. 14, no. 10 (October 1978): 29–31, 74–76.

Guttman, Robert. "The Missile with a Man In It." *Aviation History* (January 2000): 46–54, 84.

Guyton, Boone. "Old Hog Nose." *Airpower*. Vol. 1, no. 1 (September 1971): 38–53.

Heenan, Mike, with Captains Bob Ellis and Mike Zettler. "The Eagle is a Pretty Bird." *Air Classics Quarterly Review*. Vol. 3, no. 3 (Fall 1976): 66–77.

Hucker, Robert. "Seversky: Innovator and Prophet." *Air Classics*. Vol. 16, no. 5 (May 1980): 34–36, 56–61.

"The Last P-6E." *Air Classics Quarterly Review*. Vol. 2, no. 4 (Winter 1975): 43.

Linn, Donn. "Banshee: McDonnell's Flying Banjo." *Airpower*. Vol. 9, no. 6 (November 1979): 18–35.

Lord, Charles, Jr. "Crusader." *Air Classics*. Vol. 8, no. 2 (December 1971): 52–56.

McCampbell, David. "Flying the Hellcat in World War II." *Warbirds: Official Publication of the EAA Warbirds of America, Inc.* Vol. 5, no. 8 (August 1982): 20–21.

McDowell, Donald R. "Five Years in a Phantom." *Air Classics*. Vol. 9, no. 1 (January 1973): 25–31, 54–5.

Mizrahi, J.V. "Carrier Fighter: Curtiss and its Sea Going Hawks." *Airpower*. Vol. 2, no. 5 (September 1972): 18–22, 60.

———. "F4F Foreman of the Iron Works Gang." *Wings*. Vol. 2, no. 1 (February 1972): 16–32.

———. "Farewell to the Fleet's Forgotten Fighter: Brewster F2A." *Airpower*. Vol. 2, no. 2 (March 1972): 24–36, 60–61.

———. "Hawk 75: First of the Modern Falcons." *Wings*. Vol. 2, no. 2 (August 1972): 41–57.

———. "P-35 Seversky's Cadillac of the Air." *Wings*. Vol. 1, no. 2 (October 1971): 32–49.

Neal, Ronald D. "The Bell XP-59A Airacomet: The United States' First Jet Aircraft." *American Aviation Historical Society Journal*. Vol. 11, no. 3 (Fall 1966): 155–178.

O'Leary, Michael. "Lone Star's Flying Barrel." *Air Classics*. Vol. 29, no. 11 (November 1993): 21–27, 39–50.

Otto, Richard. "The Sabre Saga." *Air Classics*. Vol. 8, no. 3 (January 1972): 10–20.

"P is for Pursuit." *Wings* 6, no. 2 (April 1976): 47–52.

"P-26." *Air Classics* 4, no. 4 (April 1968): 17–21.

"P-26 Peashooter." *Air Classics Quarterly Review* 1, no. 2 (Fall 1974): 83.

"P-26: The First of the Monoplane Pursuits." *Wings* 9, no. 4 (August 1979): 50–55.

Pape, Garry R., and Ronald C. Harrison. "Dark Lady: Part II The Further Adventures of Northrop's Flying Spider Ship from P-61B through P-61 E." *Airpower*. Vol. 6, no. 6 (November 1976): 8–25, 64–66.

Phillips, Ward. "Bat Out'a Hell." *Air Classics*. Vol. 14, no 6 (June 1978): 36–41, 70–73.

Ryan, Frank. "Boeing's Fabulous Peashooter/P-26." *Wings*. Vol. 8, no. 5 (March 1972): 49–55.

"Saga of the F4B-4." *Air Classics*. Vol. 3, no. 2 (1966 Annual): 19–23.

Scarborough, W.E. "A Hellcat Comes Home." *Air Classics*. Vol. 6, no. 5 (June 1970): 44–54, 70, 72.

Schoeni, Arthur. "Crusader. Part One." *Air Classics*. Vol. 13, no. 11 (November 1977): 28–37, 94–95.

———. "Crusader. Conclusion." *Air Classics*. Vol. 14, no. 1 (January 1978): 28–33, 92–97.

Seitz, E.A. "Flying Sword: 86 was the Right Number for North American's First Jet Fighter, for It Was the Last of the Pure Dog-Fighting Breed." *Wings*. Vol. 5, no. 5 (October 1975): 8–20, 50–55.

Slaughter, Tod. "Last of the Red Hot 'Cats." *Air Classics*. Vol. 10, no. 7 (July 1974): 38–47, 78.

Tillman, Barrett. "Bearcat." *Wings*. Vol. 6, no. 1 (February 1976): 32–45, 54–55.

———. "Homage to the Big Cat." *Wings*. Vol. 9, no. 6 (December 1979): 22–39.

Trimble, Robert L. "First of the Bethpage 'Cats, Part 1." *Air Classics*. Vol. 14, no. 8 (August 1978): 34–41, 64–67.

———. "First of the Bethpage 'Cats, Part 2." *Air Classics*. Vol. 14, no. 9 (September 1978): 36–41, 70–74.

———. "Scorpion: Fully as Deadly as Its Namesake, Northrop's F-89 Seemed to Carry a Sting Everywhere but Its Tail." *Air Classics*. Vol. 14, no. 10 (October 1978): 20–28.

———. "Thunderjet Part Two." *Air Classics*. Vol. 12, no. 5 (May 1976): 52–65, 80–82.

———. " Thunderjet Part Three." *Air Classics*. Vol. 12, no. 6 (June 1976): 28–41

Various. *Air Classics Quarterly Review*. Vol. 1, no. 3 (Winter 1974).

Westerburg, Peter. "P-6E Hawk, Part 1." *Wings*. Vol. 14, no. 3 (March 1978): 18–25, 70–75.

———. "P-6E Hawk, Part 2." *Wings*. Vol. 14, no. 5 (May 1978): 18–24, 68–75.

Websites

www.boeing.com/companyoffices/history/mdc/index.htm
History of Boeing, McDonnell-Douglas, and North American

naca.larc.nasa.gov/reports/1925/naca-report-193/naca-report-193.pdf
National Advisory Committee for Aeronautics: MB3 report

www.wpafb.af.mil/museum/
U.S. Air Force Museum at Wright-Patterson Air Force Base, Dayton, Ohio

www.nasm.edu/
Smithsonian National Air and Space Museum, Washington, D.C.

www.navalair.org
The National Museum of Naval Aviation, Pensacola, FL

www.nationalaviation.org/history.html
National Aviation Hall of Fame

www.afa.org
Air Force Association

www.flightjournal.com

www.thehistorynet.com/AviationHistory/

www.pratt-whitney.com/classicengines/html/ClassicEngines.html
Pratt & Whitney

www.airventure.org/2001/thursday26/nasa.html
EAA Aviation Center, Oshkosh, WI

Photo Credits

Index

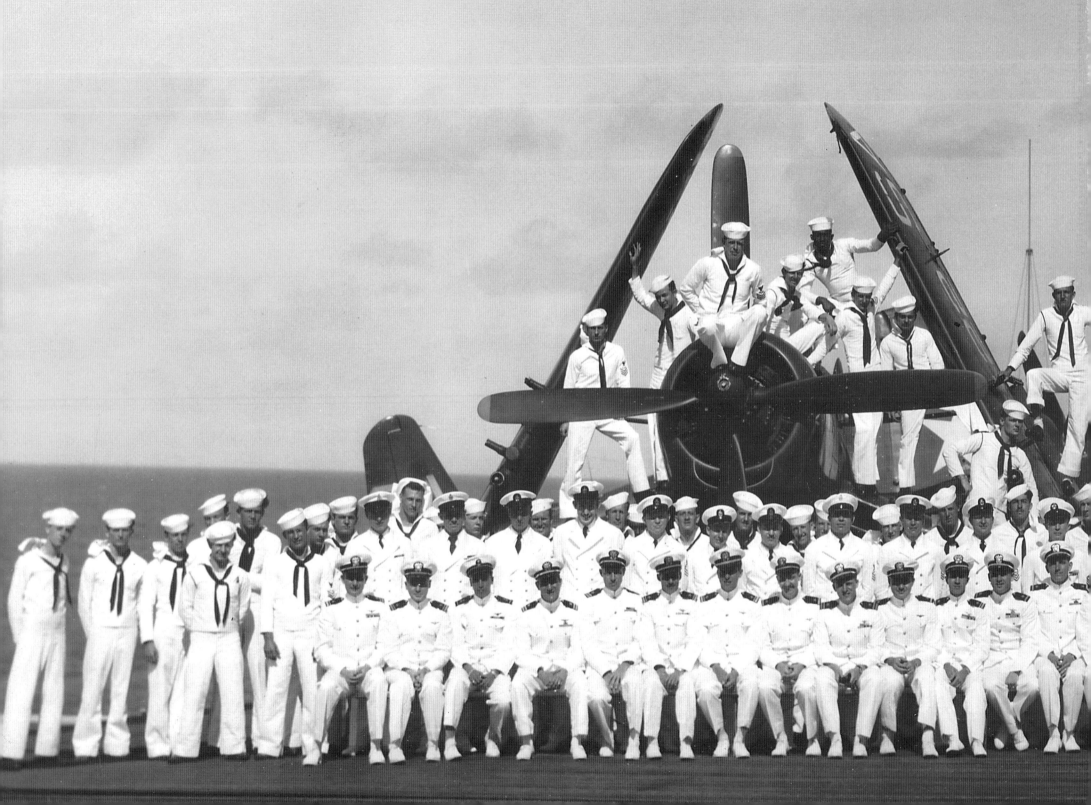